Yale Music Masterworks

BRAHMS

The Four Symphonies

Walter Frisch

YALE UNIVERSITY PRESS
NEW HAVEN AND LONDON

Published in 2003 by Yale University Press
Originally published in 1996 by Schirmer Books

Copyright © 2003 by Yale University

Printed in the United States of America

Library of Congress Control Number: 2003104448
ISBN 0-300-09965-7 (pbk. : alk. paper)

A catalogue record for this book is available from the British Library.

The paper in this book meets the guidelines for permanence and durability of the Committee
on Production Guidelines for Book Longevity of the Council on Library Resources.

10   9   8   7   6   5   4   3   2   1

For Nicholas and Simon

Contents

Foreword   *ix*

Preface and Acknowledgments   *xiii*

CHAPTER 1: THE SYMPHONY IN BRAHMS'S WORLD   1
    The "Great Symphony" after Beethoven   1
    The Symphonic "Crisis" at Midcentury   5
    The Alternative of Program Music   12
    The Symphonic Style   15
    Social and Institutional Aspects   18
    Bruch and Bruckner: A Context for Brahms   20

CHAPTER 2: BRAHMS'S PATH TO THE SYMPHONY   29
    First Attempts at Orchestral Writing   30
    Toward the C-Minor Symphony: Brahms's "First Maturity" 32
    The German Requiem   35
    Final Steps: The Works of 1873   36

CHAPTER 3: THE FIRST SYMPHONY, OP. 68   45
    First movement: Un poco sostenuto—Allegro   46
    Second movement: Andante sostenuto   52
    Third movement: Un poco Allegretto e grazioso   56
    Fourth movement: Adagio—Più andante—
        Allegro non troppo, ma con brio   58

CHAPTER 4: THE SECOND SYMPHONY, OP. 73   67
    First movement: Allegro non troppo   68
    Second movement: Adagio non troppo   75
    Third movement: Allegretto grazioso (Quasi Andantino) 80
    Fourth movement: Allegro con spirito   85

CHAPTER 5: THE THIRD SYMPHONY, OP. 90   91
    First movement: Allegro con brio   92
    Second movement: Andante   100
    Third movement: Poco Allegretto   105
    Fourth movement: Allegro   107

CHAPTER 6: THE FOURTH SYMPHONY, OP. 98   115
    First movement: Allegro non troppo   117
    Second movement: Andante moderato   123
    Third movement: Allegro giocoso   127
    Fourth movement: Allegro energico e passionato   130

CHAPTER 7: PATTERNS OF RECEPTION   141
    The Symphonies in the Concert Hall   142
    The Beethoven Problem   145
    Symphony as Chamber Music   147
    Heart vs. Brain   152
    Hermeneutic Traditions   154

CHAPTER 8: TRADITIONS OF PERFORMANCE   163
    Orchestral Size and Arrangement   164
    Orchestral Technique   165
    Interpretation: The Richter-Bülow Dichotomy   166
    The Coda of the First Movement of the
        First Symphony: A Comparison   173
    Weingartner and Brahms   177
    The First Movement of the Second Symphony: A Comparison 181
    Norrington's Brahms   185

Appendix I: A Chronology of the Brahms Symphonies   189
Appendix II: Sources and Editions   193
Notes   197
Selected Bibliography   217
Index   223

Foreword

The Yale Music Masterworks series is devoted to the examination of single works, or groups of works, that have changed the course of Western music by virtue of their greatness. Some were recognized as masterpieces almost as soon as they were written. Others lay in obscurity for decades, to be uncovered and revered only by later generations. With the passage of time, however, all have emerged as cultural landmarks.

The Masterworks volumes are written by historians and performers, specialists who bring to their accounts the latest discoveries of modern scholarship. The authors examine the political, economic, and cultural background of the works. They consider such matters as genesis, reception, influence, and performance practice. But most importantly, they explore the music itself and attempt to pinpoint the qualities that make it transcendent.

Next to Beethoven's "nine," Brahms's "four" represent the most consistently performed group of symphonies in the classical repertory. Enthusiastically received almost from the moment they first sounded, Brahms's works have enjoyed immense popularity down to the present day—as a glance at the most recent issue of the Schwann catalogue confirms. Yet at the same time, they have been subjected to a steady stream of barbs from critics claiming that they do not measure up to the Promethean grandeur of Beethoven's orchestral essays. "Strip off the euphemism from these symphonies," Bernard Shaw, for one, warned his readers, "and you will find a string of incomplete dance and ballad tunes, following one another with no more organic coherence than the succession of passing images reflected in a shop window in Piccadilly during any twenty minutes of the day." Few writers of first rank have leveled such remarks at Beethoven's symphonies. Why is it, then, that Brahms's works continually draw criticism even though their central position in the orchestral canon seems unassailable?

Walter Frisch confronts this paradox head on in his remarkable book *Brahms: The Four Symphonies*. Rather than shrug off the reservations of past writers, Frisch uses their complaints to help the reader understand both the scope of Brahms's dilemma as he approached the task of writing a symphony in the second half of the nineteenth century and the immensity of his triumph as he rose above his contemporaries to revivify a seemingly moribund genre.

In chapter 1, "The Symphony in Brahms's World," Frisch analyzes the cultural milieu in which the Brahms symphonies were written, exploring the symphonic "crisis" that enveloped Europe after Beethoven's death and showing why Brahms was better positioned than other German composers to resolve the predicament successfully. Scholars have long pointed to the fourteen-year genesis of the First Symphony as a sign of Brahms's reluctance to compete with Beethoven in the symphonic realm. In chapter 2, "Brahms's Path to the Symphony," Frisch looks at Brahms's personal development and shows why the composer needed so much time. It was not a question of extending Beethoven's symphonic technique—the route later traveled by Mahler. Rather, it was a matter of taking the symphony in a new direction. For Brahms, this meant approaching the symphony in a way that enabled him to capitalize on his gifts as a writer of chamber music. But he first had to hone his skills to the point where he could successfully sustain formal designs on a grand scale. As Frisch points out, it was only after composing tightly structured chamber pieces such as the G-major Sextet and the Horn Trio and orchestral works such as the D-Minor Piano Concerto, the German Requiem, and the Haydn Variations that Brahms was ready to dispel the ghost of Beethoven with the C-Minor Symphony.

In the central chapters Frisch looks at the music of the symphonies in detail and demonstrates how Brahms was able, time and time again, to take small gestures, beautiful in themselves, and transform them into bold architectonic strokes that sweep across movements and even complete works. As orchestrated chamber music, his symphonies capture the imagination differently than Beethoven's. Frisch shows how Brahms chose to redefine the symphony rather than repeat Beethoven's formulas.

In chapter 7, "Patterns of Reception," Frisch follows the fate of the symphonies over the course of time and surveys the issues they have raised with succeeding generations of performers and critics. And in chapter 8, "Traditions of Performance," Frisch makes what may well be the most original contribution to the literature on the Brahms symphonies: he examines the performance traditions of the works and illustrates, among other things, how the present-day quandary over "free" versus "strict" interpretation can be traced back to the first performance of the works, to the Richter and Bülow renditions heard by Brahms himself.

In another Masterworks volume, David Levy makes the case that composers after Beethoven labored "in the shadow of the Ninth." Here Walter Frisch reminds us how firmly Brahms stepped out of that shadow and into the bright sunlight with his four monumental symphonies. This is a study that delights and enlightens. Most importantly, it is a book that greatly increases our appreciation of Brahms's masterpieces.

George B. Stauffer
Series Editor

Preface and Acknowledgments

❦

The four symphonies of Johannes Brahms have been staples of the concert and recorded repertory for more than one hundred years. Some critics have carped and caviled—the works are too academic, too dense, too muddily scored—but the symphonies show no signs of vanishing from the canon or from the list of most beloved compositions. Despite their status, the symphonies have not received sustained treatment in writing. Surprisingly, not since Julius Harrison's survey-analysis of 1939 has there been a full-length study in English. There have, to be sure, been many individual articles on aspects of the works, mainly analytical and theoretical in nature (many are listed in the bibliography of the present study). There have also been various one-volume guides. Recently, a fine monograph on the Second Symphony has been written by Reinhold Brinkmann. An excellent study of the First is due from David Brodbeck in the Cambridge Handbook Series; also forthcoming, from the present publisher in the volume *The Nineteenth-Century Symphony*, is Brodbeck's elegant essay on the four symphonies.

There is thus some justification for a book that examines all four symphonies together. Within a closely prescribed word count, such an approach will, of course, bring some loss of detail, hindering the possibility of following up individual points of interest. But I hope the result will not seem too superficial to specialists, nor too forbidding for general readers. My approach is literally to surround close examination of the pieces, in chapters 3 through 6, with chapters that establish the historical, biographical, and musical contexts in various ways.

I am grateful to George Stauffer, the series editor, for encouraging me to take on this work and for his careful reading of the manuscript, and to the Schirmer editors, first Maribeth Anderson Payne and, after her departure, James Hatch, Jill Lectka, and Jonathan Wiener, for their patience and support over the years that this project gestated.

Colleagues who have been generous with their time, knowledge, and mate-
rials include Styra Avins, Mark Evan Bonds, George Bozarth, David Breckbill,
Reinhold Brinkmann, David Brodbeck, John Daverio, Joseph Dubiel, Josef
Eisinger, Virginia Hancock, Kurt Hofmann, Roger Norrington, Robert Pascall,
Ernest Sanders, Carl Schachter, Christian Martin Schmidt, and Elaine Sisman.
Professors Brodbeck and Daverio gave this book especially valuable readings.
I wish also to thank for their assistance Elizabeth Davis and the staff of the
Columbia University Music Library; John Shepard and the staff of the Music
Division of the New York Public Library for the Performing Arts; J. Rigbie
Turner and the staff of the Pierpont Morgan Library; Richard Warren of the
Historical Sound Recording Collection at the Yale University Library; and
Barbara Haws of the New York Philharmonic Archives.

Anne, Nicholas, and Simon remain among the most ardent of Brahms-
ians. After being subjected to countless CD renderings of the symphonies,
they still enjoy the works, proving that familiarity—in the truest sense of the
word—can enhance appreciation.

I am grateful to Yale University Press for permitting me to correct some
errors and make small emendations in the text for this reprinting.

Chapter 1

THE SYMPHONY IN BRAHMS'S WORLD

THE "GREAT SYMPHONY" AFTER BEETHOVEN

*I*n his authoritative *Allgemeine Musiklehre* of 1839, A. B. Marx, a leading German writer on music, defined the symphony as

> an orchestral composition in the sonata-form, but, in accordance with
> the great powers of an orchestra . . . usually constructed upon large,
> massive and well-defined proportions. It mostly consists of an intro-
> duction, allegro, andante, scherzo, and finale; all of which movements
> are more fully developed and more powerfully marked than is thought
> necessary in a sonata.[1]

Although accurate as far as it goes, this dry description scarcely begins to
account for the hallowed position the genre of the symphony assumed in
German-speaking lands in the nineteenth century.

Already in the late eighteenth century, as articulated in Sulzer's renowned
Allgemeine Theorie der schönen Künste (1771–74), the symphony was
esteemed as an important vehicle of the "sublime." A generation later, especially in the writings of literary and musical figures of the early Romantic
period, instrumental music in general, long considered inferior to vocal
music, continued its rise in status. Among instrumental genres, the symphony became the most highly valued. When in 1809 E. T. A. Hoffmann called

1

the symphony "the opera of instruments, so to speak," he was paying it the
highest possible compliment.[2] Hoffmann's remarks are prefigured or echoed
by numerous contemporary writers.[3] The distinguished lexicographer E. L.
Gerber, writing in the *Allgemeine musikalische Zeitung* in 1813, characterized the symphony as "the *non plus ultra* of the newer art, the highest and
most excellent among instrumental pieces."[4]

Twenty-five years later, during the childhood of Brahms, these views still
prevailed. In an encyclopedia article of 1838, Gottfried Wilhelm Fink suggested that the *große Symphonie*, or great symphony ("great" in scope or
intention)—by which he meant the type of piece invented by Haydn and further developed by Mozart and Beethoven—was "the highest form of instrumental music."[5] As such, it was—and could only be—for Fink a purely
German phenomenon.

Unlike the laconic and technically worded entry by A. B. Marx that
appeared the following year, Fink's remarks are worth dwelling on for the
image they give of the symphony in the decades after Beethoven. For the
symphony, Fink set extremely, almost impossibly, elevated standards that
emphasized organicism and coherence:

> It is absolutely necessary that the great symphony have as its essence,
> and in considerable abundance, the greatest potential for development,
> as does the morning dream before awakening. Thus, that which music
> alone has—melody; rhythm; harmony; character; the roundedness of
> an autonomous whole; shapes that are clear, well-formed and beautiful,
> even uniquely magical and stimulating; the setting into motion of these
> shapes—all this must be present in the highest degree within and for
> the symphony, like a life force that is ever bubbling and richly vital. All
> these things must intertwine and grow from one another without effort,
> as if by chance. They must support each other mutually, they must
> strengthen, necessitate, and condition each other until the fruit, which
> must be nutritious and refreshing, is ripe.[6]

Fink goes on to discuss many other standards and qualities that the symphony must uphold. Above all, the great symphony must be on an appropriately grand scale. Following the opera analogy of Hoffmann, Fink suggests that
the instrumental effects of a symphony must be like set designs in theater:

> There is no place for small decorations, suited to domestic paintings,
> nor for tiny, delicate figures, which in miniature paintings are exceed-

ingly pleasing. Everything must be cast more grandly, as if it were making its effect from the stage down toward listeners who are always eager
for a show and do not value, or even notice, that which lacks far-reaching impact.[7]

In other words, the symphony is fundamentally a public work, one that must
project across the proscenium.

But Fink also acknowledged what he called the *Doppelansicht*, the double aspect, of the symphony. On the one hand, the symphony is public and
large-scale, like an opera; on the other, it is like a "dramatized, well-paced
sentimental novel":

> It is a tale, developed with psychological coherence and told in tones. It
> is a dramatically developed story that captures a particular state of mind
> shared by a large group. Stimulated by some main impulse, it expresses
> their common essential feeling individually—in all respects like a repre-
> sentative democracy—through an instrument absorbed into the whole.[8]

With his characterization of the double aspect, Fink's article points up
quite neatly what came to be two almost contradictory impulses within composers of the post-Beethoven generation: on the one hand, a kind of operatic
grandioseness—what Carl Dahlhaus has called the monumental style[9]—and
on the other, romantic individualism. Few composers managed to balance the
two impulses in symphonic composition. It is no surprise that in the 1830s
and 1840s many turned away from symphonies, or at least found more congenial the realm of piano miniatures and lieder, the intimate Romantic art
forms par excellence. According to research by F. E. Kirby, the number of
symphonies published in the Austro-German sphere declined dramatically
across the first half of the nineteenth century, from 50 in the decade
1800–1809, to 20 in the decade 1830–1839, with only a slight increase to 23
in the years 1840–1849.[10]

In 1839, only one year after the appearance of Fink's article, Robert
Schumann reviewed in the *Neue Zeitschrift für Musik* works by three young
symphonists: Gottfried Preyer, Karl Gottlieb Reißiger, and Franz Lachner. His
article shows only too clearly the situation of the German symphony at the
time. "When the German speaks of symphonies, he means Beethoven," he
wrote. "The two names are for him one and indivisible—his joy, his pride."[11]
Schumann went on to observe that many contemporary composers rarely rise
above imitation of Beethoven, especially of his early symphonies:

We find many too close imitations, but very, very seldom, with few exceptions, any true maintenance or mastery of this sublime form in which, bound in a spiritual union, continually changing ideas succeed one another. The great number of recent symphonies drop into the overture style, especially in their first movements; the slow movements are there because slow movements are required; the scherzos have nothing of the scherzo about them save the name; the last movements completely forgot what the former ones contained.[12]

What Schumann identifies here seems to be precisely the lack of the more organic, coherent, large-scale great symphony called for by Fink and embodied in Beethoven's works. For Schumann, the new works by the three young composers are "sonatas for orchestra" rather than genuine symphonies in a Finkian sense. Schumann goes mercilessly through Reißiger's symphony, pointing out not only the echoes of Beethoven but reminiscences of Spohr, Mendelssohn, Bach, and Mozart. Lachner's work comes in for a more positive assessment. Indeed, Schumann is encouraged to say that Lachner "seeks to move forward on the path toward the ideal of a modern symphony, which after Beethoven's departure is destined to be arranged according to a new norm. Long live the German symphony and may it blossom and thrive anew!"[13]

It is not clear just what Schumann had in mind by the "new norm" according to which the symphony was henceforth to be shaped. As Jon Finson has observed, in the 1839 article Schumann mentions only two composers he felt had the ability to continue the symphonic tradition: Berlioz, to whose *Symphonie fantastique* Schumann had devoted an extensive analysis in 1835, and Schubert, whose "Great" C-Major Symphony he had unearthed some months earlier and about which he was to write in a famous article of 1840.[14] Neither of these figures, however, was destined to become the savior of the symphony. Schubert was, of course, long since dead; and after the *Symphonie fantastique* of 1830 Berlioz moved off in directions that led him far away from traditional symphonic composition. (And, of course, Berlioz was not German, though Schumann obviously thought well enough of his work to give him a kind of honorary status in the *Davidsbund*.) Thus, despite the praise accorded Lachner, to read Schumann's review in conjunction with Fink's article is to understand that in 1840 the symphony was indeed in something of a sad state, dominated mainly by epigones, or pale imitators, of Beethoven.

Schumann's own special double aspect, as both critic and composer, makes him at once a witness to, and an example of, this situation. Schumann had sketched some symphonic movements as early as 1829, only two years after Beethoven's death; at this time he was strongly under the spell of the master's symphonies, which he had heard in Dresden and Leipzig.[15] During the years 1832–33 he composed portions of a symphony in G minor, whose first movement met with some success when it was performed at the Leipzig Gewandhaus.[16] But Schumann turned away from the genre of symphony and toward piano music. He created, over the next nine years, his most famous cycles of character pieces, including *Carnaval* and *Davidsbündlertänze*, as well as song cycles like *Dichterliebe*. Only in the 1840s, not long after the review cited above, did he return actively to the genre of the symphony, in part out of a desire to create what among connoisseurs like Fink (and those of Schumann's own imaginary *Davidsbund*) was still considered to be the highest form of instrumental music.[17]

During the decade 1841 to 1850—and beyond, if one takes into account later revisions or retouchings—Schumann created his four mature symphonies, in which he engaged fundamentally and profoundly with the task of symphonic composition.[18] This is not the place for a survey of these pieces, but it might be said that, as splendid as they all are, perhaps only the Second— with its close interrelationship among movements and its clear and powerful sequence of ideas unfolding through the symphony as a whole—fulfills all the conditions of the great symphony.[19] In this work Schumann is able to mediate successfully between the public and private, the two sides of the double aspect, in ways that are fully satisfying. As such, Schumann's Second may stand as the finest symphony between Schubert's Ninth and Brahms's First.

The Symphonic "Crisis" at Midcentury

If Schumann himself went at least part way toward helping to create the "new norm" and to maintain the high standard of the symphony, what happened next? Kirby tabulates only nineteen new symphonies published in the Austro-German realm in the decade 1850–59, the lowest number in any ten-year period in the century.[20] It is striking to see that as late as 1890 a widely read reference work, Mendel's *Konversations-Lexicon*, implies that the genre virtually dried up after 1850. The article "Symphony" effectively ends its discussion with Schumann; in a very brief final paragraph, the author mentions Brahms as being among the "younger" Romantics who have composed in the genre. There is no discussion of Brahms's works and no mention at all of Bruckner, Dvořák, or Tchaikovsky, all of whom had composed the major part of their symphonic oeuvre by 1890.[21]

Although the viewpoint represented by this article is, to say the least, odd, it does seem to acknowledge a kind of symphonic black hole immediately after 1850. Dahlhaus has taken up this notion, suggesting that the symphony indeed entered a "crisis" at midcentury, evidenced by the fact that Schumann's Third Symphony of 1850, chronologically his last, is separated by almost twenty years "from any work of distinction that represented absolute rather than programmatic music." The period of decline was to be reversed only in the 1870s and 1880s, Dahlhaus observes, with the advent of Bruckner, Brahms, Tchaikovsky, Borodin, Dvořák, and Franck, in whose collective hands the symphony "entered a 'second age' whose legacy still continues to dominate a large part of the concert repertoire even today."[22]

It may seem a dubious historiographic practice to identify a "crisis" point for the symphony. People, composers, and perhaps even institutions can undergo crises; but how can an inanimate genre like the symphony have one? Siegfried Kross has disputed the crisis-and-rebirth picture, arguing that Dahlhaus has merely identified as a "second age" of the symphony the one dominated by those works that occupy concert programs in our own century:

> It is problematic when a history of genre equates the symphonies that determine today's repertory with "works of distinction." We must take into account the obvious randomness of such repertory formation and consider whether among the pieces that haven't been studied, or among those that have been supplanted in the market place by newer ones, we might yet find works of aesthetic distinction, whose absorption or even reabsorption into the repertory would be an undertaking as praiseworthy as it would be historically necessary.[23]

A scan of music periodicals and bibliographic sources reveals, not surprisingly, that the number of new symphonies was far smaller than that of new piano, chamber, and choral works, which poured forth from publishing houses at an astounding rate during the period 1850–75. Yet Kross is right to observe that there was no real shortage of new symphonies written and played. Indeed, Kirby shows that the number of Germanic symphonies increased significantly across the latter part of the century, from a low of 19 in the years 1850–59, to 33 in the years 1860–69, to 43 in the years 1870–79, to a high of 52 in the years 1880–89 (the most of any decade in the century), before another decline to 30 occurred in the years 1890–99.[24]

Table 1–1, based on my own research (the quantitative numbers do not always tally with those of Kirby), lists the symphonies by contemporary composers published in the Austro-German sphere during the quarter century extending between the appearances of Schumann's Third and Brahms's First Symphonies. Although forgotten today, some of the more popular ones made the rounds of regular public and court orchestras in Austria and Germany. It is out of this immediate musical context that Brahms's symphonies grew.

(text continued on page 11)

TABLE 1–1
Symphonies 1851–1877

A chronological listing of symphonies by contemporary composers published in the Austro-German sphere in the period between Schumann's Third and Brahms's First.*

1851

H. F. Kufferath (1818–96): Symphony, Op. 15, C Major
Robert Schumann (1810–56): Symphony No. 3, Op. 97, E♭ Major
Wilhelm Taubert (1811–91): Symphony, Op. 69, F Major

1852

Niels Gade (1817–90): Symphony No. 5, Op. 25, D Minor
Georg Goltermann (1825–98): Symphony, Op. 20, A Major
Richard Wüerst (1824–81): Prize Symphony, Op. 21, F Major

1853

Ludwig Spohr (1784–1859): Symphony No. 9 ("Die Jahreszeiten"), Op. 143, B Minor
J. J. H. Verhulst (1816–91): Symphony, Op. 46, E Minor

1854

Heinrich Esser (1818–72): Symphony, Op. 44, D Minor
Ludwig Spohr: Symphony No. 8, Op. 137, G Major

1855

Franz Lachner (1803–90): Symphony, Op. 100, G Minor
Fritz Spindler (1817–1905): Symphony, Op. 60, B Minor
Hugo Ulrich (1827–72): Symphony, Op. 6, B minor; *Symphonie triomphale*, Op. 9

1857

Niels Gade: Symphony No. 6, Op. 32, G Minor
Julius Rietz (1812–77): Symphony No. 3, Op. 31, E♭ Major
Joseph Street: Symphony No. 1, Op. 4, E♭ Major
Wilhelm Taubert: Symphony, Op. 113, C Minor

1858
Anton Rubinstein (1829–94): Symphony No. 2, "Océan," Op. 42, C Major

1859
Anton Rubinstein: Symphony No. 1, Op. 40, F Major

1860
Ferdinand Gleich (1816–98): Symphony, Op. 16, D Major
W. H. Veit (1806–64): Symphony, Op. 49, E Major

1861
Salomon Jadassohn (1831–1902): Symphony No. 1, Op. 24, C Major
Franz Liszt (1811–86): A *Faust* Symphony
Ernst Pauer (1826–1905): Symphony No. 1, Op. 50, C Minor

1862
Anton Rubinstein: Symphony No. 3, Op. 56, A Major
Joseph Street: Symphony No. 2, Op. 14, D Major
Richard Wüerst: Symphony No. 3, Op. 38, C Minor

1863
Carl Reinthaler (1822–96): Symphony, Op. 12, D Major
Fritz Spindler: Symphony No. 2, Op. 150, C Minor
Thomas Täglichsbeck (1799–1867): Symphony No. 2, Op. 48, E Major
Robert Volkmann (1815–83): Symphony No. 1, Op. 44, D Minor

1864
F. J. Fétis (1784–1871): Symphony No. 1, E♭ Major; Symphony No. 2, G Minor
Joachim Raff (1822–82): "An das Vaterland," Prize Symphony, Op. 96
Carl Reinecke (1824–1910): Symphony, Op. 79, A Major

1865
J. J. Abert (1832–1915): *Columbus, Musikalisches Seegemälde in Form einer Sinfonie*, Op. 31, D Major
A.W. Dreszer (1843–1907): Symphony No. 1, Op. 3, D♭ Major; Symphony No. 2, Op. 4, C Major
J. L. Ellerton (1801–73): *Wald-Symphonie*, No. 3, Op. 120, D Minor
Ferdinand Hiller (1811–85): Symphony, *Es muss doch Frühling werden*, Op. 67, E Minor
Joseph Huber (1837–86): Symphony No. 1, C Major; Symphony No. 2, C Major

1866
Woldemar Bargiel (1828–97): Symphony, Op. 30, C Major

1867
J. M. Coenen (1824–99): Symphony, B Minor
Ferdinand Vogel (1807–92): Symphony No. 1, C Minor
Robert Volkmann: Symphony No. 2, Op. 53, B♭ Major

1868

Richard Hol (1825–1904): Symphony, Op. 44, D Minor
Eduard Lassen (1830–1904): Symphony, D Major
J. S. Svendsen (1840–1911): Symphony, Op. 4, D Major

1869

Joachim Raff: Symphony No. 2, Op. 140, C Major
Georg Vierling (1820–1901): Symphony, Op. 33, C Major
Richard Wüerst: Symphony, Op. 54, D Minor

1870

Max Bruch (1838–1920): Symphony No. 1, Op. 28, E♭; Symphony No. 2, Op. 36,
     F Minor
Albert Dietrich (1829–1908): Symphony, Op. 20, D Minor
Heinrich Esser: Symphony, Op. 79, B Minor
Isidor Rosenfeld: Symphony, Op. 20, F Major

1871

J. J. Abert: Symphony, C Minor
Joachim Raff: Symphony No. 3, *Im Walde*, Op. 153, F Major
Julius Zellner (1832–1900): Symphony, Op. 7, F Major

1872

Niels Gade: Symphony No. 8, Op. 47, B Minor
C. G. P. Grädener (1812–83): Symphony, Op. 25, C Minor
Joachim Raff: Symphony No. 4, Op. 167, G Minor

1873

Joachim Raff: *Leonore* Symphony, Op. 177, E Major

1874

Julius Benedict (1804–85): Symphony, Op. 101, G Minor
August Klughardt (1847–1902): Symphony No. 1, Op. 27
Richard Metzdorff (1844–1919): Symphony No. 1, Op. 16, F Major
Joachim Raff: Symphony No. 6, Op. 189, D Minor

1875

Felix Draeseke (1835–1913): Symphony, Op. 12, G Major
Friedrich Gernsheim (1839–1916): Symphony, Op. 32, G Minor
Hermann Götz (1840–76): Symphony, Op. 9, F Major
Julius Otto Grimm (1827–1903): Symphony, Op. 19, D Minor
Heinrich Hofmann (1842–1902): Symphony (*Frithjof*), Op. 22, E♭ Major
Carl Reinecke: Symphony No. 2 (*Hakon Jarl*), Op. 134, C Minor
Anton Rubinstein: Symphony No. 4 (*Dramatique*), Op. 95, D Minor

1876

Joseph Huber: Symphony No. 3 (*Durch Dunkel zum Licht*), Op. 10, E Minor
Salomon Jadassohn: Symphony No. 3, Op. 50, D Minor
Joachim Raff: Symphony No. 7 (*In den Alpen*), Op. 201, B Major
Joseph Rheinberger (1839–1901): Symphony, Op. 87, F Major
Philipp Rüfer (1844–1919): Symphony, Op. 23, F Major

1877

Johannes Brahms (1833–97): Symphony No. 1, Op. 68, C Minor
Carl Goldmark (1830–1915): Symphony (*Ländliche Hochzeit*), Op. 26, E♭ Major
Arnold Krug (1849–1904): Symphony, Op. 9, C Major
Joachim Raff: Symphony No. 8 (*Frühlingsklänge*), Op. 205, A Major

---

* By "contemporary" composers I mean primarily those who were active in the period and whose works were published shortly after composition and/or performance. But I have also included some figures, like Ludwig Spohr, whose symphonies were published well after their creation. My table includes a number of foreign composers (Dutch, Scandinavian, English, French) whose works were issued by the publishing houses of Austria and Germany in this period.

The dates given are those of publication, which are easier to gather than those of performance but are also difficult to confirm. Many printed scores are unavailable and, in any case, bear no dates of imprint. For this table I have relied primarily on Wilhelm Altmann, *Orchester-Literatur-Katalog*, 2nd ed. (Leipzig: Leuckart, 1926), supplemented by information from other bibliographic sources. (Where possible I have sought to provide birth and death dates for the composers included in the table.) Altmann includes publication dates for parts, scores, and four-hand arrangements of symphonies. In each case in my table, I give the earliest date of publication of a symphony in one of these three forms.

Altmann's dates frequently conflict with those given in some other standard sources, including *Musik in Geschichte und Gegenwart* and *The New Grove Dictionary;* I have opted for Altmann for the sake of consistency. In addition to Altmann and the standard dictionaries, useful sources are the supplementary volumes (*Ergänzungs Bände*) of Adolf Hofmeister's *Handbuch der musikalischen Literatur*, which appeared every eight years during this period: 1852, 1860, 1868, and 1876. Because they include works published during the eight-year period without further specification of date, the Hofmeister volumes cannot be used to pinpoint publication.

For further bibliographic information on the publication of symphonies in Germany in the nineteenth century, as well as a quantitative table arranged by decade, see F. E. Kirby, "The Germanic Symphony of the Nineteenth Century: Genre, Form, Instrumentation, Expression," *Journal of Musicological Research* 14 (1995): esp. p. 197 and fn. 24.

In my table I have included only those works published as "symphonies," that is, with "symphony" in the title. This includes some works with programmatic or poetic titles and necessarily (and somewhat arbitrarily) excludes symphonic poems and other symphony-like program works. Such works are listed under a separate category in the catalogues of Hofmeister and Altmann. The bibliographic uncertainties involved in pigeonholing works as "symphonies" or "symphonic poems" reflect the genuine historiographic ambiguities surrounding the two genres at midcentury.

Kross is justified in calling for precise, or at least well-developed, historical-critical criteria before positing a symphonic corpus of "distinction." But the simple truth is that repertory or canon formation is not a result of "obvious randomness." With the great symphony, as with virtually every other genre of art music, it seems almost always to be the best music—which is what I take to be the meaning of Dahlhaus's phrase *work of distinction*—that tends to survive its own day. Of course, the use of *best* opens up further ambiguities. By "best" I mean the music that most successfully fulfills the conditions and demands created, either explicitly or implicitly, by the genre, form, and history. As we shall see in the brief examination of the symphonies by Max Bruch at the end of this chapter, there may be good aesthetic and historical grounds for separating the Bruchs from the Brahmses and the Bruckners, however much the scores of all three composers, as well as those of Klughardt and Reinecke, are entitled to space on the shelf of a responsible historiographer.

Moreover, it is important to reiterate that the act of valuation or canonization, which in turn leads to repertory formation, began not in our own century, as Kross would seem to imply, but at least as early as the 1830s. The symphonies of Beethoven became the standard by which others would be measured; from this point on they never left the active concert repertory. Thus, they maintained a continuous aesthetic and historical presence throughout the nineteenth century; they were supplemented, rather than replaced, by the later symphonic achievements of Schubert, Mendelssohn, and Schumann.[25]

A post-Schumann doldrum or decline in the symphony is not an invention of the twentieth century, but was acknowledged repeatedly by critics of the 1850–75 period in such journals as the *Neue Zeitschrift für Musik* and the *Allgemeine musikalische Zeitung*. The how-can-anyone-do-anything-after-Beethoven comments made by Schumann in his above-cited 1839 review, as well as the standards implied by Fink's article of 1838, echoed forcefully and cumulatively down through the decades. By the 1850s, any aspiring symphonic composer was made to drag behind him an impossibly heavy tradition. "The creation of a symphony nowadays," said one anonymous critic reviewing a symphony by Heinrich Esser (1818–72) in the *Neue Zeitschrift* in 1855, "is a rock on which, with only a few exceptions, most composers suffer a complete shipwreck."[26] In the opinion of the reviewer, Esser was definitely to be counted among the wrecked.

And here is how, in the *Allgemeine musikalische Zeitung* of 1863, a critic (identified only as "a") began what was essentially a positive review of a symphony by Carl Reinthaler (1822–96):

Has the symphony made "progress" since Beethoven? Has the formal aspect of this genre been expanded? Has the content been made greater, more significant in the sense in which we can say Beethoven did in relation to Mozart? All things considered—including everything subjectively new and therefore epoch-making that Schubert, Mendelssohn, and Schumann have created—the answer to this question is no.[27]

The critic continues for a full paragraph about how easy it is for composers to become mere epigones of the masters. Only then does he go on to single out for praise many aspects of Reinthaler's symphony. In 1867 the same critic ended another basically favorable review, this time of Robert Volkmann's Second Symphony, with these patronizing remarks:

We are convinced that in Beethoven the "symphony" reached its high point in spiritual and technical quality. Yet it pleases us when the best talents of today test their wings even in this difficult form and thereby at least manage to create something interesting and pretty.[28]

One can only wonder how Reinthaler and Volkmann must have felt having the symphonic deck not only stacked against them in this way but shuffled in their very faces. The situation seems not to have improved significantly by 1871, when the critic Hermann Deiters held up a new Symphony in D Minor, op. 20, by Albert Dietrich (1829–1908) as a kind of lone beacon shining over the symphonic waters: "Even the decision to write a symphony, and the fortunate outcome of this decision, must be reckoned a noteworthy event. As is well known, our era is not rich in pieces of instrumental music in the forms inherited from the classical period."[29] It is no surprise that many young composers, reading reviews like these, steered clear of the symphonic shoals altogether, charting instead a course in the more tranquil areas of chamber music and song.

THE ALTERNATIVE OF PROGRAM MUSIC

There were other, safer harbors for those Austro-German composers at mid-century wanting to write orchestral music but avoid the great symphony. Overtures, serenades, and orchestral suites were plentiful; Brahms himself tested the symphonic waters with two serenades in the late 1850s. But the most prestigious and visible alternative was program music. The years around 1850 saw not only an apparent decline in the genre of the symphony, but also the appearance of the ambitious and influential "symphonic poems" of Franz Liszt, who had established himself in Germany at the court of Weimar in 1848. Over the next decade he produced a series of twelve symphonic poems, which inspired not only countless such works among his followers but also much polemical critical and aesthetic writing.

The essence of the works emanating from Liszt and his circle is that they are based on a poetic, literary, mythical, or historical source, which is often given as a title or epigraph, or discussed in a preface, and of which the listener is supposed to be aware. Liszt was himself not interested in tone painting. Nor does his music seek to narrate a story or event, or to recreate in musical language what has been said in the original literary text; this much is clear from important contemporary statements on program music, including Wagner's 1857 "open letter" on Liszt's symphonic poems.[30] Liszt and his followers saw the symphonic poem, with its uniting of the "poetic" and the "musical," as the outcome of, and a more elevated stage in, the development of the traditional great symphony.[31]

These viewpoints color unmistakably the criticism in the *Neue Zeitschrift*, which was edited from 1845 to 1868 by the most prominent spokesman of the Liszt circle, Franz Brendel. (It was Brendel who at the end of the 1850s would coin the term *New German School* to describe the group.) In the journal in December 1854, Peter Cornelius, a composer-critic in Liszt's orbit, used a review of a prize-winning symphony by a young composer named Richard Wüerst as a platform for a new aesthetics of the symphony. Identifying what was already becoming the most important and divisive musical-aesthetic debate in German-speaking lands, Cornelius observed that the musical world was now divided into two parties:

> For one, music is a fantastic play with tones according to laws of harmony and aesthetics that are derived from the specifically musical works of Haydn, Mozart and Beethoven. . . . According to this party, music should make its effect only through itself, without the mediation of secondary ideas. . . .
> The other party sees the music left to it by the great masters as language shaped by poetry, in which they speak, and whose capacity for representation they wish to exploit; this party sees in it a created world in which man and the poetic idea wander.[32]

As might be imagined, poor Wüerst gets fried by Cornelius, who fully admits being of the "second" party. He remains "critical of Wüerst's symphony and the recognition it has received, not because it has no program, but because we neither feel the urge to find, nor envision the possibility of finding, one for it." Only by filling his skillfully crafted forms with "poetic content" can Wüerst hope to rise from his status as composer to that of "tone poet."[33]

Though he is not mentioned by name, Eduard Hanslick is clearly a target in Cornelius's review. In the same year, 1854, Hanslick had virtually written the platform for the "first" party in his pamphlet *Vom Musikalisch-Schönen* (usually translated as *On the Beautiful in Music*). The term *specifically musical* (*spezifisch-musikalisches*) used by Cornelius was coined by Hanslick, who argued that by its very nature music can never represent precisely feelings or emotions. Whatever the sources of inspiration for a piece of music, whatever images it may in turn evoke in listeners, its actual "content" or essence can be only "forms set in motion by sounding" (*tönend bewegte Formen*).[34] According to Hanslick:

> The instrumental composer does not give a thought to the portraying of any definite content; or if he does, his attitude is mistaken and 'paramusical' rather than musical, in which case his work will be the translation into music of some programme unintelligible to those who do not possess the key.[35]

It is critical to reiterate that the dividing line between program and absolute music was by no means as obvious in reality as it came to seem in the midcentury polemics. As has been shown by Dahlhaus, Walter Wiora, Ludwig Finscher, and, more recently, Anthony Newcomb, there are many grey areas in actual compositional practice.[36] From Vivaldi to Mahler and beyond, countless symphonic works, whether overtly "programmatic" or not, have been inspired (or encumbered) by epigraphs, titles, poems, stories, images, and other things verbal or visual.

To take one significant example from the period under discussion: Schumann's Third Symphony, in many respects a paradigm of the "great" symphony, was from the very first understood by critics as a work seeking to capture the spirit of the Rhine. Though he did not provide the nickname "Rhenish," Schumann himself described the symphony in a letter as "perhaps reflecting here and there a piece of life" on the Rhine.[37] One of the earliest reviews, from 1851, picks up this vocabulary, characterizing the symphony as "a piece of Rhenish life in bright gaiety." There is little question that the fourth (or "extra") movement in E♭ minor, with its broad pacing, choralelike themes, plagal cadences, powerful suspensions, and fugal textures, was informed by one of Schumann's most profound Rhenish experiences of the years around 1850: the sight of the Cologne cathedral. At the premiere of the symphony, the movement had a heading provided by Schumann—"In the character of an accompaniment to a solemn ceremony"—to which the critic cited above responded, "We see Gothic cathedrals, processions, imposing figures in the choir stalls." With all these extramusical associations, is Schumann's Third to be understood as "program" music, or not? As with so many works, the questions cannot and should not be answered simply.

To focus an image of the symphony at midcentury becomes still more complicated when one is aware that the followers of the Mendelssohn-Schumann tradition and the followers of the newer Lisztian one were not alone in claiming the legacy of the Beethovenian great symphony. The years around 1850 saw not only the composition of Schumann's Third and Liszt's symphonic poems but also the writing of *Opera and Drama*, the famous treatise in which Richard Wagner proclaimed the death of the traditional symphony altogether. Wagner declared that after Beethoven's Ninth, which resorts to the use of words in the finale, no further symphonies in the traditional mould could be written; rather, absolute music would have to be "redeemed" in the music drama.[38] Over the next quarter century—in fact, almost exactly the period between Schumann's Third and Brahms's First Symphonies—Wagner set out to create just that kind of music drama with his *Ring des Nibelungen* cycle, begun in 1848 and completed in 1876. It has been suggested that it may have been the premiere of the *Ring* at Bayreuth in 1876 that encouraged Brahms to complete at last his First Symphony, in order to reclaim the Beethovenian symphonic mantle.

THE SYMPHONIC STYLE

Amidst the bewildering variety and diversity of claimants, we may ask who *was* the real inheritor of the German great symphony after 1850: figures like Dietrich and Esser; the titans Liszt and Wagner; or, later, Brahms or Bruckner? The answer is: each of these figures. For as Dahlhaus has suggested, the "symphonic style" became more important for the legacy than the symphony as a specific form or genre. This style, derived essentially from the works of Beethoven, became grafted onto works other than "symphonies" in the strict sense, including the music drama and the symphonic poem.[39]

Because it also affects the composition and the reception of virtually all symphonies after 1850, this symphonic style deserves some discussion here. First, the style may be said to involve the dimensions of a work or a move-

ment. The expanded structures of Beethoven, in such works as the "Eroica"
or Ninth Symphonies, became the standard by which many symphonic works
would be measured. Commentators at midcentury would often remark on
whether the scale of a movement was sufficient for its symphonic context. To
take a prominent example: the middle movements of Brahms's First Symphony were criticized by the conductors Hermann Levi and Otto Dessoff and
by a Dresden critic as being too slight for their setting.[40]

Related to sheer dimension is the less readily tangible—but ultimately
more significant—aspect of what Dahlhaus calls the "monumental" style, in
which the presentation of musical ideas is intimately bound up with the
orchestral medium. One famous example of this phenomenon, adduced by
Dahlhaus, is the opening of the first movement of Beethoven's Ninth, which
is fundamentally unrealizable on the piano or in a chamber ensemble. In the
monumental style, he observes, "the medium that is drawn upon is made to
appear as the function of an aesthetic idea."[41]

Another important aspect of the symphonic style is that of thematic and
motivic processes. The notion of *thematische Arbeit*, or thematic working,
lies at the very heart of the Austro-German musical language from the
Viennese Classical era onward. In symphonic music, a high value was
placed by critics not only on the quality and the development of individual
themes within movements but also on thematic unity or relationships that act
as a binding force for an entire work. Perhaps the most famous early example of thematic criticism of this kind is E. T. A. Hoffmann's 1810 review of
Beethoven's Fifth Symphony. Hoffmann spends much time praising and analyzing the four-note basic motive from which Beethoven builds the first
movement: "There is no simpler motive than that on which the master based
the entire Allegro. With great admiration, one becomes aware that Beethoven
knew how to relate all secondary ideas and all transition passages through
the rhythm of that simple motive."[42] Later on, Hoffmann remarks on "the
intimate relationship of the individual themes to one another which produces
the unity that firmly maintains a single feeling in the listener's heart."[43]

Reviews of symphonies in the two and a half decades that precede
Brahms's First make it clear that the principles articulated by Hoffmann and
other earlier writers were still operative, and, indeed, came to be upheld
more rigidly and restrictively. The result was a kind of stranglehold on symphonic composers. Each new symphony was scrutinized—and often criticized—according to criteria that included the quality of its individual
themes; their suitability to a symphonic movement; the effectiveness of the

thematic work, including motivic development and counterpoint; and the unity or coherence demonstrated by the work as a whole.

In a review of Carl Reinecke's A-Major Symphony, the curmudgeonly critic "a," already cited above, prints the main theme—extensive musical examples were common in both the *Neue Zeitschrift* and the *Allgemeine musikalische Zeitung*—and then proceeds to trash it: "The reader will hardly dispute that this theme is more a figure or a piece of passage-work than a real 'theme'. . . . We cannot regard it as a proper theme for the first movement of a symphony. Perhaps it would have been suited for an overture."[44]

Reviewing Eduard Lassen's D-Major Symphony for the *Neue Zeitschrift* in 1869, Emanuel Klitzsch was somewhat more tolerant of what he took to be weak thematic ideas, but he firmly upheld the standards of symphonic development. He confessed to finding Lassen's themes "not particularly new or striking" in invention. Nonetheless, "as regards the grouping of the main ideas, their development and the subsidiary motives with which they are intertwined, this movement fulfills all the conditions that one is accustomed to expect from the first movement of a symphony."

Even when most of the main elements of the symphonic style were in place, critics could find reasons to carp. In the *Allgemeine musikalische Zeitung* in 1871, Selmar Bagge found a new symphony by Julius Zellner to be sufficiently deft in orchestration, poetic in mood, noble in demeanor, and solid in thematic working. "Yet," he said—and the reader of the present chapter can guess what kind of judgment follows this conjunction—"we believe we may not withhold our opinion that the work seems not really rich enough, its form occasionally not plastic enough, for a *symphony*, the highest genre of instrumental music."[45]

In a sense, all these critics are identifying a situation, and are articulating a value, that Dahlhaus has labeled a "problem" for composers in the symphonic style after Beethoven: how to create effective large forms out of a very small amount of basic thematic material. In Beethoven, Dahlhaus claims, there remained an ideal balance between the formal structure and the individual musical "idea" or basic inspiration. But after Beethoven, musical form became less a "system of formal relations" than "a consequence drawn from thematic ideas."[46] The composers who could best cope with the larger instrumental forms were those who could draw those consequences with the greatest logic and coherence. This "problem" is, of course, somewhat oversimplified, but as we have seen, critics of the mid–nineteenth century were well aware of its existence.

SOCIAL AND INSTITUTIONAL ASPECTS

The notion of symphonic style is useful not only for an understanding of the compositional-technical aspects of the symphony and how they were perceived by critics, but also for exploring the broader aesthetic and sociological dimensions, which are equally important in establishing a background for Brahms's symphonies. As Dahlhaus has shown, symphonic style—and the symphony itself—were powerful expressions of the "autonomy" principle of music that came to dominate the nineteenth century. Essentially, the autonomy principle posited a purely contemplative aesthetic experience that was free of any external or extramusical ties.[47]

The autonomy principle became the leading aesthetic value for the educated middle classes (*Bildungsbürgertum*) in the nineteenth century. This group, which included scholars, doctors, merchants, and others, was the social core that supported the symphony concert as an institution. For them, the symphonic style represented the highest, noblest, and purest form of art. The historian William Weber has labeled this phenomenon "musical idealism," which created "the pantheon of great composers against whose music . . . all new works had to be judged."[48] It is in the context of, and as a result of, the desire of the bourgeoisie to cultivate autonomous or idealist music that public concert institutions grew.

As is well known, Beethoven and Schubert had no regular orchestra or public for their symphonies. Each symphonic, or mixed, concert had to be planned individually, with money raised for the players and the hall. The most famous such concert of the early nineteenth century was that at which the premiere of Beethoven's Ninth Symphony took place, in May 1824.

By the 1830s a more permanent situation began to evolve in each of the major cities of Germany and Austria, a process that extended well into the latter half of the century. In Vienna, the Gesellschaft der Musikfreunde had been presenting orchestral concerts since its founding in 1812; a new hall specifically intended as a public performance space was completed for the Gesellschaft in 1870. In 1842 the Vienna Philharmonic began concerts under its first director, Otto Nicolai.[49] In Berlin, there were at midcentury a number of private orchestras, or *Kapellen,* one of which, the Bilse Kapelle, was founded in 1867 and became the Berlin Philharmonic Orchestra in 1882. In Hamburg, the founding of the Philharmonic Society in 1828 led to the formation of a professional orchestra. In Leipzig, the concerts of the Gewandhaus dated well back in the eighteenth century and reached a new prestigious status with the appointment of Felix Mendelssohn as director in 1835. In Cologne, a Concert Society was formed in 1827.

For the concert hall, and for the educated public that filled it, more demanding music tended now to be written, music of aesthetic autonomy that, as Alexander Ringer has pointed out, depended for its understanding on repeated performances. Ringer observes:

> Beethoven's works made intellectual and emotional demands on musicians and audiences alike that no single performance was likely to satisfy. Conversely, once repeat performances became standard practice, composers felt free to require even greater efforts on the part of all concerned. The result was an expanding repertory of concert works written for large paying audiences whose members were not necessarily as well informed as their noble predecessors.[50]

Included in this expanded repertory are the works of Mendelssohn, Schubert, and Schumann as well as the later symphonists Brahms and Bruckner.

One ironic but far-reaching result of the emphasis on repeated hearings was that, from 1830 on, orchestras tended increasingly to fill programs with older works, leaving little room for the genuinely new. This process is, of course, that of canon formation, of making the concert hall into a museum for the preservation and contemplation of great works of the past, rather than a platform for new compositions.[51]

In Berlin in 1848, Christoph-Hellmut Mahling points out, only three new symphonies were played, while there were fifty-three performances of symphonies by Beethoven (from among the First through Eighth), twenty-six of Haydn, and twenty of Mozart.[52] A similar situation prevailed in Vienna, where Hanslick reported that in a hundred Gesellschaft concerts given between 1815 and 1830 the symphonies of Beethoven and Mozart dominated; only a handful of symphonies by new composers were premiered.[53] Things had not changed much a quarter century later: in the 1852–53 season, in eight Gesellschaft concerts, there were three symphonies by Beethoven, three by Mendelssohn, one by Mozart, and only one by a living composer, none other than the above-mentioned—and shipwrecked—Heinrich Esser.[54] In the second volume of Hanslick's history of Viennese concert life, which covers the two decades 1848–68, only ten new symphonies are reviewed.[55]

By 1870, the situation had evolved in Austria and Germany to the point that Chrysander could comment regretfully in the *Allgemeine musikalische*

Zeitung on inequities in the reception of what he deemed two worthy symphonies completed in 1868, the Symphony in D Major by Eduard Lassen (already mentioned above) and the Symphony No. 1 in E♭, op. 28, by Max Bruch (to which we return below): "The circumstance that the latter found performances rather quickly in the major venues worked somewhat to Lassen's disadvantage, for most of our orchestras believe they have discharged their obligations entirely if they perform one new symphony in a season."[56]

The "crisis" of the symphony at midcentury is thus a complex phenomenon that requires a complex diagnosis taking into account technical, aesthetic, psychological, and sociological dimensions. Many new symphonies were epigonic and of inferior quality; orchestras became gradually less inclined to play new works; and many composers seemed to avoid the genre altogether. The extreme disincentive to compose a great symphony—it might not be played or published, and if it were, it would likely be torn apart by critics—must have discouraged all but the most thick-skinned. In this light, the emergence of Bruckner and Brahms as strong and successful symphonists in the 1870s and 1880s seems all the more remarkable.

BRUCH AND BRUCKNER: A CONTEXT FOR BRAHMS

It is the task of chapters 3 through 6 of the present volume to assess and analyze in detail Brahms's four contributions to the tradition of the great symphony. But to understand how special his achievement was, it may be helpful to assess in more detail the immediate musical background against which he composed. There can, of course, be no such thing as a completely representative symphonic composer—or symphony—from the third quarter of the nineteenth century, the interregnum between Schumann's Third and Brahms's First. Even a "control group" would be difficult to construct persuasively from those listed in table 1–1. But among those composers who shared Brahms's basic aesthetic values and compositional outlook, Max Bruch (1838–1920) might come closest to a "typical" figure. There is even the possibility that Brahms borrowed a symphonic idea or two from Bruch.

Although he was to outlive Brahms by many years, Bruch was a close contemporary. Having studied in his native Rhineland with Ferdinand Hiller, an eminent figure in the Schumann circle, Bruch went on to take a series of positions as music director at Koblenz, Sondershausen, Liverpool, and

Breslau. Bruch moved in many of the same professional circles as Brahms, and they shared a publisher, Fritz Simrock.[57] Although it comprises only fifteen items, the surviving correspondence between Bruch and Brahms extends across thirty years, 1864–94, and suggests a commonality of outlook and experience.[58] In later years Bruch came to resent Brahms's success and often felt snubbed by the more famous composer, who was notorious for letting slip dismissive remarks. Nonetheless, Bruch clearly viewed Brahms as a compositional soulmate. In 1868 Bruch described himself in a letter to Brahms as a *mitstrebender Kunstgenosse*, a mutually striving comrade-in-art.[59] Writing to Simrock in 1890, he remarked wistfully, "I belong to the few who now, along with Brahms, maintain the true, organic essence of music."[60]

Bruch completed the first of his three symphonies, op. 28 in E♭ Major, in 1868; it was given its premiere that summer and published with a dedication ("in friendship") to Johannes Brahms, who also received a copy of the score. Brahms attended the Viennese performance of Bruch's symphony in February 1870 and reported to the composer that "it went really very splendidly."[61] (Brahms characteristically drew a veil of silence about the work itself.) Bruch's Second Symphony, op. 36 in F Minor, dedicated to Joseph Joachim, appeared later that year, in the fall of 1870; this score was also sent to Brahms.[62] Brahms thus saw—and in the case of Bruch's First, definitely heard—both works during the gestation of his own First Symphony. This exposure is significant because there are suggestive points of contact between Brahms's symphonies and Bruch's. (Bruch's Third Symphony, op. 51 in E Major, was written in 1882, considerably after the other two, on a commission from Leopold Damrosch and the Symphony Society of New York.)[63]

A hearing of his symphonies and a study of the scores reveal that Bruch was a genuinely gifted composer and fine craftsman but also that the relative oblivion suffered by these works—in comparison to the canonical status enjoyed by Brahms's symphonies—is no mere historical accident. For all his skill, Bruch lacks in the end a real mastery of the symphonic style, especially the ability to work out or develop musical ideas effectively in the context of sonata or sonata-related forms. It is this balance between individual idea and control of the larger span that can make Brahms so compelling and Bruch so disappointing.

Bruch's First has an opening that in itself is as magnificent and promising as that of any post-Beethoven symphony (ex. 1–1a.). Emanuel Klitzsch reviewing the work in the *Neue Zeitschrift*, rightly called the initial idea "genuinely symphonic" and "significant enough for a first movement that is passionate in content."[64] This theme, emerging in m. 5 from a backdrop of

Example 1–1: Max Bruch, First Symphony, op. 28, I

horns, bassoons, and low strings, begins on the tonic and rises majestical-
ly to the fifth and the tenth, before sinking down through the notes of the
tonic triad to settle on the third. This gesture strikingly anticipates the
"motto" of Brahms's Third Symphony, especially the form that Brahms's
motto takes in the development section of the first movement, where it
appears in the same key of E♭ and has a similar melodic profile (ex. 1–2).
(Bruch's theme is also close in spirit to the opening of Brahms's G-Major Sextet,
op. 36, of 1864.)

Example 1–2: Brahms, Third Symphony, I

The harmonic unfolding of Bruch's main theme is as impressive as its
initial profile. The theme comes to a tidy pause in its eighth measure (m.
11), on the tonic; in the next measure it moves to the dominant, B♭ major,
where by convention we might expect a counterstatement to begin. The
three-note head motive duly appears, only to be sent off on a splendid
detour: after two measures the dominant turns to minor, B♭ minor, which
moves downward by thirds to G♭ major in m. 17 and E♭ in mm. 20–21. A
series of chromatically shifting chords leads eventually back in m. 27 to the
dominant, the starting point of the digression. The dominant harmonies and
the timpani roll on B♭ create (despite the continuing E♭ pedal in the double
basses) a strong build-up toward resolution on the tonic, which arrives in
m. 31. Though Brahms would have had other models in the works of
Schubert, he may well have studied and admired the thirds-related harmonic shifts in Bruch's first theme. The first movement of Brahms's Third
Symphony is built on similar harmonic premises.

The first thirty measures of Bruch's Allegro can hold their own with any
other symphonic opening of the nineteenth century. The problem is what follows. At the cadence to the tonic in m. 31 (ex. 1–1b), Bruch lapses or lurch-
es into a thoroughly ordinary theme, with awkward dotted rhythms and
clumsy cadences. In that it outlines basic tonic and dominant triads, this
theme can be said to be derived from the initial idea; but the relationship is
weak, unmotivated. Bruch has broken the spell of the opening, and the

magic is not regained when the first theme reappears in m. 47, serving as transition to the second group.[65]

For all his talent, Bruch can legitimately be criticized by the standards that were applied, by such critics as those cited above, to symphonic movements of his time. The Allegro disappoints because Bruch fails to do justice to his opening idea; he fails at the kind of thematic work, transformation, and development that lie at the heart of the symphonic style and that Brahms employed so effectively in his own symphonies.

In the *Allgemeine musikalische Zeitung* in 1869, Friedrich Chrysander criticized Bruch's First Symphony rather relentlessly (and, to my mind, excessively) along these lines. The nine-measure opening theme itself was deemed problematic for being too "longwinded" and unmemorable. A shorter initial idea would be more advantageous for the symphonic first movement Bruch is seeking to write in that "it would make easier an organic unfolding and extension."[66] For Chrysander, Bruch's technique of isolating the three-note head motive in later developmental passages gives the entire movement a "somewhat unmotivated roughness, recalcitrance, and abruptness, especially at the very beginning."

The finale of Bruch's Second Symphony, op. 36, highlights more directly than the opening movement of the First the compositional problem identified by Chrysander: how to build a movement, not from a relatively short motive, but from a broad, closed melody. Bruch's spacious main theme (ex. 1–3a), introduced by the strings, extends a full sixteen measures and is then granted a complete counterstatement in the woodwinds. The general cut of the theme, its meter, its opening motive, and its scoring—strings for the first statement, winds for the counterstatement—seem to anticipate directly the main Allegro theme of the finale of Brahms's First. Both themes, moreover, are prefigured motivically before their appearance, Bruch's in eighteen introductory measures leading in from the third movement, Brahms's in a full-fledged slow introduction. As in the case of the motto of his Third Symphony, Brahms may well have had Bruch's music (as well as, of course, the common source, Beethoven's Ninth) in his ear when composing the finale of the First.[67]

Bruch's is indeed a well-crafted melody, in most ways intrinsically as good as Brahms's. (The principal objection one might raise is that in the middle of its consequent phrase, mm. 24–25, it descends into the lower range, to the G below middle C, from which Bruch must then leap abruptly, and awkwardly, up an octave to continue in the original register.) But much as in the opening movement of his First Symphony, Bruch fails to sustain the

Example 1–3: Bruch, Second Symphony, op. 36, IV

level of inspiration. After the 32–measure double presentation, Bruch lapses into dotted rhythms and into figuration that sounds empty, arbitrary (ex.
1–3b). By contrast, Brahms in the finale of the First goes on to build a powerful symphonic structure from the materials of his opening theme.

It may seem that Bruch is being unfairly criticized here for not being
Brahms; after all, no one but Brahms *could* be Brahms. But my main point is
that the symphonic style, as defined above, carried with it certain obligations, or raised certain "problems," that only composers of the very first rank
could meet. Brahms was neither the first nor the only composer after 1850 to
do so. In this regard, it may be useful to conclude this chapter with a brief
consideration of the figure who was to become Brahms's real symphonic
antipode in the Vienna of the 1870s and 1880s, Anton Bruckner (1824–96).

Bruckner's symphonic output is not only larger—and longer—than that of
Brahms, but extends over a much greater portion of his career. His
"Studiensymphonie" in F Minor was completed in 1863, not long after Brahms
had composed the first movement of what was eventually to be his First
Symphony. By the time Brahms managed to complete the First in 1876,
Bruckner had already finished five of his nine numbered symphonies,
although only two had been performed in public and several were yet to under-
go extensive revision.[68] At Bruckner's death in 1896, long after Brahms (and
Bruch) had ceased symphonic composition, his Ninth was still in progress.

Any meaningful comparison of Brahms and Bruckner as symphonists would take us well beyond the scope of the present study.[69] Although each saw himself, and was seen by respective partisans, as the heir to the Viennese symphonic tradition, their aesthetics and compositional styles are very different. Briefly put, what most distinguishes the mature Bruckner—that is, Bruckner from the Second Symphony on—from the Brahms-Bruch tradition is his sense of musical time. For Bruckner, the symphonic sonata form was a vast expanse in which themes were to be set out at a magisterial pace. As such, the symphonic style took on unprecedented dimensions in his works.

As a comparison with the opening of Bruch's First presented as ex. 1–1, we can consider the opening of Bruckner's Fourth in the same key. Bruch's movement, even with the repeat of the exposition, takes just over ten minutes in performance. In scale, this movement is even smaller than most of the comparable symphonic first movements by Brahms. The first movement of Brahms's Second Symphony, his most expansive, takes fourteen to fifteen minutes without a repeated exposition and nineteen to twenty with the repeat (see the timings in table 8–1 in chapter 8). The first movement of Bruckner's Fourth, in which the exposition is not indicated for repetition, clocks in at twenty minutes and is thus twice as long as Bruch's and in some sense a third again as long as the opening Allegro of Brahms's Second.

But beyond clock time, it is experiential time that sets Bruckner apart. In both Bruch and Bruckner, the main theme enters with great self-possession in the horns over a quiet, steady pedal point; both composers are clearly aiming for a "monumental" effect. But there the resemblances end. Bruckner's first theme group comprises two separate ideas (ex. 1–4a and b) that are in themselves very brief, but whose initial unfolding is extended by means of repetition and sequence to seventy-four measures (about two and a half minutes) in a moderate tempo. Where Bruch abandons his principal theme and lapses into aimless figuration, Bruckner sticks determinedly, indeed obsessively, to his material. Not a single measure within the first group is without thematic content. Brahms too tends to adhere closely to his thematic material, but he works, varies, and develops it much more intensively than Bruckner, who relies more on sequence and repetition. Brahms's musical time thus seems more eventful and compressed.

Bruckner's harmony is as expansive and distinctive as his thematic processes. The tonal endpoints of the first group of the Fourth Symphony are conventional: respectively, the tonic, E♭ major, and the dominant of the dominant, F major, which is reached in m. 67 (only to resolve deceptively onto D♭ major in m. 75). In between, the pacing and the scale are broad. Despite

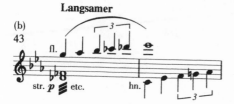

Example 1–4: Bruckner, Fourth Symphony, I

chromatic inflections, the first thirty-two measures remain rooted on the tonic. After a detour that passes through many different harmonic regions, E♭ returns again, *fortissimo*, in m. 51. Here Bruckner begins a still more extensive modulatory journey, which reaches its conclusion with the arrival of F major.

Bruckner's harmonic procedures bear little resemblance to the conventions of the Beethoven-Mendelssohn-Schumann symphonic tradition that Brahms inherited. Although they owe something to Schubert and even more to Wagner, who—together with Beethoven—was Bruckner's great idol, these techniques also represent an idiosyncratic use of what were aptly characterized by the early twentieth-century writer Ernst Kurth as "symphonic waves."[70] It is these waves or wave forms, rather than conventional Classic-Romantic phrase structures and harmonic progressions, that in Bruckner's best music fill the musical space (another Kurthian metaphor) so compellingly.

Given the relatively complex picture of the symphony at midcentury, it may seem naïve to say that Brahms and Bruckner arrived on the scene at the right time. But it is clear—or, as far as Brahms is concerned, should become clear in the following chapters—that they were better equipped than most to grapple with the thematic, harmonic, and formal issues that so preoccupied both composers and critics of the symphonic repertory in the latter half of the nineteenth century.

Chapter 2

BRAHMS'S PATH TO THE SYMPHONY

*A*s has been suggested in the last chapter, from the 1830s on the "symphonic style" came to comprise the most elevated set of compositional procedures and priorities in Austro-German music and as a result penetrated into genres other than the symphony *per se*. In this light, Brahms may be said to have displayed symphonic ambitions and skills early on, even though his actual First Symphony was completed only in his forty-fourth year.

Brahms's first surviving instrumental compositions, written between 1851 and 1853, are three imposing piano sonatas, opp. 1, 2, and 5, and the E♭-minor Scherzo, op. 4. It was the first two sonatas, composed in the reverse order of their eventual publication, that the young Brahms apparently played for the Schumanns upon his arrival in Düsseldorf in the fall of 1853 and to which Schumann referred as "veiled symphonies" in the famous article "Neue Bahnen."[1] By this Schumann probably meant that the sonatas displayed a richness of texture, an intensity of thematic working, and a large-scale approach to form that were characteristic of the symphonic style. Indeed, the first movement of the C-Major Sonata, op. 1, is an expansive sonata form that unfolds with a wide variety of timbres and voicings that are in many respects unpianistic, at least by comparison with much contemporary piano music of the Liszt-Chopin school. It is probably fair to say that the thematic working in this movement is as elaborate and dense as in any sonata since Beethoven.[2]

First Attempts at Orchestral Writing

In "Neue Bahnen" Schumann predicted that Brahms would soon begin to compose for orchestra; in such a context, a prediction is tantamount to a mandate. Brahms's response was characteristically cautious: he began not with the orchestra directly, but with an attempt to unveil some of the symphonic possibilities of his piano music, specifically a two-piano sonata in D minor he had begun shortly after Schumann made his fateful leap into the Rhine on February 27, 1854; three movements appear to have been completed by early April. The medium suggests that Brahms had already found the solo piano too limited to contain his ideas. By the summer, even doubling the forces seemed inadequate; having gotten no further with the new work, Brahms wrote to his friend Joseph Joachim that "two pianos just aren't really sufficient for me."[3]

It may have been largely as a tribute to the now disabled Schumann that Brahms made a decisive turn in the direction his mentor had pointed him the previous year: toward the orchestra. Within a few weeks Brahms set about orchestrating the first movement of the two-piano sonata and turning it into a symphony.[4] But the symphonic medium—and perhaps the demands of the symphonic style—proved not entirely congenial, and by the following winter Brahms found a compromise between his original keyboard work and the symphony: he recast the piece as a piano concerto. During the years 1855–57, the first movement of the work was to evolve into the opening Allegro of the Piano Concerto No. 1 in D Minor, op. 15.

Although there are references in the correspondence and memoirs of the Brahms circle to both prior versions of the concerto, two-piano and symphonic, no manuscript materials or sketches of any kind survive.[5] Thus we can never know precisely what shape Brahms's first projected symphony might have taken. In many respects, it would probably have been similar to the concerto we know today; but much of the symphony was also jettisoned in the process of transformation. The original slow movement of the sonata and would-be symphony was replaced by the present Adagio of the concerto. The original scherzo was set aside entirely—the concerto has none—and later resurfaced in greatly altered form as the second movement of the German Requiem. It would appear, too, that the Rondo finale of the concerto is different from any finale Brahms may have contemplated for the sonata-symphony.

In attempting to reconstruct the basic outlines of the D-minor symphony, Christopher Reynolds has speculated that since its scherzo survived in the German Requiem, other portions of the work may have ended up there as well. He suggests that the Requiem's fourth movement, "Herr, lehre doch mich," which features a baritone soloist, might have originally served, in the same key of D minor, as a choral finale to the symphony. The obvious precedent for such a finale was Beethoven's Ninth, a work to which the concerto as we now know it is still strongly indebted. Reynolds bases his argument on some of the many references to both Clara and Robert Schumann that are musically encoded into the concerto and the Requiem.[6] Reynolds's argument is clever but ultimately unpersuasive. It rests almost entirely on circumstantial evidence. We know too little about the sonata-symphony itself, and too little about the compositional process of the early Brahms, to propose any particular shape for the work.

In any case, Brahms kept revising the D-minor sonata-turned-symphony-turned-concerto even well beyond its premiere—and a disastrous second performance—in January 1859. By this time, though, he had already rerouted his symphonic ambitions in yet another direction, that of the orchestral serenade. As was suggested in the last chapter, this was a path around the symphony often taken by composers of the time. Brahms's two serenades, op. 11 in D major and op. 16 in A major, were composed during the years 1857–59 for the small court of Detmold, where Brahms served as conductor and teacher for three successive seasons. In the case of op. 11, as in that of the concerto, the work changed medium as it evolved. Perhaps inspired by the fine wind playing of the Detmold orchestra, Brahms first wrote a chamber work for winds and strings, which soon evolved into a D-major serenade for these forces, in which form the work had its premiere in March 1859 in Hamburg. During the following winter, in December 1859, Brahms told Joachim that he hoped to turn the serenade into a symphony and set out to do that, expanding the size of the playing forces and giving the work a hybrid title, "Symphony-Serenade."[7] In this form it was performed under Joachim in Hannover in March 1860. As in the case of the sonata/symphony/concerto, however, the concept of the "symphony" surfaces temporarily only to be transformed or set aside. Brahms struck off the "Symphony" portion of the title, and the work was published as Serenade for Large Orchestra in December 1860.[8]

Thus in two cases in the 1850s—those of the First Concerto and First Serenade—Brahms approached but then skirted the genre of the symphony. We can never know the exact cause of what might be called his generic insecurity. But among the factors must certainly be counted the kinds of critical standards constantly evoked in contemporary symphony reviews, as cited in the last chapter, as well as Brahms's own inherently cautious nature, which would only have been further affected in light of the expectations raised in the critics and the public by Schumann's "Neue Bahnen" article of 1853.

Although they are not symphonies, the two serenades and the First Piano Concerto mark Brahms's first engagement with orchestral writing and as such mark a significant stage on his road to the symphony. The concerto in particular engages with aspects of the "symphonic style," as adumbrated in the preceding chapter. Its opening Maestoso, which must be the longest concerto movement up to that time, is laid out on a massive scale, with several theme groups in the orchestral exposition alone. Brahms is clearly aiming at the monumentality of Beethoven's Ninth.

That Beethoven's opening was the direct model for Brahms's takes little away from the latter's originality (ex. 2–1). The D pedal is Brahms's analogue to Beethoven's hovering A–E fifths. But Brahms's tonal and thematic strategy is very different. Beethoven's theme emerges gradually, almost imperceptibly out of the tonal background. Brahms's strides boldly onto the symphonic stage with a triadic figure that asserts its independence from, rather than allegiance to, the continuous D pedal. The first ten measures unfold instead an augmented, or "German," sixth harmony, here a $B\flat^7$, which serves as a substitute for the tonic chord we would have expected over the pedal. Regardless of the specific genre into which it eventually settled, the first movement of Brahms's D-Minor Concerto, op. 15, is one of the most powerful utterances in the symphonic style since Beethoven.

Example 2–1: First Piano Concerto, I

TOWARD THE C-MINOR SYMPHONY: BRAHMS'S "FIRST MATURITY"

Within two years of the appearance of opp. 11, 15, and 16 in print, Brahms felt emboldened enough to give the "great symphony" another attempt. By June 1862 he had completed the first movement of a symphony in C minor, which he sent to Clara Schumann, who reported on it in some detail in a now-famous letter of July 1 to Joachim:

> Johannes sent me a little time ago—only fancy how surprised I was—the first movement of a Symphony with this bold opening: [Clara includes a musical example of mm. 38–42, the beginning of the Allegro].
>
> ٫ That is rather tough, certainly, but I soon got used to it. The movement is full of wonderfully beautiful passages, and the motives are handled in the masterly fashion which he is making more and more his own. It is all interwoven in such an interesting way, and yet it goes with such a swing that it might have all been poured forth in the first moment of inspiration; one can enjoy every note of it without being reminded of the work there is in it. He has succeeded in making another splendid transition from the second part [development section] back again to the first [recapitulation].[9]

The musical example included by Clara makes it clear that this was the work, minus the slow introduction, that would evolve eventually into the first movement of the First Symphony. Her description of the retransition (the "splendid transition"), though not precise, also seems to correspond closely to the work as we know it.

Despite much interest in the symphony from the Brahms circle over the next four years, including Clara, J. O. Grimm, Albert Dietrich, and Hermann Levi, the symphony seems not to have advanced significantly. Once again, Brahms deflected or displaced his symphonic ambitions and, during the first half of the 1860s, devoted himself primarily to chamber music. This period marked what Tovey aptly called Brahms's "first maturity," a six-year span that produced the B♭ Sextet, op. 18 (1859–60); the two Piano Quartets, opp. 25 and 26 (1861–62); the Piano Quintet, op. 34 (1862–64); the G-major Sextet, op. 36 (1864); and the Horn Trio, op. 40 (1865).[10] In this magnificent · series of works Brahms becomes fully the master of large-scale instrumental form and of thematic-motivic development—what Schoenberg was later to call "developing variation."

There can be little question that some of the musical techniques worked out in the compositions of the first maturity come to inform Brahms's symphonies, as one brief example may suffice to show. The Piano Quintet in F Minor, op. 34, is remarkable for the way in which small motivic and harmonic details presented at the very opening come to play a larger role in the piece as a whole. The first theme, set out in octaves and unison, places in special relief the half-step D♭–C, representing the scale degrees ♭6–5 (ex. 2–2). Over the course of the first movement, this half-step idea becomes reiterated and expanded. It forms a part of several themes, and the pitch D♭ is raised to a higher structural level when the second key area, which would normally be A♭ in an F-minor exposition, is placed by Brahms in C♯ minor and its enharmonic equivalent D♭ major. The scherzo movement, also in F minor, is permeated with the ♭6–5 relationship, especially in its powerful final cadences.[11] The finale of Brahms's Third Symphony is built, much like the opening of the quintet, from a theme presented in F minor, in unison and octaves (see chapter 5, ex. 5–15). As in the quintet, the relationship ♭6–5, highlighted in the theme, comes to play a structural role in the movement, and the D♭ becomes likewise "writ large" at several moments as a harmonic region.[12]

Example 2–2: Piano Quintet, op. 34, I

In an important sense, the relationship between the chamber music of the early 1860s and the symphonies of the late 1870s in Brahms is not only compositionally very close, but also chronologically closer than it may at first appear. For if the version of the first movement of the C-Minor Symphony that Brahms sent to Clara Schumann in the summer of 1862 resembled the work as we know it in its final version—and, based on the musical example in Clara's letter there no reason to think it might not, apart from the slow introduction added later—then Brahms was likely engaged with a symphony *concurrently* with the chamber works of the first maturity. More precisely: although there is no hard evidence before June and July of 1862, the composition of the first movement of the First Symphony would have fallen between that of the two piano quartets in the fall of 1861 and the Piano Quintet, originally composed as a string quintet, in August 1862. This chronology makes more plausible and logical the appearance of "symphonic" techniques in the Piano Quintet and other works of the first maturity.

We might expect that after having mastered certain aspects of large-scale composition in the series of chamber works culminating in 1865, Brahms would seek to reapply them to the genre of the symphony, either by returning to the languishing work in C minor or by starting a new one. Instead, he continued his detour around the symphony. The only hint of possible work on the C-Minor Symphony is Brahms's well-known letter of September 12, 1868, in which he sent to Clara the Alphorn melody that would appear in the finale of the First Symphony.[13] Brahms makes no mention, however, of any symphonic context for this melody; at this point he may well have had no such use in mind.

THE GERMAN REQUIEM

The latter part of the 1860s and beginning of the 1870s are dominated in Brahms's oeuvre by massive choral-orchestral works, notably the German Requiem, op. 45 (1861–68), and a series of shorter works, including the Alto Rhapsody, op. 53 (1869), the *Schicksalslied*, op. 54 (1868–71), and the *Triumphlied*, op. 55 (1871). The Requiem put Brahms's name on the musical map; within a few years of its Bremen premiere in 1868, the piece was performed in dozens of Austro-German locales.[14] The Requiem marked Brahms's first return—or his most successful return—to orchestral writing since the First Piano Concerto and the serenades. For many critics, the work also marked the real fulfillment of Schumann's prophecy that Brahms would reach greatness when he directed "his magic wand where the powers of the masses in chorus and orchestra may lend him their forces."[15]

The completion and popular success of the Requiem helped pave Brahms's path toward the symphony in another, still more important sense. The Requiem was the first work of his that could be said to be truly "society-forming," or *gesellschaftsbildend*, in the sense articulated by Paul Bekker in 1918 and echoed by Theodor Adorno in 1962.[16] The context for Bekker's remarks was a discussion of Beethoven's symphonies, which he felt were the first—and, in his opinion, the only—symphonic works created in the nineteenth century that communicated effectively to a broader public. In earlier times, said Bekker, this social function had been fulfilled in music by masses, oratorios, and passions, which had, however, lost this role as organized religion declined in influence in the later eighteenth century. What Bekker admired about Beethoven's symphonies was their unique ability "to organize the new humanity of the years around 1800 into artistic form, and thereby give to that humanity the opportunity to recognize itself as an entity capable of feeling."[17] Bekker saw the problem of all the post-Beethoven symphonists (until Mahler) as their inability or lack of desire to achieve this sense of identification and communication with society as a whole.

It could be suggested, following Bekker's line of thought, that Brahms was well aware of the sociological problem of the symphony after Beethoven. Despite his attempts to complete a symphony in the 1850s and 1860s, he, like most of his contemporaries, could not hope to achieve the society-forming spirit Beethoven had breathed into the genre. The German Requiem, begun in 1865 and completed in 1868, gradually took on this role for Brahms. In it, Brahms eschewed liturgical function and avoided the traditional Latin words of the Mass for the Dead, choosing his texts instead from various parts of the Bible in Martin Luther's German translation. He sought thereby to appeal not simply to Catholics—nor only to Protestants, nor to churchgoers in general. Rather, his intended audience was the broader society that shared his native tongue and culture.

National consciousness was, of course, prevalent in Germany in the 1860s, as the various states and principalities moved toward unification, which was achieved at last in 1871. Yet the title of Brahms's Requiem was not intended as narrowly nationalistic. For the composer, the language and culture were less important than the larger message of comfort and faith. "I'd happily give up the 'German' in the title," Brahms told Carl Reinthaler, "and just put 'Human'."[18] The kind of secular humanism displayed in the Requiem was undoubtedly one reason for its immediate and wide popularity. With the Requiem, Brahms had achieved precisely the kind of society-forming work that had eluded him—and, indeed, that he realized was perhaps unattainable—in the realm of the symphony.

FINAL STEPS: THE WORKS OF 1873

After the Requiem and the other choral-symphonic works that followed in its wake in the late 1860s and early 1870s, the path to the completion of the First Symphony may be said to have been paved directly by two other, purely instrumental compositions of the year 1873: the String Quartet in C Minor, op. 51, no. 1, and the Variations on a Theme by Haydn, op. 56. Like its symphonic counterpart in the same key, the quartet had a lengthy gestation. It was begun as early as 1865, thus in the context of the chamber works of the first maturity and the first movement of the First Symphony. But, like the symphony, the quartet advanced only in fits and starts.

The genre of the quartet was perhaps second only to that of the symphony in terms of prestige and historical weight. Perhaps for this reason Brahms had difficulty completing what was to be his first published work in the medium. (He claimed to have composed and rejected twenty string quartets before issuing his op. 51 set.) By 1869 he felt sufficiently confident about the state of the two quartets in C minor and A minor to assign them an opus number, op. 51. This number is immediately prior to that of the *Liebeslieder* Waltzes, op. 52, which were composed and published in 1869. But Brahms withheld the quartets and released them to his publisher only four years later, in September 1873, by which time his published opus numbers had reached 59 and the quartets had, according to Brahms's own private catalogue of works, been "written for a second time."[19]

Because no earlier version of the C-minor quartet survives—not even a thematic incipit, as in the case of the symphony—we cannot know how extensively it was rewritten in 1873. But it is indeed striking, and in my view significant, that in musical style the C-minor quartet comes so close to that of the first movement of the C-minor symphony that had been drafted in 1862. Especially in the first movement of the quartet, Brahms achieves an extremely dense motivic style unprecedented in his earlier published works. The sonata form of the first movement of the quartet is far shorter and more compressed than in other chamber works of the 1860s. Rather than settling into broad, tuneful themes, as in those works, the individual motives tend to remain confined to almost breathless units, very much as in the first movement of the C-minor symphony. Principal thematic elements of the two works even have similar profiles, characterized by triadic arpeggios that surge continually upward (ex. 2–3; cf. chapter 3, ex. 3–1, motive *z*) and by stark, angular downward leaps of a diminished seventh (quartet, m. 2; symphony, mm. 51–52).

Example 2–3: String Quartet, op. 51, no. 1, I

As a kind of corollary to the fluid motivic-thematic technique, the harmonic processes in both works frequently fail to settle down into stable areas. In both expositions, the second key area is the conventional E♭ major (reached in m. 63 of the quartet, m. 121 of the symphony); and in both, that key does not arrive in root position and is continually side-stepped. Both works turn instead to a more turbulent E♭ minor (m. 75 in the quartet, m. 160 in the symphony), in which key the expositions conclude.

The completion of the C-minor quartet in 1873 may have finally opened the way for Brahms's return to the symphony. Or, to put it differently—since the first movement of the C-minor symphony preceded that of the quartet in the same key—the successful completion of the quartet confirmed for Brahms the viability of the kind of language that he had already begun to explore in the symphony movement but with which he had remained unsatisfied.

What the C-minor quartet achieved in the realm of form and thematic technique, the Haydn Variations accomplished in the realm of orchestration. In this work, conceived virtually simultaneously in the versions for orchestra and for two pianos in the summer of 1873 (and published as opp. 56a and b, respectively), Brahms shows a mastery of orchestral forces well beyond that of the two serenades completed some fourteen years earlier.[20] Walter Niemann notes that "to an infinitely greater degree than the two serenades," the Haydn Variations "may claim to be the first truly symphonic work of Brahms."[21] Niemann's grand statement is plausible, but in light of the discussion devoted to symphonic style in this and the preceding chapter, we may, and should, legitimately ask just how the Haydn Variations are more "symphonic" than the serenades. In what ways do they really constitute, as is so often asserted, one of "the final steps" toward the First Symphony?[22] In the Brahms literature, there is surprisingly little about the symphonic aspect of the Variations beyond this kind of generalization.

In actual instrumentation the Variations go only a small way beyond the First Serenade. Both works are built upon the traditional Classical and early Romantic complement of double woodwinds (two each of flutes, oboes, clarinets, bassoons), four horns, two trumpets, timpani, and strings. To these forces, Brahms adds in the Haydn Variations piccolo, contrabassoon, and triangle, instruments that are to appear as well in the symphonies but that do not substantially alter the earlier configuration.

It is less the instrumentation *per se* than the treatment of the orchestra that makes the Haydn Variations a step on the way to the symphonies. Especially symphonic are the ways in which the rich counterpoint of the composition is realized through the orchestra, not only in devices like canons and invertible counterpoint, of which there are numerous examples, but also more generally in the polyphonic movement of parts. In the First Serenade, a less polyphonically conceived work, the winds and strings tend to be set off against one another in blocks; in the Haydn Variations there is far greater interpenetration and interaction between the two groups. The delicate exchange in variation 3, for example (mm. 108ff., corresponding to the second half of the theme), in which portions of the melody are divided soloistically among instrument groups, would have been unthinkable in the earlier work.

Perhaps nowhere is the orchestration more subtle than in the mysterious, fleeting Presto variation, no. 8. The dynamic remains mostly *pianissimo* and never rises above *piano;* the strings are muted throughout. The initial thematic statement is given to the medium-low strings, violas and cellos, playing in octaves (ex. 2–4). In the fourth measure they are joined at a third octave by the first violins, which serve as a kind of transitional timbre to the reply or counterstatement of the theme in inversion, beginning at m. 327. The woodwinds—here piccolo, clarinet, and bassoon—also play in three different octaves and are accompanied by independent obbligato lines in the violin and viola. At its return in m. 350 (corresponding to m. 19 of the original chorale), the theme is now presented simultaneously with its inversion. The initial instrumental groupings and registers are preserved: viola and cello play the theme, piccolo-clarinet-bassoon the inversion.

The final measures of the variation (mm. 356–60; ex. 2–5) contain some of the eeriest and most unusual sonorities in all of Brahms. Pedal points on B♭ are sounded by the piccolos and double basses at the distance of six octaves—thus at the very extremes of the orchestra—and by other instruments, including timpani, at several octaves in between. Among or around the pedals, the thematic content slithers to a pause—one can hardly call it a cadence—in the flute, clarinet, bassoon, and middle-range strings. The final chord comes, unexpectedly, on the last, normally weak beat of the measure. Brahms accentuates the chord by bringing in the second flute, clarinet, bassoon, and both trumpets for the first and only time in the variation. The effect is that of a no-nonsense punctuation point. With this chord, Brahms seems abruptly to shoo away what Niemann calls the "shadowy and phantom-like" spirits that have dominated the eighth variation,[23] and thus clears the air for the imposing finale.

Niemann suggests that the Presto variation is "a preliminary study on a small scale for the finale in F minor of the F major Symphony."[24] Indeed, the finale of the Third Symphony opens with a theme that is strikingly similar, played in unison and octaves by the strings and bassoons (see chapter 5, ex. 5–15). For the second phrase and the half-cadence to the dominant, the strings divide into parts. For the counterstatement of the theme beginning in

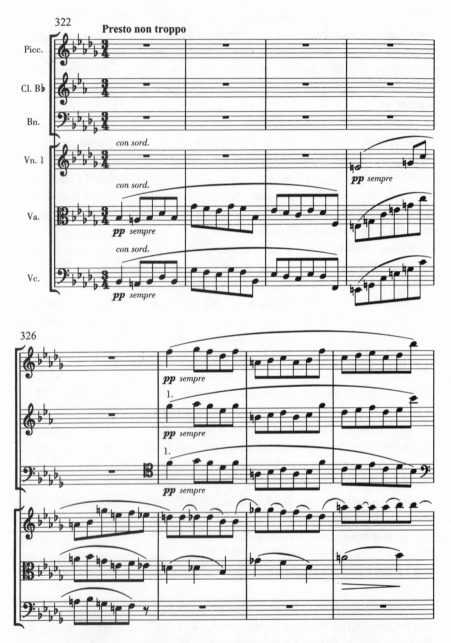

Example 2–4: Haydn Variations, op. 56a, var. 8

Example 2–5: Haydn Variations, op. 56a, var. 8

41

m. 9, the texture has evolved further, as the clarinets take up the melody in
thirds and sixths and the strings provide an arpeggiated accompaniment.

This kind of textural evolution across a theme was not new in Brahms:
something very much like it occurs in the second movement, a scherzo, of
the First Serenade (ex. 2–6). Here, as in the Third Symphony, a dark and
fleeting theme is presented first by strings and bassoons in octaves and unison. Part-writing begins as the cellos drop down in m. 5 to become the real
bass. In m. 10 the strings continue to divide, playing the melody in thirds,
doubled an octave lower by the clarinets. The orchestration of the scherzo is
competent, even elegant, but it is no match for either the sophisticated
Presto variation in the Haydn Variations or the finale of the Third Symphony,
both of which can count as more genuinely "symphonic."

Two principal works of 1873, the C-Minor Quartet and the Haydn
Variations, are therefore each in their own way significant precursors of
Brahms's symphonies. But they were not the final instrumental works completed before the First Symphony. They were followed in 1873–74 by the
resumption and completion of the Piano Quartet in C Minor, op. 60, and in
1875 by composition of the String Quartet No. 3 in B♭ Major, op. 67. Like the
Quartet, op. 51, no. 1, and the symphony with which it shares a key, the

Example 2–6: First Serenade, op. 11, II

Piano Quartet in C Minor had a lengthy, fitful gestation. It was begun in fact in 1855 or 1856, much earlier than either of the other works, as a piano quartet in C♯ minor, portions of which appear to have survived in the first and second movements of the final version.[25] The work shows some affinity of style to the other C-minor pieces, including a concentration on terse, brief motives in the first group of the first movement and, as in the First Symphony, a slow movement set in the key of E major.

In some respects the B♭-Major String Quartet stands in relation to the C-Minor Piano Quartet as do the first two symphonies to each other. In both cases, a gruffer, grittier work that took long to assume its final shape is followed within a very short time span by a work that is overall sunnier and more approachable. To be sure, the creative rhythm that produced works like opp. 60 and 67 in close succession had already been manifested earlier in Brahms, in the case of the two previous piano quartets, opp. 25 and 26, and to some extent in that of the first two string quartets, op. 51, nos. 1 and 2. But coming immediately after the great compositional triumphs in the instrumental realm represented by the String Quartet in C Minor and the Haydn Variations, the succession of opp. 60 and 67 may at last have given Brahms the confidence to emerge as a symphonist in the truest sense of the term, with the resumption and completion of his First Symphony.

Chapter 3

THE FIRST SYMPHONY, OP. 68

$\mathcal{T}$he First Symphony has a distinctive large-scale structure that belies to some extent the protracted and discontinuous genesis of the work. There is a parallelism between the slow introductions to the first and last movements, and the finale works out and brings to resolution tonal and thematic processes set in motion in the first movement. As critics have often pointed out, Brahms's First follows an expressive and technical trajectory of *per aspera ad astra;* this quasi-narrative scheme can be, and has been, also interpreted as a journey through darkness to light, pain to joy, struggle to victory. Beethoven's Fifth Symphony—in the same key as Brahms's—and, later, his Ninth, were the models for this influential symphonic "plot archetype," as Anthony Newcomb has called it.[1]

The trajectory in Beethoven's Fifth can be said to include a motivic-thematic process, involving the opening "Fate-knocks-at-the-door" motive, that spans all four movements. So, too, is Brahms's path *ad astra* paved in part by the evolution across the symphony of a rising chromatic motive, called x below and—surely by analogy to Beethoven's Fifth—dubbed the "Fate motive" (*Schicksalsmotiv*) by Brahms's biographer Max Kalbeck.

Brahms's symphony is characterized by a key plan that proceeds upward by major thirds between movements: C–E–A♭–C. This kind of symmetrical division of the octave, which avoids the traditional dominant and subdominant areas, was not new by 1876; Liszt and Chopin, and before them Schubert, had explored such possibilities, often in radical ways. But it is important—and characteristic of Brahms—that the third relations that are writ large in the tonal scheme also feature on the more local level in each of the movements, in some of the following ways:

the shift at the beginning of the development in the first movement from Eb minor down to B major (mm. 188–89).

a similar shift for the trio of the Allegretto from Eb to B major (mm. 70–71).

the appearance, quite suddenly, of C major in the midst of the E-major theme of the Andante (m. 7).

the strong presence of E minor in the closing group of the finale (mm. 148ff.) as a transition between the dominant of the second group and the C major of the start of the development (m. 186).

First movement: Un poco sostenuto—Allegro

The first movement of Brahms's First surges and churns almost without pause. On the largest level it has the conventional divisions of sonata form, but these are not readily articulated by a musical style that rarely settles down into areas of harmonic, melodic, or rhythmic stability. The few moments of stillness—as at m. 155 in the second group of the exposition or m. 290 in the development section—are achieved less through resolution or release than through the halting of forward motion. Much of the power of the first movement derives from the way in which its gritty chromaticism, dense motivic style, and complex rhythmic language work in tension with, or actually carry to extremes, traditional Classic-Romantic techniques.

One such technique is motivic-thematic coherence, which, as we saw in chapter 1 was considered a *sine qua non* of the symphonic style. Brahms builds his movement almost exclusively—obsessively, one might say—from three basic motives, or really motivic families, that contrast sharply with each other (ex. 3–1). One (x) consists of extremely restricted chromatic stepwise motion usually presented in equal or even rhythmic values, but often beginning in a syncopated manner, with the first note tied over the barline. Another (y), which grows out of x but is often treated independently, is a more sharply profiled rhythmic figure consisting usually of a longer note and three sixteenth notes leading to a downbeat. The third (z) comprises more wide-ranging and mobile triadic figuration. The three motivic types are manipulated, combined, varied, and transformed with an intensity that carries this movement well beyond even the most motivically taut creations of Beethoven. Especially characteristic of the First Symphony is its contrapun-

Example 3–1: First Symphony, I

tal richness, apparent from the very beginning. The chromatic *x* is presented, together with its inversion, at the start of both the slow introduction and
the Allegro. Motives *x* and *y* then both serve as a counterpoint to *z*.

The asymmetry of phrase structure in the Allegro is another way in which
Brahms forcefully reshapes Classic-Romantic models. Many first groups in
the Classic-Romantic tradition end with a full cadence on the tonic before
beginning the modulatory process or transition that leads to the second
group. Beethoven's First Symphony represents a kind of *locus classicus* of
one compositional tactic (ex. 3–2). The first group consists of three phrases,
of which the first two are parallel and the third (although based on the same
rhythm) contrasting: the plan might be represented as *a a' b*. (Often, such
phrase groupings in Classic-Romantic music have the proportions 1:1:2, a

Example 3–2: Beethoven, First Symphony, I

structure that Schoenberg called a sentence.) In the Beethoven, phrase *a* begins on the tonic and moves to the dominant of ii, the supertonic; phrase *a'* restates the material beginning on ii and moves to V^7. The third phrase, *b*, serves to expand on, or develop, the previous two and make a definitive cadence to I in m. 21.

Brahms expands his first group in part by giving it a ternary design: A (mm. 38–51); B (mm. 51–70); A' (mm. 70–89). The opening measures of A, mm. 38–42 (as seen in ex. 3–1), constitute a cadential figure moving from i (represented only by the tonic note) through V/V and V, to land emphatically on the tonic triad on the downbeat of m. 42. Only at this point does there appear in the violins something we might identify more readily as a theme, presented as an antecedent-consequent structure (mm. 42–46, mm. 46–51). We might thus represent A as having three phrases: phrase 1 (mm. 38–42); phrase 2 (42–46); phrase 3 (46–51).

Because of its cadential nature, phrase 1 lies *outside* the more traditional structure of mm. 42–51, whose two phrases (2 and 3) thus correspond roughly to phrases *a* and *a'* from Beethoven's First Symphony: a statement beginning on the tonic is followed by a parallel one beginning on the dominant, in this case the dominant minor, in m. 46. Phrase 1 takes on an

ambiguous status, constituting in itself a kind of extra introduction that
throws us off balance. The contrapuntal density of the "theme" that follows
in mm. 42–51 continues to keep us off balance; it is less a melody—one
does not come away humming the first theme of the first movement of
Brahms's First Symphony—than it is a motivic-thematic complex.

Brahms plays on these ambiguities at approach to A' (ex. 3–3). He folds
the chromatic ascent x (now modified to E–F♯–G) and a single statement of
the rhythmic motive y (there were two in the original phrase 1) into the end
of B such that the return, A', begins in m. 70 *not* with the cadential phrase
1, but directly with phrase 2: phrase 2 (mm. 70–78); phrase 3 (mm. 78–89).

Phrase 2 now lasts nine measures (as against five in mm. 42–46), and
motives x and y are inverted. Brahms also achieves expansion by harmonic
means. Phrase 3 had initially centered only on the dominant, the goal of the
half cadence at m. 51. Now phrase 3 begins on the *subdominant* (m. 78) and
stretches over twelve measures, twice its original length, to form a large-
scale cadence, iv–V–i.

Example 3–3: First Symphony, I

The development section of the first movement contains a fine example of
another characteristically Brahmsian device, what might be called the procedure of thematic fulfillment, whereby a previously fragmentary or jagged
motive becomes smoothed out and regularized into a genuine theme. The
rather innocuous-sounding three-note motive that marked the beginning of
the transition in the exposition, where it appears in a detached form, is now
smoothed out to dotted quarter notes and forms the head of a more lyrical and
regular melodic phrase in G♭ major of essentially four measures (ex. 3–4).

In some ways Brahms's procedure here reverses that of the Classical
sonata-form model, in which themes are more stable in the exposition and

Example 3–4: First Symphony, I

become fragmented or "liquidated," as Schoenberg called it, in the development section. It is Brahms's tendency—nowhere more evident than in the
opening movement of the First Symphony—to "develop" his material so
extensively within the exposition that new tasks, like thematic fulfillment,
must be found for the development section proper.

Also striking in the development of the first movement of the C-Minor
Symphony is the lull of mm. 289–93. Here action and movement have virtually ceased as the strings meditate quietly on a remnant of motive x. A distant model for this moment may be found in the first movement of
Beethoven's *Eroica*, where the forceful syncopations of the development section die down to quiet chords in mm. 280–84, which in turn give way to a
quiet new theme in E minor. Brahms's gesture is more extreme, and the
build-up to the subsequent retransition is far more gradual. The idea of a
development section having a kind of still center—an eye of the storm—is
perhaps not entirely new with Brahms. But no composer exploited it as dramatically, as fully, as in the First Symphony, which redefines the traditional
notion of "development section" as a place where only modulation, fragmentation, and constant motion take place.

The other aspect of the development section that Brahms reconceived is
the retransition, or the passage that leads back to the recapitulation. After
the uneasy repose of mm. 289ff., the tail motive of y is heard above a pulsating dominant pedal point on G (ex. 3–5a). Brahms builds steadily toward
what we assume, when we reach m. 321, will herald the return. By m. 334,
we expect the pedal point to resolve to C and the recapitulation to begin.
Instead, the bottom literally drops out of the dominant; the G falls to F♯,
which underpins a B-minor triad (ex. 3–5b). Now the motivic material of the
first group floods in, as the harmonies ascend restlessly by minor thirds,
from B minor, to D minor, to F minor.

Example 3–5: First Symphony, I

Above these harmonic shifts, the three-note motive x rises in sequence, as if in search of a foothold at the right pitch. That point is reached on the C–C♯–D♮ of mm. 339–41, at which moment x magically becomes phrase 1 of A, thus beginning the recapitulation. Brahms has subtly altered the harmonization of this phrase. At the opening of the Allegro, in m. 38, the C was underpinned, first, by a diminished chord (F♯–A–C), of which the lower dyad moved to F and A♭, thus forming a minor triad. Now Brahms provides only the latter, F-minor chord, which in itself has formed part of the sequential progression of minor thirds leading out of the development.

The coda, beginning at m. 474, is relatively brief, but not at all perfunctory. It is here that motive x is accorded for the first time thematic fulfillment of the kind we saw in the development section (ex. 3–6). Indeed, mm. 478–95 form one of the most regular thematic statements in the entire movement, quite close to standard sentence structure, with proportions approximating 1:1:2: mm. 478–81 = a (4 measures); mm. 482–85 = a' (4 measures); mm. 486–95 = b (10 measures).

We get only one full statement of the "fulfilled" theme. The Meno Allegro then returns us to something close to the tempo and the material of the slow introduction; the timpani pedal points, the chromatic presentation of motive x reappear. Although Brahms now abandons the regular melody of mm. 478–95,

Example 3–6: First Symphony, I

there is a significant element of completion or closure in the addition of the note C to the presentations of motive x in the woodwinds and strings in mm. 495–501. After the final appearance of x, extended or augmented in the strings of mm. 501–05, the completing note C is delayed until m. 508 by—and actually serves as culmination of—the emergence of the triadic motive z.

Deviating significantly and boldly from the model of Beethoven's Fifth and Ninth Symphonies, Brahms ends his first movement in the major mode. Because it arrives with so little harmonic preparation, at the end of a movement that has been almost relentlessly in minor, C major has little power of resolution or of closure. The C-major chords accompanying the final statement of z seem remote, even cold. Giving at best a distant glimpse of the triumph of the finale, they indicate that there is still much unfinished expressive and technical business to take care of.

Second movement: Andante sostenuto

As performed in Germany, Austria, and England during its premiere season, 1876–77, the Andante of the C-Minor Symphony had a rondolike form (ABACA).[2] Before publication, Brahms compressed the movement into a ternary structure with coda—A (m. 1) B (m. 27) A' (m. 67) Coda (m. 100)— by eliminating the central return and uniting the original B and C into a single middle section. He thus brought the Andante into line with the majority of his other slow movements.

Within the apparently conservative E-major frame of section A unfolds one of Brahms's most sophisticated thematic groups, a splendid example of what Schoenberg was to call "musical prose," by which he meant thematic statements that avoid mere repetition or predictable patterns.[3] Brahms pours forth no fewer than five different thematic ideas (labeled a through e in ex. 3–7). The coherence of the large group depends to some extent on the reappearance of the second, b (mm. 3–4), as a cadential or half-cadential gesture, roughly at the two-thirds point, in mm. 15–17, and at the end, in mm. 24–27.

Brahms wastes no time in linking the Andante to the larger narrative of the symphony. Between phrases a and b, which stand to each other in a kind of antecedent-consequent relationship, three repeated Bs in the horns recall, as if in a dream, the throbbing pedal points from the slow introduction to the first movement. These pedal points had been recalled, also by the horns, only moments earlier in the previous coda. Indeed, although the meter differs—$\frac{6}{8}$ in the first movement, $\frac{3}{4}$ in the Andante—the *rhythm* of three eighth notes leading to a downbeat is identical in both cases.

Example 3–7: First Symphony, II

The somber mood introduced by the horns immediately affects phrase *b*, which is colored by the minor third, G♮, instead of the expected G♯. Simultaneously in the bass, C♮ appears as a chromatic passing tone between the C♯ and B, and a full C⁷ chord appears on the third beat of m. 3. Although this chord functions as an augmented sixth, or enhanced dominant preparation, within E major, its tonal orientation also provides, in light of what has preceded (the horn pedals) and what follows (phrase *c* in mm. 4–6), an echo of the first movement, which has ended in C major.

The chromatic motion in the bass across mm. 3–4, C♯–C♮–B, is an inversion of motive *x* from the first movement. A moment later *x* in something very close to its original form—beginning as a syncopation and underpinned by a chromatic descent, or inversion, in contrary motion—emerges to form phrase *c* in the violins and violas. Memory has now flooded to the surface: *c* constitutes a direct intrusion of the material from the first movement. In purely local terms, *c* also interrupts or derails the regular 2 + 2 phrase structure of the theme. There is no bass at all underneath the first measure of *c*. With a strong entrance in m. 6, the bass initiates its own pattern of 2 + 2, which is displaced from, or out of phase with, that of the upper parts. The response of the melody to the bass's apparent usurpation of the phrase structure seems to be to present a short one-measure "catch-up" unit in m. 7, followed by a two-measure continuation that brings the two elements, melody and bass, back into phase. The overall phrase design of the upper parts in mm. 5–9 can thus be represented 2 + 1 + 2, that of the bass 0 + 2 + 2, where 0 is the gaping emptiness underneath *c* in m. 5.

The upbeat figure of phrase *d* echoes the rising chromatic *x* figure heard in *c*. The oboe melody of m. 18 (phrase *e*) is at once a new idea and grows out of the previous ones. Its three-note upbeat derives from the identical rhythmic figure repeated prominently in phrase *d* as an echo of *x* but now fully diatonicized, and the dotted-eighth–sixteenth figure leading to a downbeat comes quite clearly from phrases *b* and *c*. Underneath the fifth measure of *e*, phrase *a* returns in a particularly elegant and unexpected reappearance. The final three notes of *e*, the descending scale in the oboe in mm. 22–23 (D♯–C♯–B), parallel a third higher the B–A–G♯ that concludes phrase *a*, making it seem as if the two melodies were destined to coincide (end of ex. 3–7).

The art of Brahms's orchestration is particularly apparent here. The horns, which at the opening had been heard only as a transition to phrase *b*, have returned to play a prominent role—again as pedal points—in phrase *e*. They continue to sound with the return of *a* in mm. 22–23. But then they drop out on the final beat of m. 23, at precisely the point where they had *entered* at the opening of the movement.

The central or B section of the Andante veers from the tranquil E major of m. 27 toward the relative minor, C♯. Brahms gradually, over eight measures, mirrors this harmonic process by transforming the dotted-eighth–sixteenth rhythm (common to most of the themes in section A) from the gentle lilt of the transitional m. 27 into the anguished funeral march of mm. 34–35. Accompanying this transformational process are further recollections of motive *x*, in the first violins in mm. 29 and 33. The technical and expressive metamorphosis, achieved before our very ears, so to speak, represents Brahms's art of developing variation at its most refined. (We might call it Brahms's answer to Wagner's "art of transition.")

In what follows at m. 39 (comprising what had been the C section in the original rondo form of the Andante) the accompanimental rhythm is further transformed to a syncopated pulsation. Over this figure, the oboe and clarinet trade long, supple, but uneasy melodies. The emotional process of the movement has "modulated" yet again, from despair to a more suppressed, persistent agitation.

The approach to A' is fashioned with no less elegance than the analogous retransition/recapitulation in the first movement. Where in the first movement Brahms relied on the sudden harmonic displacement of the dominant pedal, here he employs metrical displacement. The first half of the downbeat of m. 63 is empty, and on the second eighth note the woodwinds begin a stepwise ascending thematic pattern that is echoed by the strings; a complementary descent follows. These patterns fall into a $\frac{2}{4}$ meter that has been displaced by an eighth note from the notated meter (ex. 3–8).

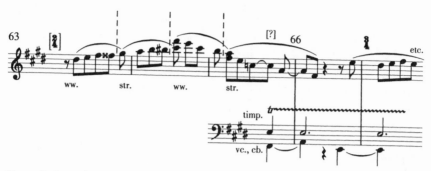

Example 3–8: First Symphony, II

Harmony is also involved in this process. In an exquisite moment on the
last beat of m. 65, the horns, bassoons, second violins, and timpani play the
note E, which, however, forms part *not* of a tonic chord, but of a ii^7 chord,
underpinned by the low F♯ in cellos and double basses. On the last beat of
m. 66 the tonic harmony enters directly in the full orchestra, without any
dominant preparation, thus ushering in the recapitulation. The note E, only
moments earlier the dissonant seventh of a ii harmony, has magically redefined itself as tonic.

There are numerous modifications in A', the most evocative of which is
an otherworldly woodwind cadenza in mm. 84–87 (ex. 3–9), which delays
the second return of *b* and the arrival of phrase *e*. The thematic material can
be derived from phrase *a* and from motive *x* as filtered through phrase *c*. But
the use of sequence and the scoring give this passage an anachronistic feeling, as though a phrase from a Baroque piece for winds had crept into a
Romantic symphony. The solo violin, emerging with oboe and horn for phrase *e*
in m. 91, closes the window on this gnomic utterance and brings us back to the
late nineteenth century by personalizing—and even sentimentalizing, in a manner unusual for Brahms—the discourse of this movement.

The coda readdresses the larger-scale issues of the symphony. In m. 116
the solo violin reemerges to introduce motive *x*, which appears as E–E♯–F♯

Example 3–9: First Symphony, II

and now leads after four measures to its own resolution. The final melodic statement, in the high winds in mm. 122–24, E–F♯–G♯, represents a satisfying resolution of x, which is diatonicized in a manner—as commentators have suggested—not unlike the "Longing" motive in the final moments of Wagner's *Tristan*. If this moment and the final cadence do not ease all the tensions generated by the motive since its appearance in the first movement, they nonetheless achieve a level of resolution—and manage to clear enough expressive space—to allow the Allegretto to emerge in tranquility.

Third movement: Un poco Allegretto e grazioso

The Allegretto of the First Symphony presents an almost complete change of mood from the preceding movement. Where the Andante rarely has continuous rhythmic flow—the first theme, we recall, was a succession of dissimilar phrases, punctuated by silences and pauses—the Allegretto is characterized virtually throughout by a steady pulse of eighth notes, often presented as gentle pizzicato accompaniment. Digressive, introspective musical prose seems to have given way to a more symmetrical and "verse"-like discourse. Indeed, the Allegretto proper is built from balanced pairs of themes, whose arrangement might be represented as follows:

Theme A, mm. 1–10
Theme B, mm. 11–18
Theme A', mm. 19–32
Theme B', mm. 33–45
Theme C, mm. 45–49
Theme D, mm. 50–53
Theme C', mm. 54–57
Theme D', mm. 58–61
Theme A", mm. 62–70

There is a broader ternary aspect to this design: the C, D, C', and D' themes form a kind of contrasting or central unit, which is followed by a truncated return of the opening segment. This plan is, in turn, nested within the movement's still larger ternary structure of Allegretto–Trio–Allegretto.

Brahms's urge to symmetry is further evident in both the harmonic plan of the movement and the actual melodic structures. The thematic pair C–D is in F minor, which lies a minor third below the tonic A♭ of the A–B themes.

The Trio is in B major, lying enharmonically a minor third *above* A♭ (though a major third below the dominant E♭, where the Allegretto actually closes in mm. 69–70). The two parallel phrases of theme A (mm. 1–5, 6–10) are exact melodic inversions of one another. Inversion in a different, contrapuntal sense is also present in theme C'. Here a slightly modified theme C is placed in the bass, underneath the pulsing accompaniment; mirroring it above (in the oboe, mm. 54–57) is a free inversion of the original C.

Despite the multilayered balance and symmetry in the movement, all is not "normal," and therein lie the connections between the Allegretto and the symphony as a whole. By sustaining the final melodic note, Brahms extends both phrases of theme A from the expected four measures to five. In the second appearance of this theme (A', mm. 19–32), each phrase is elongated to seven measures, thus stretching the whole to fourteen. Underneath these sustained notes Brahms introduces stepwise chromatic motion and a dip to remote harmonies that immediately bring us back to the larger drama of the symphony. The melodic F–F♯–G motion across mm. 30–33 appears to constitute a direct reference to motive *x*.

The transition back to the Allegretto (m. 109) is made by means of a four-note descending stepwise figure that will appear at the very opening of the finale. In other ways, too, the apparently independent Allegretto looks both ahead to the movement that follows and back to the first movement. When it returns after the Trio, theme B, which at the opening of the movement was a precise inversion of A, takes on an entirely new melodic profile that directly anticipates a prominent figure of the main theme of the finale (ex. 3–10). Moreover, the transition or link from A in mm. 118–20 is transformed to make a fleeting but unmistakable reference to motive *x* and its attendant counterpoints from the first movement.

At m. 144 the A theme returns for the last time, now in mysterious unison and octaves in the lower strings. Above this, in the first violins (mm. 148–50)

Example 3–10: First Symphony, III/IV

emerges yet another quotation of the three-note chromatic motive x from the first movement (ex. 3–10). Like the reference in mm. 118–20, this gesture brings us back to the symphony's main drama moments before it is about to resume full force in the finale.

Fourth movement: Adagio—Più andante— Allegro non troppo, ma con brio

Though there is no direct evidence, it may well have been the composition of the finale that held up the completion of Brahms's First for so many years.[4] For if it was difficult enough to write a symphony after Beethoven, it was especially difficult to create an appropriate finale. Scholars have often pointed to a "finale problem" in the post-Beethoven symphonic era, when many composers felt the need to make their finales not the last-but-equal movement among four, but the real goal or climax of the symphonic process. In this respect, the paradigms to be either imitated or avoided, but not ignored, were the end-weighted Fifth and Ninth Symphonies of Beethoven.

Perhaps nowhere in Brahms's symphonic music are we more aware of those models than in the finale of the First. Like Beethoven's Fifth in the same key, Brahms's First is an end-weighted symphony; as in the Fifth, the bright C major of its final movement is meant to be heard and felt as a reversal of the C minor of the first movement. But Beethoven and Brahms proceed quite differently in achieving these effects. In Beethoven, the scherzo movement revisits the opening key of C minor. In its last appearance, the scherzo theme cadences deceptively onto A♭ major, which becomes a pedalpoint underpinning the famous, tension-building transition that connects the third and fourth movements.

In Brahms, C minor has been pretty much absent since the first movement. Brahms's Allegretto is in the key of A♭ major, and as such may be said to stand in for the sustained A♭ pedal of Beethoven's transition. Indeed, the A♭ is made to descend clearly and distinctly in the very opening gesture in the bass of the finale. But rather than recreating Beethoven's drama of minor-major and tension-release in a process leading from the third into the fourth movements, Brahms relies on a slow introduction to the finale. In adopting this strategy, he thus turns to the other Beethoven paradigm, the Ninth Symphony.

Tovey called the preface to Brahms's finale "the most dramatic introduction that has been heard since that to the finale of Beethoven's Ninth Symphony," and it is hard to disagree.[5] Of course, the introduction is in many ways more compact and restrained than its predecessor; there is no "Horror Fanfare," no attempt systematically to review and reject the themes of all the preceding movements before introducing the "Freude" theme.

The first four notes in the bass, C–B♭–A♭–G, serve to lead us from the world of the Allegretto to that of the finale. The four-note descending figure has already been heard in the transition from the Trio back to the Allegretto; now it makes the next transition, to the finale. The four-note descent seems to be a direct response to the ending of the Allegretto, the elegant triplet triadic descent to the tonic A♭. At the opening of the finale, Brahms seems to dismiss that cadence as too light, too easy. He begins on the third of A♭—and the tonic of this movement—and instead of a quick downward swoop, as at the end of the Allegretto, comes a measured stepwise descent to the dominant.

The spacious introduction divides on the largest scale into two sections, marked off by the change of key signature and tempo in m. 30. On the one side are agitation, chromaticism, thematic fragmentation, and the minor mode; on the other, hope and redemption, conveyed by the major-mode tuneful themes. The minor section of the introduction makes obvious reference to the introduction to the first movement. The accompanying voices descending chromatically in thirds in mm. 2–5 recall, of course, the similar accompaniment to motives x and y at the opening of the symphony. And the strong Neapolitan chord on the downbeat of m. 12 directly evokes the similar moment in m. 19 of the first movement.

Also recalling the first movement is the way Brahms builds this part of the introduction in "waves" that break onto contrasting material. Through m. 29, the introduction to the finale has three such parallel segments, which might be represented as A (mm. 1–5) B (mm. 6–12) // A' (mm. 12–15) B' (mm. 16–19) // A" (mm. 20–21) B" (mm. 21–29). In each case an ever more laconic lyrical, sustained line gives way to an increasingly longer passage characterized by detached, disjunct motion.

The Più andante segment of the introduction (mm. 30–60), which moves to the major mode, is based on the radiant Alphorn melody that Brahms had sent to Clara Schumann in 1868 and a solemn theme that Giselher Schubert has aptly called an "imaginary chorale."[6] Together they create a small rounded binary form with the shape: A (mm. 30–38) A (mm. 38–46) B (mm. 47–52) A' (mm. 53–60). As Schubert has suggested, these two themes bring a new dimension into the symphony—or bring the symphony into a new dimension: "The horn theme has associations of the sphere of ideal nature, the chorale that of religiosity. At this moment the music not only changes suddenly its expressive character, but this character itself becomes more concrete."[7]

When the broad Allegro theme emerges in m. 62, it sounds at once familiar and new ("Es klang so alt, und war doch so neu," as Sachs says of Walther's Trial Song in *Meistersinger*). It is new because it opens the finale proper as a first theme. It is familiar in part, of course, because of the apparent allusion to the "Freude" theme of Beethoven, but also because it is the result of a compelling thematic evolution that has unfolded across the whole symphony, most intensively in the introduction itself.[8]

As shown in ex. 3–11, the first three movements have featured themes that descend through an actual fourth or through four notes that outline a portion of the chromatic scale (the inversion of motive x). The introduction to the finale with a portentous four-note descent in the bass, C–G, that announces that the thematic process is now to be taken up in earnest. The minor-mode prefigurement of the Allegro theme in mm. 13–14 is clearly

Example 3–11: First Symphony, thematic evolution

based on the same C–G fourth, now filled in somewhat differently. In the second segment of the slow portion of the introduction (B') we hear in the oboe a *three*-note descending motive (m. 20) that in this context seems to derive or evolve from the stepwise four-note version. It is this figure, E–D–C, that then builds to a climax in B" at mm. 25–26 (as E♭–D–C and G♭–F–E♭). At the change of tempo and key signature in m. 30, the figure becomes transformed into the Alphorn melody.

The Alphorn melody can be said to combine both elements of the preceding thematic evolution: the descending E–D–C third, and the outline of the C–G descending fourth. These are taken up and further transformed in the main theme of the Allegro. The chorale remains somewhat apart from this evolution, although its initial fourth, A–E, might be said to derive from the prominent C–G fourth.

The overall structure of the Allegro portion of the finale of Brahms's First is a modification of sonata form, in which there is no separate development section but rather a developmental expansion within the recapitulation's transition:

EXPOSITION
    First theme, m. 62
    Counterstatement of first theme, m. 78
    Transition, m. 94
    Alphorn theme, m. 114
    Second group, m. 118
    Closing group, m. 142

RECAPITULATION
    First theme, m. 186
    Counterstatement of first theme, m. 204
    Transition, with development, m. 220
    Alphorn theme, m. 285
    Second group, m. 301
    Closing group, m. 326

CODA, m. 367

Although this type of structure is not unique to the First Symphony, it seems particularly well suited here.[9] A sonata-form finale with a full development section might have overwhelmed, or drawn our attention away from, the higher-level thematic-motivic "development" across the symphony, a process that becomes most intense within the finale. It comes as little surprise that in the String Quartet in C Minor, op. 51, no. 1 (1873)—the chamber piece most closely associated with this symphony, as I have suggested in the previous chapter—Brahms fashions a finale with a similar form. In that quartet, as in the symphony, Brahms wishes us to focus on the higher-level thematic process, which likewise culminates in a finale for which a separate development would seem superfluous.[10]

As can be seen in ex. 3–11 and the formal analysis above, the process in Brahms's symphony does not end with the arrival of the Allegro theme. As if to signal the fact that the higher-level evolution is still underway, the Alphorn theme returns at the end of transition (m. 114) and leads directly to an elegant transformation in the main theme of the second group. The melody of this second group (m. 118) takes over from the Alphorn theme the E–D and the descent to G; underneath, as shown in ex. 3–11, the bass line is an ostinato created from the now familiar C–G stepwise descending fourth.

The tonal modifications make this double transformation especially subtle. Both figures, melody and bass, remain at the pitch level with which they were first associated, when they were oriented around C major/minor; yet they are now heard in the context of G major, the key of the second group. Thus the note G, which was by its nature as a dominant unstable both in the bass descent at the opening of the introduction and in the Alphorn theme, has become the local tonic, and thus a point of repose, in the second group.

The whole transformational process is taken up again in the recapitulation. The end of the developmental extension in the transition (m. 279) recalls directly the conclusion of the B" segment of the slow introduction, with its syncopated rhythms and three-note motive forms. As in the introduction, this high level of tension breaks onto the Alphorn theme. Now, however, in one of the most remarkable modifications in the movement, the tension actually carries over into the theme, whose head motive is accompanied by a diminished seventh chord (ex. 3–12). Only in its third measure, m. 287, does the theme—now beginning on the original note, E—arrive on the tonic major. This splendid transition, juxtaposing two forms of the Alphorn theme—tragic and hopeful—encapsulates in a few measures the thrust of the symphony as a whole, from unrest and agitation to peaceful resolution.

As in the exposition, the Alphorn theme is poised to become the second theme and its four-note ostinato accompaniment. But at m. 297, Brahms injects a remarkable *calando* or decrease in dynamics and tempo (ex. 3–13). Two measures later the music has almost come to a complete halt, as if a moment of doubt or forgetting has crept into the progression toward confident resolution. At the *animato* of m. 301, the music begins to right itself; the four-note ostinato appears in the violins. Yet this moment, too, is

Example 3–12: First Symphony, IV

"wrong": the proper place for the ostinato figure is in the bass, to which it in fact moves in the next measure, underneath the arrival of the second theme. This is one of the most exquisite moments in the symphony, in which technical and expressive devices seem in complete unity. At the *animato*, the ostinato theme emerges in what might be called the conscious level of the texture, the melody. It then migrates to the unconscious, to the bass, where it becomes a repeating pattern.

Up to this point I have been describing the main theme of the Allegro as one of the principal evolutionary goals in the symphony. But a somewhat different interpretation is suggested by the modification of sonata form used by Brahms in this movement. After the beginning of the recapitulation in m. 186, which precedes the development, the main theme is never heard again in its original form. Building on the analysis of this process by Giselher Schubert, Reinhold Brinkmann asserts that across the finale this theme comes to be replaced or "effaced": first, at the end of the development, by the Alphorn theme (m. 285), and then, in the coda, by the chorale theme (m. 407).[11] Brinkmann notes these other themes appear where, according to a more conventional sonata scheme, we would expect the main Allegro subject. Having

Example 3–13: First Symphony, IV

fashioned a subject with a direct reminiscence of Beethoven's Ninth, Brahms now seeks twice to push it aside, in a gesture of "emphatic alienation from Beethoven."[12]

Tovey, who normally had no interest in thematic associations or allusions between pieces, observed about the similarity of Brahms's theme to Beethoven's "Freude" theme, "If the resemblance were confined to generalities, no sensible person would worry about it; but there is here a certain provocative element."[13] It is this provocation that Brinkmann explores. Where Beethoven's symphony had culminated in a choral movement that was a paean to freedom and brotherhood, Brahms's moves in a different direction. By giving an obviously similar theme an instrumental setting, Brahms reclaims the purely instrumental realm of the symphony that Beethoven had renounced in the finale of the Ninth. Borrowing the words of Adrian Leverkühn, Thomas Mann's composer figure in *Doktor Faustus*, Brinkmann observes that in this way Brahms "takes back" the Ninth (Mann's word is *Zurücknahme*). Brinkmann suggests that for Mann the category of taking back derived from the experience of an exile in the middle of the twentieth century, but that "it was the musing, melancholy Brahms . . . who had already *composed* the artistic 'taking back' in the nineteenth century, and who did so from right within the Viennese tradition."[14]

There is considerable force to these remarks. But the notions of Brahms "effacing" and "alienating" Beethoven are too extreme. Although Brahms's main Allegro theme does not reappear intact after the opening of the recapitulation, there is little question that the principal idea of the coda (m. 391; ex. 3–14) is based on the head motive, including the rhythm, of the original theme of m. 62. Brahms seems far from "taking back" the Ninth here: the treatment of the Allegro theme in the coda, where the head motive is isolated and jubilantly reiterated, is not dissimilar from that of the "Freude" theme in Beethoven's coda.

Moreover, Brahms's coda theme, as a final transformation of the Allegro theme, now reintegrates a feature of the Alphorn theme as heard at the end of the developmental transition in the recapitulation. The woodwind and

Example 3–14: First Symphony, IV

brass chord that is sustained in m. 392 (as shown in ex. 3–14) is exactly the same diminished seventh (C–D♯–F♯–A) that was heard in what I called above the "tragic" evocation of the Alphorn theme (ex. 3–12). As in the earlier occurrence, it resolves as a neighbor chord back to the tonic triad (m. 393). Thus, *pace* Schubert and Brinkmann, the main Allegro theme is less displaced or effaced by the Alphorn theme than reabsorbed into or united with it. Similarly, the chorale, which makes its second and grandest appearance at m. 407, seems fully assimilated into the spirit of the coda. From the solemn chorale melody, Brahms distills a simple neighbor-note motive, G–A–G (m. 417), which bounds away confidently in triplet rhythms.

Perhaps the oddest moment in the coda is the kind of stop action in mm. 431–39, where the orchestra blares forth in unison and octaves what seems to be a new thematic idea, C–A–A♭–F♯–G. In fact, this theme harkens back directly to the first Allegro theme of the first movement, to the tail of what was above called phrase 3 of theme A (mm. 48–51; see ex. 3–1). Brahms now prefixes a C to the original shape, thus outlining for the last time the C–G fourth that has played so germinal a role in the symphony and in the finale. The theme also functions as an echo of a figure from the second group of the finale (see m. 303, B–A–F♯–G, in ex. 3–13).

As a whole, then, the First Symphony hardly seems the work of a skeptic intent on turning away from Beethoven. Rather, Brahms has reworked the paradigms of Beethoven's Fifth and Ninth, and of the "Freude" theme in particular, into a wholly original symphonic synthesis that can with some legitimacy claim to assume, rather than reject, the Beethoven mantle.

Chapter 4

THE SECOND SYMPHONY, OP. 73

The genesis of the Second Symphony seems to have been as uncomplicated and swift as the First's was tortured and protracted. Although we do not know how much sketching or creative thought might have preceded the writing out of the score, all the available evidence points to a relatively smooth process of composition in the summer of 1877, when Brahms was also busy correcting proofs and preparing the four-hand arrangement for the First.

Commentators have often suggested that the prevailingly sunny character of the Second—at least the first, third, and fourth movements—owes something to the natural surroundings in which it was composed, at Pörtschach by the Wörther See in the Kärnten region of southern Austria. Brahms himself described the symphony to Eduard Hanslick as "so cheerful and lovely that you will think I wrote it specially for you or even your young lady! That's no great feat, you will say, Brahms is a smart fellow and the Wörther See virgin soil, with so many melodies flying about that you must be careful not to tread on any."[1]

Near the end of the summer Brahms moved to his customary vacation lodging in Lichtental, near Baden-Baden, where the First Symphony had been completed the preceding year. There he played the first movement of the Second and part of the last to Clara Schumann, who found the new work more original than the First and predicted a "more telling success" with the public.[2] The remarks of Clara, as well as those of the Karlsruhe conductor Otto Dessoff, who also apparently heard only the first movement and part of the finale at this time, have led some writers to suggest that Brahms wrote

the outer movements of the symphony first, and only later that fall turned to
the inner ones.[3] As Brinkmann has observed, however, the pagination, gath-
erings, and paper types in the autograph manuscript (today in the Pierpont
Morgan Library) suggest a more complicated picture: Brahms may well have
begun to put down the second and third movements before the first was complete, and the finale may have been written out before the third was finished.[4] What the comments by Clara and Dessoff *do* show—and this is no
less significant than the actual order of composition—is that to give his
friends an "idea" of the Second Symphony, Brahms chose to play them the
outer movements, which share a key and much thematic material.

Dessoff, enthusiastic about the new work, may have sought to persuade
Brahms to allow its premiere in Karlsruhe, as with the First Symphony.[5] But
this time the composer, perhaps buoyed by the general acclaim accorded the
First during its first year and by the favorable initial reaction to the Second,
chose the more visible and prestigious venue of Vienna. The first performance, given by the Vienna Philharmonic under Hans Richter, was originally scheduled for December 9, 1877. But in one of those little ironies of
music history, it had to be postponed until December 30 because the players
were so preoccupied with learning Wagner's *Rheingold*.[6]

First movement: Allegro non troppo

Perhaps no movement among the symphonies shows quite so well as the first
movement of the Second how Brahms combines two apparently contradictory compositional impulses: expansive lyricism and dense motivic-thematic
working. Historically, this synthesis reflects the dual heritage of Schubert
and Beethoven. The result is pure Brahms.

Lyrical counterpoint, as it might be called, is apparent at the very opening of the movement, which, like that of the First Symphony, grows out of a
small group of contrasting motives (ex. 4–1). As with the First, we must
speak less of an opening "theme" than of a thematic complex, or, as
Brinkmann calls it, a "configuration."[7] The principal three motives are: in
the cellos and basses, a neighbor-note alternation D–C#–D (x) falling to A
(the A is not always part of the motive); in the horns, the triadic F#–A–A figure (y); and in the woodwinds, the small stepwise scale segment, A–B–C#–D
(z). The two lines or parts that carry these motives do not stand to each other
in the traditional relationship of melody to bass; they are virtually equal elements. They are also closely related: the third measure of the horns' phrase
presents motive x in inversion (E–F#–E).

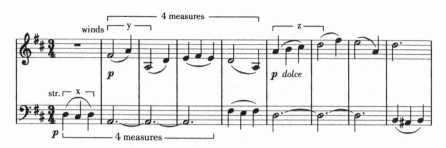

Example 4–1: Second Symphony, I

The lyricism of this opening is tempered by an underlying—and, for Brahms, characteristic—tension created by the independent phrase structure of the two lines. As indicated in ex. 4–1, each falls comfortably into four-measure units that are one measure out of phase. The ambiguous status of m. 1—we are not sure whether to hear it as a weak or strong measure—is a feature of the opening complex that Brahms will exploit.[8] The harmonic corollary to this rhythmic-metrical ambiguity is the absence of any firm tonic triad in root position until m. 44. Although its force is never in doubt, the tonic is obscured in m. 2 by the implied third inversion and, in both mm. 2 and 6, by a metrical position in the weak second measure of the bass's phrase.

The almost surreptitious entry of violins and violas, *piano*, on the last beat of m. 17 adds a new timbral element and disrupts the apparent symmetry of the phrase structure. When the upper strings begin motive *x* in m. 19, we might believe they are to take up the thematic thread from the cellos and basses. Instead they drift downward in a series of arpeggios and octave alternations that seem literally to unravel the preceding material. When the middle and lower registers are reached in m. 26, the strings wander as if lost among the notes of the dominant seventh chord and then break off, in m. 31, on the diminished triad B–D–F♮.

There has been no cadence, no thematic closure—only a receding into silence. This gesture, whereby the movement has come to a halt after barely a minute, is probably unprecedented in the symphonic literature before Brahms. The timpani roll on D that follows in m. 32, *pianissimo*, is no conventional tonic resolution, but an ominous rumbling that ushers in a new sound world of trombones and bass tuba, timbres quite distinct from any of the three—low strings, woodwinds, high strings—that we have heard to this point.

The conductor Vincenz Lachner was sufficiently struck by the change in tone of this passage to ask Brahms in a letter of 1879,

> Why do you throw into the idyllically serene atmosphere with which the first movement begins the rumbling kettledrum, the gloomy lugubrious tones of the trombones and tuba? Would not that seriousness which comes later, or, rather, that assertion of vigorous youthful manliness, have had its own motivation without these tones proclaiming bad news?

In an unusually revealing reply for so tight-lipped a figure, the composer defended the use of the trombones, which he says he "wanted to manage without" in the first movement. But, he explained, "I would have to confess that I am, by the by, a severely melancholic person, that black wings are constantly flapping above us."[9]

The virtual dissolution represented by the timpani-trombone passage of mm. 32–43 is only the most obvious manifestation of Brahms's extraordinary approach to sonata form in this exposition. The first forty-three measures come to seem less like a traditional first theme than a kind of introduction, lying outside the exposition proper. This ambiguity of function is fundamental to Brahms's strategy in the first movement of the Second Symphony.

On the downbeat of m. 44, the tonic at last arrives in a metrically strong, root position. As if in celebration, a new theme unfolds (ex. 4–2), distilling all three motives from the opening: the neighbor note of x, the triadic aspect of y, and the stepwise motion of z, which is here retrograded. Unlike a real first theme, however, this one does not remain stable for long; it evolves rapidly into what we hear as "transition." This process of thematic-formal conflation, by which several functions of the traditional sonata form are compressed, is the logical complement of the earlier blending of "introduction" and "first theme" in mm. 1–43.

In the Second Symphony Brahms draws to some extent on the Schubertian model of the three-key exposition, whereby an intermediate theme and key area—here the broad lullaby in F♯ minor (m. 82)—appear between the tradi-

Example 4–2: Second Symphony, I

tional endpoints of tonic and dominant.[10] But the whole process is invested with greater urgency and continuity than in Schubert. As Carl Schachter has shown in a sensitive analysis, the F♯-minor theme is really a subsidiary phenomenon on the way to the dominant of the dominant: over the longer span of the passage, the F♯ can be heard to move in the bass to F♮ (m. 114), which then underpins an augmented sixth chord and resolves down to E.[11]

The dominant would seem to be at hand, but a Brahmsian detour again forces us to reinterpret the sonata structure. In m. 134, as if in harmonic regression, the second group suddenly freezes on V/V, or E major, and the prevalent rhythmic figure of an eighth note and two sixteenths congeals into a pulsating syncopation. In m. 136 the bassoons and lower strings begin a new theme, based on a rising stepwise motive, z, heard at the opening of the movement but not exploited by Brahms until now. This theme begins on the notated second beat and unfolds as a canon between lower strings and bassoon with upper strings. Because of the syncopated accompanimental figures and the lack of any clear articulation of the downbeat, the listener begins to lose metrical orientation and the notated second beat comes to sound like a downbeat or strong beat.[12] The dominant is reached only twenty measures later, in m. 156.

Development sections normally ratchet up the tension; here Brahms heads initially in the other direction. At the second ending (m. 183), the bass A of motive x is magically reharmonized to form not the dominant of D but the third of F major. The exposition has exploited almost exclusively keys that lie on the "sharp" side of the tonic: F♯, B, E, and A. The sudden shift to F major, which resolves ten measures later to B♭, represents an opposite move—three steps on the flat side of the circle of fifths.

After an energetic fugato based on z, Brahms creates an especially striking transformation in which x is given a rounded melodic shape, or what was in the preceding chapter called thematic fulfillment. From m. 234 on, almost everything has proceeded in phrases or units of two or four measures that alternate thematic units. At m. 274 Brahms changes the large-scale rhythm by creating from x an eight-measure melody comprising a four-measure antecedent and four-measure consequent (ex. 4–3). (This thematic shape

274

Example 4–3: Second Symphony, I

had already been anticipated with the inversion of *x* near the beginning of
the development section at mm. 195–98.) This is followed by another eight-
measure unit based on motive *y*. Immediately thereafter, at m. 290, Brahms
suddenly, and again to great effect, shrinks back to two-measure units.

The moment of recapitulation is a masterful display of Brahmsian harmonic legerdemain (ex. 4–4). In the first movement of the First Symphony,
we recall, Brahms had to a large extent undercut the extensive dominant
preparation of the retransition by means of an abrupt harmonic detour, out
of which—or through which—the recapitulation emerged. In the Second,
he adopts a different, but related, strategy that again manages to circum-
vent the dominant-tonic relationship. The recapitulation proper begins at
m. 302, the moment that the E in the bass resolves to A, the dominant, and
motive *y* enters in the oboes. The tonic is absent: the progression V/V–V
(E-A) ends up one step on the circle of fifths short of where we would expect
it to be.

Thematic-formal conflation complements this harmonic process. The
opening motive *x* does not appear as part of the recapitulation proper, but is
embedded, in augmented form, into the final measures of the retransition in
the first trombone (mm. 298–301). The melody from m. 44, which had

Example 4–4: Second Symphony, I

appeared to be the main theme in the exposition, is now also incorporated into the introduction, which is expanded by means of broad sequences: the initial statement at m. 319, plus the sequences of mm. 327 and 335, the latter being compressed. A magnificent series of modulations—which, over nineteen measures, lead from the dominant of A directly to the second group in B minor—elegantly assimilate the flat tonal regions into the recapitulation; as we have seen, these regions were specifically avoided in the exposition but were featured at the beginning of the development section.

The melancholic passage for timpani and trombones is also modified significantly in the recapitulation. In the exposition it had consisted of three four-measure units (mm. 32–35, 36–39, and 40–43), in each of which one measure of timpani was completed by three of trombones. Now, the first two timpani rolls (mm. 342 and 344) elicit no response whatsoever from the brasses, only continuing downward arpeggiations in the violins. The third roll, in m. 346, brings forth at last the awaited three-measure response with, however, an important timbral change. The trombones and bass tuba are joined by the horns, which carry more pastoral connotations. It is this sonority that began the movement with motive y and that will also initiate its coda.

The first movement of the Second Symphony contains Brahms's most splendid and variegated symphonic coda. The first segment, mm. 447–77, is dominated by the solo horn's nostalgic reverie on an inversion of motive x (from m. 4). In the next segment, the violins attempt to make a genuine melody out of the opening material—to realize fully its lyrical potential—by bringing motives x and y into a new relationship. At the beginning of the movement, we recall, motive x began alone in the bass, followed by the entry of y in the horns; each motive generated its own four-measure phrase, and these phrases were out of phase by a measure. Now, by adding a melodic D above x and before y, as well as a rocking, syncopated accompaniment (ex. 4–5), Brahms throws yet another light on the metrical-rhythmic qualities of the thematic complex. By its first-measure position in the phrase and the fact that it is supported by a tonic harmony, the treble D of m. 477 almost sounds like the strong measure of a two-measure unit. And yet because of our previous perception of motive y as having its own downbeat quality, the D dotted half note and its complement, the A two measures later, remain weak; the real eight-measure unit of the melody is formed by mm. 478–85.

From free reverie to structured melody to lilting dance: the final, scherzando segment of the coda (from m. 497) changes mood yet again. Thematically, it draws directly upon the transition between first and second themes (mm. 66–78) that was heard in the exposition but *not* in the recapit-

477

Example 4–5: Second Symphony, I

ulation. The absence of this transition passage in the recapitulation makes
its emergence and transformation in the coda all the more compelling.

Brahms adds a new element here: the flutes and oboes in mm. 502–5 play
a modification of motive *x* (ex. 4–6a) that alludes, as Brahms himself acknowledged, to one of the composer's own songs in the same key, D major. *Es
lieb sich so lieblich im Lenze!* ("Love is so lovely in spring"), op. 71, no. 1
(ex. 4–6b), was composed in the same summer as the Second Symphony.
There is directly shared melodic material in the upward melodic leap B–E at
the words "die zärtlichen." And the harmonic progression, moving through
the circle of fifths toward the tonic (B–E–A–D, or vi–V/V–V–I), is common to
both song and symphony.

Overall, the first movement of the Second Symphony presents two very
different moods, the more melancholic one hinted at in the appearance of the
timpani and trombones—and perhaps again in the disorienting developmental canon in the second group and the fugato of the development—and the

(a)
502

(b)
10

win - det die zärt - lich - sten   Krän - ze

Example 4–6: (a) Second Symphony, I; (b) *Es liebt sich
so lieblich im Lenze!*, op. 71, no.1

brighter, more pastoral one suggested by the other main themes of the exposition and recapitulation and the beginning of the development. The third segment of the coda seems to confirm the happier mood. But the final cadence, in mm. 521–23, brings back the timpani and trombones specifically associated with a darker side that cannot—and will not, in what follows—be ignored.

Second movement: Adagio non troppo

The Adagio is constructed as a modified sonata form. A full, expansive exposition, with first (mm. 1–32), second (mm. 33–44), and closing (mm. 45–48) groups in the conventional key areas of tonic and dominant, is followed by a brief development (mm. 49–68) that grows directly out of the closing group; in the recapitulation, the second group is omitted but a further, "secondary" development (mm. 87–91) is inserted.[13] The closing group reemerges (mm. 92–96), followed by a coda based on the first group (mm. 97–104). When listening to this movement one has little sense of a predetermined larger form but rather of the form growing moment by moment, section by section out of the thematic material.

The low strings, woodwinds, and trombones at the opening take us back immediately to the more somber world of the first movement. The twelve-measure main theme (ex. 4–7) begins in a cloud of metric-harmonic ambiguity, on a weak beat (beat 4) and over a "weak" note (the dominant F$\sharp$). Beats 4 and 2, rather than the expected 1 and 3, continue to receive the emphasis so that until the arrival of the tonic on the downbeat of m. 3, they appear to determine the meter.

This theme unfolds by means of "developing variation" in that most of its components derive from a continuous reshaping of the descending line of m. 1. As if to allow the proselike developing variation maximum comprehensibility, Brahms forgoes real variety of tone color in the presentation of the theme, which appears only in the cellos.

The first half of the theme presents three distinct ideas in the form $aa'bcc'$. The twofold presentations of the outer figures serve to balance the single inner one: like the uniform tone color, the phrase symmetry helps to make the musical prose intelligible. Figures a and b are both built from a descending scale; b begins with a rising fourth (B–E) that is to become a critical motive in this movement. Like a, the triadic figure c is repeated (c') and cadences in a way that alludes to but does not state the tonic; the initial melodic note D$\sharp$ of m. 6 is unaccompanied. The chord that emerges on the second beat is in fact iii, or D$\sharp$ minor.

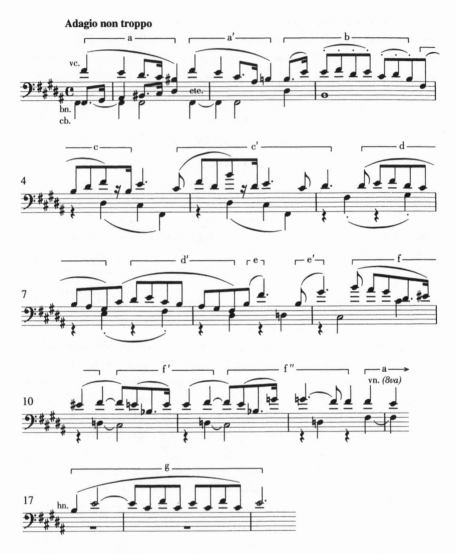

Example 4–7: Second Symphony, II

Now begins idea *d*, which relates closely to *a* in that it is built from a descending scale and stresses the second and fourth beats. Like *a*, figure *d* is repeated sequentially and gives way to a fifth component, *e* and *e'*, which consist of upward striving two-note groups that clearly are related to previous gestures but are now isolated. A cadential phrase, *f*, is given a threefold presentation (*f*, *f'*, and *f"*), more than any previous phrase—as if the triple iteration is necessary to bring such a wide-ranging, irregular theme to close. Yet like previous cadences, this one too is avoided: the melodic F♯ of m. 10 is harmonized with D major, a harmony that remains in force through the closure on this chord in m. 12.

Now comes the first real pause or break in the prose: a counterstatement or repetition of the theme begins in the full orchestra on the last beat of m. 12. This counterstatement begins with figures *a*, *b*, and one statement of *c*, but then deviates from the original. The tail of *c*, the rising fourth motive B–E, now generates a new continuation, which we might call *g* (m. 17, shown in ex. 4–7). This gesture is the first strong indication of the powerful developmental role that the rising fourth motive plays in this movement. Figure *g* is introduced by the horn, then taken up as an extended fugato by oboe, flute, and cellos. In m. 27 the fugato dissipates as quickly as it had arrived; *b* resumes its familiar course almost as though nothing had happened, builds to a large climax, and resolves to the dominant, F♯, at m. 33.

In this key begins the second group of the movement, whose main theme represents a remote but recognizable variation of figures *c* (rising triadically) and *a*, *b*, and *d* (descending stepwise) from the first theme. The second theme is almost dancelike after the brooding ambiguities of the first group. It is followed by a closing theme in which the rising fourth motive, transposed to F♯–B, is now filled in with stepwise motion; this is a transformation of the motive that is to have far-reaching implications.

Instead of coming to a quiet cadence as might a conventional closing theme in a sonata exposition, this closing theme swells outward, after only four measures, into a powerful development. As Tovey expressed it, "A child may say the word that makes history; and so this unpretentious theme startles us by moving, with a rapid crescendo, into distant keys, and blazing out in a stormy fugato."[14] The fugato theme really has two forms: the original fourth, rising stepwise B–E, which is presented in the woodwinds; and the modified version presented in the strings, in which the motive rises initially a third, from B to D, and the D is tied over, resolving to E in the next beat (ex. 4–8).

Example 4–8: Second Symphony, II

One can hardly emphasize enough the fluidity and originality of Brahms's thematic-formal techniques at this point in the movement. When the filled-in fourth motive moves into the energetic development section at m. 49, Brahms is fulfilling a process he has already begun earlier, when the same basic motive, as part of phrase *g* in the first theme, gave rise to a developmental fugato (mm. 17–27). Whereas the earlier fugato was a mysterious interruption or parenthesis in the middle of the exposition, the new one, again generated by the fourth motive, "blazes out" in a more forceful manner to form the real development section of the movement.

Yet like earlier thematic ideas, this fugato is short-lived; after only six measures, it comes to an abrupt halt on a diminished seventh chord, sustained *tremolando* by the strings. Among the woodwinds drifts a transformation of the fourth motive in which the fourth, or final note of resolution, is missing (ex. 4–9). This transformation to a rising third proves to be a profound one, for in m. 57 it is suddenly overlaid by phrase *a* of the first theme in the violins. This moment, as well as similar ones in mm. 62 and 65, associates the rising scalar figure in dotted rhythms, played by the bassoons as counterpoint to *a* (shown in ex. 4–7), with the triplet, rising-third version of the fourth motive. The main theme of the movement thus seems to be reborn or recreated out of a motivic element that it helped to generate in phrases *a* and *b* at the opening. There is in the symphonies perhaps no more impressive example of Brahms's powers of thematic development and association, nor of his ability to integrate motivic development with formal processes.

Example 4–9: Second Symphony, II

Although the main theme makes its first tentative reappearance at m. 57, this moment does not constitute the start of the recapitulation. The key, G major, is wrong; and as if in acknowledgment of this fact, the theme breaks off in m. 59 and resumes its developmental wanderings. The actual recapitulation begins on the last beat of m. 67, where the theme is embellished in triplets (ex. 4–10). This transformation of *a* associates the theme with the triplet figuration—and the $\frac{12}{8}$ meter—of the second group, figuration that

Example 4–10: Second Symphony, II

has also dominated the development section. This triplet rhythm, which through the development has also come to be associated with the fourth motive, continues to permeate the recapitulation.

In the recapitulation at m. 87, phrase *g* throws off its original modest demeanor; the fourth motive explodes *forte* into a brief but bold secondary development based on phrase *b*. This developmental passage lasts six measures before subsiding onto the closing theme. The surprising "extra" developmental passage seems to be an explicit reaction to the fugato. Twice before, a version of the fourth has given way to a fugato; now that path is rejected by an impassioned phrase *b*.

The closing theme (m. 92) now churns with the chromatic turbulence of the secondary development that has preceded it. Just before the coda, in m. 96 (ex. 4–11), Brahms again associates the main theme with the transformed fourth motive, now in a still more direct fashion than at the recapitulation. This motive, in the form of the rising third that dominated the development section, appears isolated in the bassoons. A moment later at the start of the coda (m. 97), and with the change of meter to **C**, the same instruments take up the counterpoint in dotted rhythm to phrase *a*. Although the

Example 4–11: Second Symphony, II

powerful developmental motive of the fourth has now been brought home, the main theme has not returned—and cannot return, after such a remarkable journey—to its original state. In the coda, it is tinged unavoidably with the solemn triplet rhythm of the second group and development, which now appears as a muted but persistent figure in the timpani.

Third movement: Allegretto grazioso (Quasi Andantino)

Although at barely five minutes it is Brahms's briefest symphonic movement, the Allegretto of the Second Symphony is also one of his most original creations. The basic outline of scherzo-trio-scherzo that is maintained in the Allegretto of the First here recedes much farther into the distance. Indeed, this movement could be said to break the mold.

From one perspective, the movement might be heard as a scherzo with two trios, like those of Schumann's symphonies, in the form A (m. 1) B (m. 33) A' (m. 107) C (m. 126) A" (m. 194) Coda (m. 219). For ease of reference we may stick with these designations, but the interpenetration and variation of material among the segments of the structure are really too extensive to permit even so general a schematic formulation. Some commentators have suggested that the movement resembles a Baroque suite of dance movements. There is some plausibility to this idea in that the main theme undergoes metrical-rhythmic variation characteristic of the suite. Furthermore, the scoring of the opening is a throwback, an evocation of a Classical or Preclassical woodwind ensemble accompanied by pizzicato cello. This sense of homage to the past is particularly striking after the Adagio, one of the least historically retrospective movements in all of Brahms.

The elegant first theme of A (a in ex. 4–12) unfolds within a traditional eight measures, dividing into 4 + 4 and moving from the tonic to the dominant. But the continuation from m. 9 lifts us out of the past directly into the world of Brahms, who extends the phrase by repeating its little E–D tail an octave higher, then again in the original register. When the melody returns to the upper octave in m. 11, we expect this to be a further repetition of the first phrase. In fact, however, this E–D serves to begin the next theme (b).

For the B section of the movement the meter changes from $\frac{3}{4}$ to a rapid $\frac{2}{4}$, marked Presto ma non assai. The Presto has a more complicated structure than the Allegretto, but one that can be ultimately characterized as a b a'. Initially, the a theme reproduces with astonishing exactness the structure of the a theme from the Allegretto (ex. 4–13), including the alternating octave "echoes" of the E–D, now embedded in the eighth-note figure, F♯–E–F♯–D.

Example 4–12: Second Symphony, III

Then Brahms brings his developmental and variational powers to the fore. Instead of immediately generating a *b* theme, Brahms inverts the two-note tail so that the descent becomes an ascent (A–B, B–C; mm. 45–46) that spirals chromatically away from the key of G.

In m. 51 the *b* theme of the Presto begins in C major; the once languid E–D motive has been whipped up into a vigorous, stomping peasant dance over an insistent pedal. The extension and registral alternation of the E–D motive after m. 93 may lead us to expect yet another appearance of the stomping dance. Instead, the earlier chromatic climb is halted, and we are guided gently back into the original Allegretto at m. 107.

Brahms accomplishes the transition from the duple-meter Presto to the triple-meter Allegretto by means of what, in the later twentieth century, would

Example 4–13: Second Symphony, III

be called a *metrical modulation*. This involves changing meter at a specific proportion or ratio, while keeping a continuous pulse across the shift. The Presto has unfolded mainly in phrases of even numbers, but mm. 101–06 are cast as two *three*-measure phrases (ex. 4–14). At the ratio specified by Brahms—that a half note or full measure of the Presto is equal to a quarter note, or one beat, of the Allegretto—three measures of the Presto would be equivalent to one full measure of the Allegretto. Brahms makes the transition not only metrically, but thematically and instrumentally: the Allegretto *a* theme is directly anticipated by the repeated melodic Bs and the scoring of mm. 101–6, which employs oboes, bassoons, and pizzicato cellos.[15]

Example 4–14: Second Symphony, III

The Allegretto melody returns at its original pitches, but its first two measures are now harmonized in A minor rather than the original G major. G major appears in m. 109, but it is initially over a dominant, or D, pedal; the tonic returns in the bass only in m. 110. In the next measure, the theme seems to start over again, as if trying to restore the proper harmonic decorum. But it still refuses to unfold as before. Now it becomes stuck, so to speak, in its fourth measure (m. 114). Instead of moving ahead to its second four-measure phrase, the melodic figure of the fourth measure is repeated an extraordinary ten times in mm. 115–24. The tonality has turned from G major to a darker E minor.

Then suddenly at m. 126, after a closure on E major, the spell is broken, the clouds are dispersed, and we return to a Presto, now in $\frac{3}{8}$ meter. The first four measures, a downward scalar run in eighth notes, can be heard as a direct transformation of the circular triplet figures of the preceding Allegretto. This "trio" returns not to the main Allegretto theme but to the earlier Presto's *b* theme in the form it took in C major at m. 51.

In the final appearance of the Allegretto, Brahms takes even further the practice of beginning out of the key. The main or *a* theme enters in the remote key of F♯ major and modulates in its fifth and sixth measures to the dominant,

B major. And here a remarkable thing happens (ex. 4–15). As the *a* theme cadences on the dominant, or B, in mm. 200–201, its profile *and* its key recall the second phrase or unit, *a'*, of the main theme of the second movement of the symphony, the Adagio (see above, ex. 4–7). The effect is uncanny in a movement that has seemed so little preoccupied with its own immediate past within the symphony.

Example 4–15: Second Symphony, III

This recollection triggers another one. The *b* theme of the Allegretto is based, as we have seen, on the two-note descending figure (originally E–D, in m. 11) taken from the tail of the *a* theme and developed in a brief transition. In the final Allegretto, Brahms refines this process. In the last phrase of *a* in m. 201, Brahms *inverts* the figure, here to A♯–B; the inversion is answered in the woodwinds by the original descending form, and the dialogue continues until, in m. 205, the strings alter the two-note descent into a three-note neighbor figure that seems to recall motive *x* of the first movement.

The reference seems to make explicit what was already implicit in theme *b* earlier on: we realize that all along it has incorporated a neighbor-note figure. Because of the original rhythm (quarter–dotted quarter–eighth) and the fact that there was a whole step (E–D) rather than the characteristic half step of motive *x*, we have not been aware earlier of any relationship to *x*. But with the additional transitional measures between *a* and *b* added by Brahms in mm. 205–6 in the final Allegretto, which present motive *x* in something closer to its original form (in quarter notes, with a half step between the notes), Brahms makes the association for us in the most elegant fashion imaginable.

But more surprises are in store. At the shift to E♭ in m. 225, where, by analogy to m. 29, we would expect merely the sustaining of chords in the woodwinds, there blossoms a glorious new melody, *molto dolce*, in the violins (ex. 4–16), consisting of a four-measure phrase that cadences in G minor. The strings drop out and the consequent is taken up by the woodwinds (m. 229), who transform it into a linear, chromatic figure moving in contrary motion between flutes (descending) and oboes and bassoons (ascending). One of the darkest moments in the movement, this perhaps hints at the melancholic mood of the first two movements.

Example 4–16: Second Symphony, III

In its final appearance (m. 233), the *a* theme gets only as far as its third measure, whence it freezes on a sustained half-diminished seventh chord (ex. 4–17). This pause, whose last beat is held out by a fermata, seems unusually long in a movement that has flowed along at a decent clip. It is as if the preceding chromaticism, in the consequent of the new G-minor melody, has opened up another world that cannot easily be shut out.

Example 4–17: Second Symphony, III

This conclusion is essentially the shadowy world of the Adagio, which has been glimpsed earlier in the thematic and tonal reference to the slow movement at mm. 200–201. The Allegretto cannot escape that world, as the prolonged half-diminished chord of mm. 235–37 seems to confirm. As if acknowledging that closure must nevertheless take place, Brahms breaks off the chord and makes a highly stylized cadence to G major. This cadence (ex. 4–17) is like a gesture from a Classical minuet; it is as if the Allegretto has had to reach outside itself, to the musical past, to achieve an ending.

Fourth movement: Allegro con spirito

The finale of the Second Symphony is structurally and expressively the most straightforward of the four movements. It is in a broad sonata form, with a full exposition (mm. 1–155), which is not repeated; a development section (155–244); a recapitulation (244–353); and a substantial coda (353–429). Despite its prevailing cheerfulness and the genuine jubilation of its ending, the finale is by no means all lightness and joy. As if acknowledging the difficulty of casting off the shadow of the sustained chord near the end of Allegretto, the movement begins *sotto voce*, with a theme whose first two measures unfold in tightly controlled octaves (ex. 4–18).

Example 4–18: Second Symphony, IV

That both main themes of the exposition (mm. 1, 78) are based on motive *x* is an indication of how actively the finale resumes the larger business of the symphony. In the first theme, the motive comes complete with the D–C♯–D neighbor note and the drop of a fourth, D–A. The second four measures of the theme and the consequent phrase, beginning in m. 9, develop the descending fourth, which is to become a key element in this

movement. Rather than rising in volume, the theme shrinks in m. 13 to
pianissimo. Then, in m. 18, the harmony, which has held closely to the
tonic and dominant, slips to outline a remote C^7, or augmented sixth chord,
and then recedes through chromatic voice-leading to total silence in m. 22
(ex. 4–19a).

Example 4–19: (a) Second Symphony, IV; (b) Second Symphony, I

The world of the Adagio, evoked by similar means near the end of the
Allegretto, has resurfaced and brought the finale to a reflective halt. The
strategy is also analogous to the long unwinding through arpeggiated descent
near the beginning of the first movement (mm. 20ff.). Indeed, the bass line
([C]—B♭—A—G♮) and the chromatic voice-leading in contrary motion in the
finale distinctly recall—though in a different scoring—the solemn trombone
passage in the first movement (ex. 4–19b).

As before, the silence must be overcome if the movement is to go forward. In m. 23, after a startling "extra" beat of silence, the full orchestra
bursts forth with the dominant of D, banishing chromaticism and silence,
and leading to the tonic and a *forte* counterstatement of the main theme in
m. 24. The counterstatement unleashes all the energy suppressed at the
opening. Now the theme bursts its original structural framework: the
antecedent generates its own new continuation that extends all the way to
m. 44, where the consequent phrase, based on the descending fourths,
begins. It too has been expanded from its original, rather spindly, legato
form (m. 9) into a robust theme.

Just as he had reworked the antecedent and consequent, Brahms expands
the mysterious, chromatic conclusion of the opening theme from mm. 18–22.
Now the C^7 generates or stabilizes its own key area, F major, in mm. 62–65.

As before, Brahms brings the remote region back to the tonic, here the tonic minor, and finally prepares the second group, which arrives in the dominant at m. 78.

The development section of the finale divides into two large and parallel segments, each of which treats consecutively the two phrases of the main theme. The second segment, marked *tranquillo* (m. 206), begins in F♯ major and moves slowly toward the dominant, A, reached in m. 227. We might expect this A to shape the retransition and resolve to D at the start of the recapitulation. Instead, a Brahmsian detour is opened.

On the first beat of m. 234, Brahms has modulated up another third from A, to C major. Then, as seems to happen so often in this symphony, comes a portentous silence. By analogy to the first section of the development (m. 184) and the first segment of the second section (m. 214), we would expect the descending-fourths motive here. The phrase indeed appears, now with pedal points on C sounding in the strings; but the fourths are augmented to become solemn, choralelike half notes, played *pianissimo*. (One can be certain that Mahler had this striking passage in his ears when writing the slow introduction to his First Symphony in the same key some ten or eleven years later.)

Participating in the fourths chorale in m. 234 are the trombones and tuba, which emerge as featured instruments for the first time in this movement. Up to this point the associations with the first two movements of the symphony have been principally motivic-thematic in nature; now, a timbral connection suggests a more significant relationship, one that is to be deepened still further in the coda.

As the fourths motive unfolds downward from C, then from D, the entire original consequent phrase from mm. 9–11, expanded in augmentation, reconstructs itself before our ears (ex. 4–20). The detour has led us, at last, back to A, but to an A that has little of the feeling of a normal dominant. There is no leading tone (C♯) to propel us toward D, and the F♮s and B♭s in the phrase in any case inflect toward D minor, rather than major. As in the first movement, to which this one alludes in so many ways, Brahms's challenge here was to prepare the recapitulation of a quiet, understated main theme. Boisterous or sustained dominant preparation would have ruined the return. In the first movement, Brahms bypassed the dominant by approaching the recapitulation directly from the half-diminished ii⁷ chord. In the finale, the dominant is not so much avoided as it is stripped of some of its most characteristic traits.

The recapitulation begins in m. 244, where, as Tovey so aptly expresses it, "the original key is reached in darkness, and the cold unison of the first

Example 4–20: Second Symphony, IV

theme meets us like the grey daylight on a western cloud-bank opposite the sunrise."[16] Brahms seems to avoid the moments and gestures that so distinctly allied the exposition and development to the preceding movements, especially to the first. Gone are the mysterious diversions or temporal unravelings created by the C[7] chords (m. 17 and m. 63). Now the abbreviated counterstatement of the main theme, beginning at m. 265, moves directly to the second theme (m. 281).

The real surprises in this movement are reserved for the large coda (m. 353), which proves fully worthy of its counterpart in the first movement and serves genuinely to "wrap up" the symphony as a whole. The mode turns from major to minor, and the trombones and tuba, emerging here for the first time since the retransition, initiate a powerful transformation of the second theme (ex. 4–21). Where in the exposition and recapitulation the second theme has been a regularly constructed, rounded eight-measure melody (mm. 78–85, 281–88), this transformation isolates the initial syncopation of the theme and creates from it a highly energized six-measure unit. The unit is treated in overlapping sequences (beginning at mm. 353, 358), which are then reduced to five-measure units (mm. 363, 367), before breaking off at m. 371.

The large-scale harmonic component of this passage is equally dynamic. Brahms moves boldly down by whole step from D minor (m. 353), to C major

Example 4–21: Second Symphony, IV

(m. 358), to B♭ major (m. 363). In m. 371 the B♭ chord is reinterpreted as a seventh, thus forming a German sixth in D major, the tonic. But the chord in fact refuses to behave or resolve in that way. Instead, in another gesture of delay or unraveling in the symphony, the harmonic-motivic element of this B♭⁷ chord is augmented (ex. 4–22a), suspended in time.

Example 4–22: (a) Second Symphony, IV; (b) Second Symphony, I

This moment returns us once again to the larger tale of the symphony, for its bass line, B♭–A–G♯, and its three-note shape recall the trombone and timpani passage near the opening of the first movement (m. 37, as shown in ex. 4–22b). Like the passage earlier in the movement at mm. 20–22 (see above, ex. 4–19), the reference to the first movement is subtle but unmistakable, not just because of the now identical bass line and identical final chord (G♯–D–F: the B♭ of the augmented sixth is dropped in m. 374), but because the compositional-formal impulse is similar: in both the first movement and the finale, the gestures bring things to a meditative halt.

In each case, the movement must gather momentum to continue. In the coda of the finale, this is accomplished by bringing back the triplet, *tranquillo* transformation of the main theme heard in the development. At its first appearance this theme, by virtue of its neighbor-note figure, resembled not only the main theme, but also the second theme (m. 78), which likewise features a neighbor-note figure and the upward leap of a third. As if to reinforce this latter association, the transformation is now, in m. 375, played directly over the second theme in its original form in the lower strings and woodwinds.

The transformation builds up to a *forte* statement of the main theme's head motive (m. 387), which in turn leads to an exhilarating passage of scales. Although resolution is clearly at hand, Brahms provides two more brief moments of delay, as the scales come to an abrupt halt in the second half of m. 408, and again in m. 412. Pauses of this kind are not uncommon in the finales of Classical symphonies, especially those of Haydn. But in Brahms's Second, these brief interruptions to the jubilation of the finale serve not just as witty compositional asides, but as the last reminders—and then overcomings—of the gestures of delay or silence that have been heard throughout the symphony.

In a conclusion to his thoughtful monograph on Brahms's Second Symphony, Brinkmann confesses that he finds the scherzo and finale of the work lacking in depth: they are both "a little too 'lightweight' after the profundities of the first two [movements]." The finale, especially in comparison with the first movement, strikes him as being "almost devoid of mysteries, without real complications, very directly optimistic."[17] He misses any sense of a "breakthrough" from the more reflective world of the first two movements.

Brinkmann may be asking too much of Brahms's symphony, whose expressive and structural universe could not sustain a cataclysmic breakthrough like that in the finale to Mahler's First, where D major emerges in a triumphant chorale. (The German term for breakthrough, *Durchbruch*, was coined in this sense by Paul Bekker in his monograph on Mahler's symphonies and later taken up by Adorno.) But that does not mean that there is no larger design for which the finale acts as fulfillment or completion. As I have suggested, Brahms builds a sequence of ideas across the entire Second Symphony, through motivic-rhythmic and timbral associations as well as more purely gestural ones, such as silence. No apology is needed for the last two movements, which fulfill their appointed roles quite comfortably.

It might even be said that in this regard the finale of the Second surpasses that of the First. In the First, Brahms supplied the finale with a slow introduction in order to regain the somber mood of the first movement and thus to reenter the larger process of the symphony, for which the C-major Allegro con brio then serves as resolution. In the Second, Brahms gives up the "crutch" of a slow introduction and relies on other means to make the finale an effective conclusion to the symphony.

Chapter 5

THE THIRD SYMPHONY, OP. 90

———————————————— ✺ ————————————————

$\mathcal{V}$ery little hard information survives about the genesis of the Third Symphony. As Christian Schmidt has observed, "All we know are the place and time of its completion: Wiesbaden, Geisbergerstraße 19, c/o Frau von Dewitz, where Brahms spent the summer of 1883."[1] Six years had elapsed since the composition of the Second Symphony. The interregnum was by no means devoid of orchestral activity on Brahms's part: it included the Violin Concerto, op. 77 (1878); the Academic Festival Overture, op. 80, and the Tragic Overture, op. 81 (both 1880); and the Second Piano Concerto, op. 83 (1881). Each shows Brahms at the height of his powers as a composer of large-scale works. But none prepares us for the highly original way in which Brahms seems to rethink symphonic form in the Third Symphony.

The Third is by far the briefest of Brahms's symphonies, in most performances lasting about half an hour.[2] Moreover, the relative durations of its individual movements are closer to being equal than in any of the other three symphonies. The more compact dimensions and balanced proportions seem intended to point up the aspects of the symphony that transcend its individual movements.

The Third Symphony as a whole is governed by three processes, all interrelated to some extent. First, there is a *thematic* process, the most obvious manifestation of which is the return of the opening theme and the three-note "motto" at the conclusion of the finale. Another theme that plays a similar, if less prominent, role is the choralelike second theme of the Andante (m. 41), which is replaced by a different theme in the recapitulation of that movement and then resurfaces three times in the finale.

The second process is a more purely *harmonic* or tonal one that orients the entire symphony around F. The outer movements are in F: the first in F major, the finale beginning in F minor and ending in major. There is, of course, nothing surprising in that tonal scheme. But a special aspect of the Third Symphony is that *both* inner movements are in the key of C, major and minor respectively. This design, with two inner movements unfolding in the key of the dominant, is, to my knowledge, without precedent in the Classic-Romantic repertory. In the Third Symphony Brahms sets up a dominant "plateau" that creates a tonal tension somewhat analogous to that of sonata form.

The third large-scale process at work in the Third Symphony is in essence both tonal and thematic: it involves a *pitch conflict* between A♮ and A♭, respectively the major and minor third degrees of F. Across the symphony, especially in the outer movements, this conflict is worked out both harmonically, through juxtapositions of the key areas of F major, F minor, A major, and A♭ major; and thematically, in that the two pitches are also incorporated prominently into the themes of the individual movements.

First movement: Allegro con brio

The first movement begins with a striking gesture that has no exact parallel in any other work by Brahms. Many of his compositions—the First and Second Symphonies are, as we have seen, fine examples—begin with a motive or motives that become integral elements of the principal themes. The Third begins instead with what may be called a motto, an upward striving F–A♭–F figure announced by the brasses and woodwinds (ex. 5–1). What is unusual about this gesture, in comparison with, say, the germinating motive *x*, D–C♯–D, of the Second Symphony, is that it recurs virtually unchanged throughout the movement; it is not developed or transformed in any traditional sense. The motto tends to form not the substance of the actual themes, but their sonic background.[3] Perhaps the boldest thing about the motto—and the aspect of its tonal constitution that will be most important for the symphony as a whole—is its juxtaposition of the pitches A♮ and A♭ through the framing of the diminished seventh chord of m. 2 by the F-major chords of mm. 1 and 3.

The main theme proper of the first movement enters in the violins in m. 3 simultaneously with the last note of the motto, which then goes "underground" to begin its own restatement in the double basses. As the theme continues to expand outward in m. 7, the motto adheres to it as if clinging to a raft surging on the rapids. Now the motto returns to the winds (the double

Example 5–1: Third Symphony, I

basses take on an independent bass line) and appears three times in diminution: on the dominant in mm. 7–8, the tonic in mm. 9–10, and the subdominant in mm. 11–12. The motto has changed in one significant respect: at the
opening, it had three notes, of which the last overlapped with the first of a
restatement; the motto now unfolds in a four-note form (1–♭3–8–♮3) that is
fully contained within a two-measure unit.

In m. 15, Brahms begins a new theme that functions as a transition to the
second group. For the first four measures the motto is absent, as though it
has been somehow banished by the cadence to F major. But in m. 19, it
returns in its original form, beginning on A. The motto is now used to prepare a modulation by means of sequence to the eventual key of the second
group, A, which is reached by a series of descending major thirds characteristic of Brahms's tonal practice: F–D♭–A. The enharmonic respelling of the
D♭ as C♯ in m. 29, followed by the change of key signature in m. 31, signals
the arrival of the second key area.[4]

The choice of the mediant for a second group was certainly not without
precedent in sonata-form movements by 1883, although it was much more
common in minor-mode pieces than in major-mode ones. In the latter, moreover, the mediant itself often appears in minor and serves as an intermediate

step on the way to the dominant, as in the three-key expositions in the first movements of Schubert's "Great" C-Major Symphony (C–e–G) or of Brahms's Second (D–f♯–A).

In Brahms's Third, the choice of A major, which turns to minor at the end of the exposition, forms part of the larger-scale strategies outlined above. First, it shows Brahms avoiding C, the dominant of F, at a place—the second group—where it might be expected to appear. This absence is part of the plan to "save" it for the coda of the first movement and for the middle movements, where it forms the dominant plateau within the symphony. Second, the choice of A projects the motivic aspects of the opening motto onto the larger harmonic dimension of the symphony. Schoenberg was impressed enough with this technique to discuss it in his *Theory of Harmony*, a book in which pieces from the standard repertory are seldom analyzed:

> When Brahms introduces the second theme of his Third Symphony (F major [first movement]) in the key of A major, it is not because one "can introduce" the second theme just as well in the key of the mediant. It is rather the consequence of a principal motive, of the bass melody (harmonic connection!) f–a♭ (third and fourth measures), whose many repetitions, derivations, and variations finally make it necessary, as a temporary high point, for the progression f–a♭ to expand to the progression f–a (F, the initial key, A, the key of the second theme). Thus, the basic motive is given by the initial key and the key of the second theme.[5]

In other words, the key area of the second group represents an expansion of the interval of the third in the opening theme, and it partakes of the juxtaposition of A♭ and A that lies at the heart of the symphony.

The exposition ends in the key of A minor, thus replicating on a new tonal level (with the pitches C♯ and C♮) the F major-minor conflict within the first group. As if to reinforce this association, Brahms brings back the motto in the key of A minor at m. 49. The motto continues to saturate what may be called the first closing theme, beginning at m. 61 (ex. 5–2). Here the motto is rhythmically displaced across the barline, appearing both in its original three-note form and in embellished diminution. The second closing theme (m. 70; ex. 5–3) can be said to combine elements of both the motto and the first theme, or to confirm their close relationship, a relationship that becomes especially apparent when the repeat of the exposition is taken, bringing us immediately back to the motto and first theme in their original form. The bass at m. 70 is like a filled-in version of the motto, while the

Example 5–2: Third Symphony, I

Example 5–3: Third Symphony, I

melody has something of the outline of the descending arpeggiation of the first theme.

The exposition has thus used the motto as a way of exploiting and exposing some of the tonal processes that lie at the core of the movement—and symphony—as a whole. The third relations, the ♭3–♮3 conflict, and the octave span—all set out so compactly and boldly in the motto—become the very substance of much of the movement. When the second theme reappears at the start of the development in C♯ minor (m. 77), the cycle of third relations is continued: F–A–C♯.

Before turning to the development section, we should return to the opening of the exposition to examine another crucial element that affects the first movement—that of meter and rhythm. Perhaps in no other first movement by Brahms does the development of these elements play so critical a role. The first movement of the Third is cast in $\frac{6}{4}$ meter, a duple meter that is also open, through internal recasting as $\frac{3}{2}$ (a so-called hemiola). Metrical ambiguity arises in the very first appearance of the motto, which thus comes to embody not only a tonal conflict but a metrical one as well (see above, ex. 5–1). The first two chords are sustained for a full measure; unless listeners are actually watching a conductor, they will have no clue as to the internal articulation of the measure.[6]

The real ambiguity or contradiction arises when the latent duple meter of the motto is confronted in m. 3 with the first theme, which has a profile much closer to $\frac{3}{2}$ or triple articulation of the measure. The accompaniment pattern in the violas and cellos (shown in ex. 5–1) does little to resolve the ambiguity. Only the trombones and timpani, which cut off their chord and roll, respectively, on beat 4, support the notated $\frac{6}{4}$ meter. The notated meter at last prevails in m. 7, where the motto appears in diminution—thus two notes to a measure—and other parts unequivocally support duple articulation.

The metrical "problem" of the movement is further explored in the second group, which is cast in $\frac{9}{4}$ meter (ex. 5–4). Here the duple $\frac{6}{4}$ is in effect expanded into a triple meter by the addition of another half measure, or three beats. It could be said that the metrical expansion here is the direct corollary to the harmonic "expansion" that Schoenberg identified in the A-major tonality of the second group.

Example 5–4: Third Symphony, I

The second theme consists of a one-measure "module" that is continually reinterpreted within the basic 37-beat unit. The downbeat of the first measure remains empty, in the melody. In the next measure the downbeat is filled with a quarter-note F♯, and the thematic figure that occupies the last three beats is altered by diminution. In the third measure, the downbeat is now occupied by a half note, F♯. This displaces the E–F♯ neighbor motion from beats two and three onto beats three and four. The first part of the module is altered yet again in m. 39, where the F♯–E neighbor motion is given in a diminution that also incorporates the A formerly restricted to beat 6. The whole process of this little theme is so fluid, so malleable, that it virtually defies either verbal description or graphic representation.

At the return to $\frac{6}{4}$ (m. 49) for the transition to the closing group of the exposition, Brahms sets in motion another metrical process, which involves the *displacement* or shifting of the notated meter. At m. 50, the notated sixth beat begins to take on an accent or emphasis because it becomes the first beat in a three-beat grouping that extends over the bar line. This grouping becomes still clearer in mm. 55ff., where Brahms even creates a hemiola within the shifted groupings: two groups of three are recast as three groups of two. The notated downbeat is firmly restored at m. 59, but the metrical grid again begins to shift backwards, or visually toward the "left" (see above, ex. 5–2), so that one tends to hear a $\frac{6}{4}$ beginning on the sixth beat. Beginning at m. 69 (see above, ex. 5–3), the sixth and third beats are tied to the successive beats such that notated strong beats are suppressed and the $\frac{6}{4}$ meter seems fully displaced.

Only at m. 77, where the development section begins with a version of the second theme in C♯ minor, is the notated meter restored. The weak sixth beat of m. 76 comes as a surprise; it sounds like an extra beat within the prevailing displaced $\frac{6}{4}$ framework. It is an example of what music theorist David Lewin has called a transformational beat, one that mediates between two metrical frameworks.[7]

In the development section, at m. 101, the motto returns for the first time since the transition to the closing group of the exposition. Here, in a splendid example of the kind of thematic fulfillment we have identified in the development sections of the first two symphonies, the motto for the first time becomes a melody or a more extended theme. Its normal three-note form is expanded by a falling stepwise line that is appended to the last note (see chapter 1, ex. 1–2). This gesture has the effect of humanizing or softening the motto. But even in its new lyrical form, the motto still, as it turns out, retains its original basic function of introducing the main theme, which returns (still within the development) *pianissimo* in the somber and remote key of E♭ minor at m. 112. The theme at last follows its natural tendency to unfold in $\frac{3}{2}$.

In the final measures of the development section, as the dotted rhythms of the theme pulsate steadily, Brahms seems be preparing not the tonic key, F major, but rather B♭ (ex. 5–5). The harmonic progression of mm. 116–19 suggests that the E♭ minor functions as subdominant, and the F of m. 118 as dominant. The last beats of m. 119 seem to confirm this reading, as the notes form a sonority that behaves like a so-called Italian sixth chord (G♭–B♭–E♮) within the key of B♭. This chord resolves as expected to F on the downbeat of m. 120. But the F harmony here is asserted as *tonic*, not as dominant, and the recapitulation is suddenly underway. As in the first two

Example 5–5: Third Symphony, I

symphonies, Brahms has bypassed altogether the dominant (here, C) at the moment of recapitulation. In the Third, this avoidance is just one part of his larger tonal strategy.

The harmonic juxtaposition of F as dominant and F as tonic across mm. 118–20 mirrors the metrical one, whereby at the moment of recapitulation in m. 120 the perceived $\frac{3}{2}$ is abruptly redefined as $\frac{6}{4}$. Moreover, since the entire last segment of the development is marked *un poco sostenuto*, and the last two measures *ritardando*, we hear at m. 120 not only a juxtaposition of the two metrical frameworks but a compression. Brahms does not specify the *proportion* of tempo between the end of the development and the Tempo primo of the recapitulation, but if a half note, or single beat of the $\frac{3}{2}$, were to

119

Example 5–6: Third Symphony, I, metrical process at recapitulation

be equivalent to a dotted half note, or half measure, of the ensuing $\frac{6}{4}$, the aural result would be a compression from $\frac{3}{2}$ to $\frac{2}{2}$, as shown in ex. 5–6.

However this passage is performed, the effect is (or should be) that of a metrical and harmonic paroxysm. This paroxysm seems to affect not only the arrival of the recapitulation but the recapitulation itself. The motto is harmonically exploded, as it were, so that the original F-major–F-diminished-seventh–F-major succession of mm. 1–3 now is spread over five measures to include a detour to Db: F-major–Ab⁷–Db–F-diminished-seventh–F-major. The first theme emerges in the tonic only at m. 124.

By dipping back down in m. 122 to Db, the enharmonic equivalent of C♯, Brahms brings forcibly to our ears the larger cycle of thirds on which this movement has been built, and through which the tonic of the recapitulation has been reached, to the virtual exclusion of normal dominant relationships. The final component of the chain, between C♯ and F, has been extended or filled in stepwise on the large scale by the harmonic area Eb of mm. 101–12 in the development. The entire chain is thus: F (m. 1)–A (m. 36)–C♯/Db (m. 77)–[Eb (m. 101)]–F (m. 120).

The coda (m. 183) is remarkable for an extended emphasis on C major, the previously absent dominant. Near the very end, at m. 202, Brahms also provides a new and significant transformation of the main theme (ex. 5–7). The F–C descending head motive of the theme, which originally lay in the first part of the measure, now occupies the second half and is preceded by a motive of a descending third (G–F–E) that has featured strongly in the coda and is derived from the main theme. We have seen in the coda to the first movement of the Second Symphony how Brahms fashioned a "new" lyrical theme out of the materials of his first group. The process in the Third is more globally significant, since the "new" coda theme also proves to be a direct anticipation of the main theme of the Andante movement that is immediately to follow (as shown in ex. 5–8 below). The falling fourth in the second half of both themes is, of course, the most direct similarity. The resemblance between the respective first halves of the themes remains one essentially of rhythm, not of contour or pitch. But especially striking—and to my mind, it clinches the association—is the way in which each theme is played together with its inversion. (In the Andante, the inversion, in the inner or tenor line above the bass, is a free one.) The thematic association can be said to be a corollary to the harmonic link between the coda of the first movement and the Andante. The Andante is in the key of C, a harmony that comes to prominence only in the coda of the first movement.

Example 5–7: Third Symphony, I

Second movement: Andante

Where the Second Symphony turned from an elegiac first movement to a brooding Adagio, the Third maintains more continuity of tone, of mood, and of technique between the first two movements. The Andante has essentially a sonata-form structure with a full exposition (first theme, m. 1; second theme, m. 41; closing group, m. 63). There is no separate development section; rather there is what might be called a developmental extension added to the closing group from m. 71. The recapitulation, beginning at m. 85, is exact or literal until m. 108, when it too sprouts an extension in place of the original second theme. The coda, based on the first theme, begins at m. 122.

As already suggested, the main theme of the Andante (ex. 5-8) has strong points of contact with that of the first movement. It also, in its third measure, makes an allusion to the motto of the Allegro, specifically as that motto appeared in the development section. The rising E–G–D, followed by the stepwise resolution of the D to C, recalls the presentation of the motto on similar scale degrees, 3–5–3–2, in mm. 101–3 of the first movement. If the transformation of the motto in the development of the first movement was one stage in its evolution into a lyrical melody, the Andante theme can be said to represent a further stage.

The opening theme, played by woodwinds, imparts the tranquil feeling of a serenade, like the Allegretto theme from the Second Symphony. But the

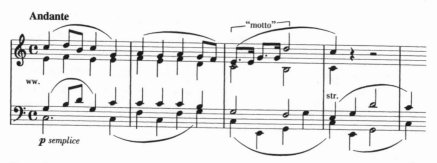

Example 5–8: Third Symphony, II

echoing figure in the low strings that closes off each phrase (mm. 4, 8, 13–14) adds a hint of unrest, of "otherness." Despite its apparently unruffled surface, the theme too contains elements of both metrical and harmonic instability. The former involves the role of the notated fourth beat, which, like the sixth beat in the previous movement, becomes gradually displaced in the exposition. The strikingly parallel metrical processes between the two expositions provide a further significant element of continuity throughout the symphony beyond those thematic, harmonic, and pitch-related aspects discussed above.

The phrasing of the main theme of the Andante poses the "problem": the melody, phrased or slurred within the measure, interprets the fourth beat as a concluding element. But in the three lower parts, the fourth beat is slurred over to the next measure; the beat is thus a forward-pushing element. The stage is thus set for the displacement of the meter, whereby the "sore" fourth beat assumes the status of a downbeat.

The harmonic corollary to this rhythmic conflict is presented by the root-position tonic triad articulated on the last, normally weak beat of the first measure and again on the second beat of m. 2. In each case this tonic leads to, or alternates with, a IV triad. Because of the slurring and the strength of the root position, we are made aware of the potential dual role of the tonic harmony: as I, it can be strong and stable; as V of IV, weak and unstable.

The strong presence of F major in this theme—and again at the theme's reappearance in the coda—represents more than merely a plagal emphasis. It imparts to the Andante another direct link with the preceding Allegro, which was in the key of F and in which C appeared only in the coda. With its frequent inflection toward F in a C-major theme, the opening of the Andante becomes an afterglow—or perhaps a hazy mirror image—of that first-movement coda. However we choose to describe the effect, it is one that only a composer with mastery of tonal forms like Brahms could achieve.

In the transition to the second group Brahms exploits the metrical ambiguity much as he did in the first movement. Beginning with m. 29, the notated second and fourth beats become strongly accented; harmonic support is
also shifted to these beats from the first and third. By mm. 32–34, we really
lose our hold on the notated meter as harmony and slurring seem fully to
support a displaced $\frac{4}{4}$ in which the notated fourth beat sounds like the first
(ex. 5–9). Although the original metrical grid seems to be restored with the
V–I bass cadence to A in m. 40, the ambiguity continues to haunt the second theme, one of the most elusive in all of Brahms.

32

Example 5–9: Third Symphony, II

Very much as in the first movement, these metrical and harmonic procedures are brought to climax at the end of the development—here, the
developmental extension. From m. 75, the harmonic focus is on F. The association with the Allegro is especially strong in m. 76, in which F alternates
with D♭ in ways reminiscent of the transition in the first-movement exposition, mm. 15–30, and the beginning of the recapitulation, mm. 120–24.
    In m. 80, a boldly articulated version of the head motive (C–D–B–C) on
the tonic announces not, as we might expect, the recapitulation, but a kind
of freezing of thematic and harmonic motion over the C, which is still heard
as V of F (ex. 5–10). The bass remains glued to C, while the same fragment
of the head motive, whose first note is now tied over the barline from the
fourth beat to the first, appears successively in the woodwinds.
    In the fourth statement of the theme fragment (m. 84), the eighth-note
figure D–B is augmented to two quarter notes, which delay the C until the
fourth beat. Simultaneously with that C, flute and oboe begin another statement of the head motive, which is still further modified. The tie across the
barline is removed so that D now appears on the downbeat of m. 85. When

Example 5–10: Third Symphony, II

the second motive of the main theme follows (G–A–G–A), we suddenly realize that the preceding C–D–B–C figure has stood in for the original motive
and that the recapitulation has in fact begun. The phrasing still, however,
shows the influence of the preceding retransition, for both the melodic voice
and the accompaniment are slurred across the bar line. Not until the next
measure, m. 87, are the proper downbeat and original phrasing restored.

Moreover, not until the downbeat of m. 87 is the tonic established. What
we have heard through the retransition and beginning of the recapitulation is
a fulfillment or expansion of the harmonic ambiguity implied in the opening
theme, in which C major had a partial identity as V of IV. It is this identity
that is assumed from m. 76 on and that is essentially sustained through the
long pedal of mm. 80–85. Thus, as the recapitulation begins in m. 85, this C
is not yet perceived as *tonic*; it resolves to F with the second motive of the
main theme on the downbeat of m. 86. Only on the last beat of m. 86 does
the dominant of C emerge to stabilize C itself as tonic; this "tonic" C arrives
on the downbeat of m. 87.

Again, the parallels with the first movement are striking. There, we
recall, the F harmony emerges in m. 118 *before* the start of the recapitulation, functioning as V of IV. At the moment of recapitulation, in m. 120, the
F must assert itself as tonic. C major fulfills a similar, though expanded, role
in the Andante.

After C is confirmed as tonic, the recapitulation proceeds normally up until
m. 107. Here, where by analogy to m. 24 we expect a transition to the second
theme group, Brahms introduces at m. 108 a new melody derived from the very
last "echo" phrase of the main theme in the preceding measure (ex. 5–11).
Although beginning stably in C major, this theme is nevertheless "infected" by
the same harmonic ambiguity that has characterized the movement as a whole.
The C moves immediately in the second measure to F, the subdominant, and
by the end of the new theme in m. 114, the introduction of B♭ and D♭ (as seventh and ninth) serves to turn the C once again into its alter ego, V of IV.

Example 5–11: Third Symphony, II

The new theme has built slowly to one of the grandest climaxes of the
movement, at mm. 112–13; but the climax is short lived, and the mysterious
repeated notes and dissonant chords of the second theme return at m. 116.
This passage, analogous to that in m. 56ff. of the exposition, is all that is left
at present of the second theme, which in the recapitulation thus plays a far
less substantive role than in the exposition. By substituting the broad theme
of m. 108 for the second theme, Brahms creates an expectation that is fulfilled only in the finale. The drama of this theme is, as was suggested above,
one of the main large-scale processes shaping the symphony.

The coda, beginning at m. 122, also plays a role in the broader drama by
alluding to the preceding Allegro. As we have seen, the first movement is
largely built from third relationships around F. These return in particularly
vivid form at the end of the Andante, where F–A♭ is directly recalled, at its
original pitch level, in the final progression of the movement: A♭–F minor–C
major in mm. 131–33. Plagal cadences are not rare in Brahms, but the conclusion of the Andante takes on special qualities in the light of the rich and

ambiguous tonic-subdominant relationships throughout this movement and the previous one.

Third movement: Poco Allegretto

As in his First Symphony, in the Third Brahms writes a three-part Allegretto movement instead of a full-fledged scherzo or minuet. The movement is distinctive among the symphonies for being the only Allegretto in the minor mode. The key of C minor serves both to extend the dominant key area of the middle movements of the symphony and to expand the web of F–C relationships explored in the first two movements.

The main portion of the Allegretto has a simple ternary form (A, mm. 1–24; B, mm. 24–40; A', mm. 41–53), in which the A section is in minor, the B in major. In this way, Brahms touches on the major-minor conflict at the heart of the symphony. The harmonic structure of the main theme brings us back even more directly and immediately into the larger harmonic drama (ex. 5–12). Like the theme of the preceding Andante, the Allegretto theme inflects strongly in its second and fourth measures toward a subdominant-related sonority, here a ii$^6_5$ chord whose bass is F. The C–F–C–F bass line that underpins this phrase in mm. 1–4 is a direct adaptation of the C–F–C–F, tonic-subdominant oscillation in mm. 1–2 of the Andante. In the Allegretto phrase, the second and fourth

Example 5–12: Third Symphony, III

measures receive the greatest melodic stress through the placement of the high notes G (m. 2) and B♭ (m. 4) and of the crescendo–decrescendo markings. The remarkable effect is that the dissonant ii⁶₅, subdominant-type chords of mm. 2 and 4 come to sound *more* stable than the understated tonics of mm. 1 and 3.

This harmonic design is the result of, or the corollary to, the distinctive phrase structure of the Allegretto theme. In an illuminating discussion, Christian M. Schmidt demonstrates how a folklike regularity is strongly modified by Brahms's own compositional personality. Schmidt posits a "normal" theme (an *Urbild*, as he calls it) that a lesser composer might have written: eight measures dividing readily into 4 + 4 and ending on the tonic (ex. 5–13).[8] Brahms may be said to turn this putative model into a supple creation of twelve measures by constantly changing the relationship between the dotted-rhythm figure and the sustained note. The first downbeat lasts for a full measure, thus displacing the next "upbeat," or dotted-rhythm figure, to the downbeat of the second measure; this downbeat contains the ii⁶₅ chord discussed above, now in a strong metrical position. A sequential repetition of this pattern brings the first half of the theme to rest on the second beat of m. 4. The continuation or second half now begins with the upbeat restored to its proper metrical position, where it remains up to m. 9. Here, where we might expect—with the melodic D—a half cadence to the dominant, Brahms extends the phrase another four measures: the half cadence comes only with the G at m. 12. The first two measures of this extension, mm. 10 and 11, turn out to be a further transformation of the downbeat-upbeat succession, which in the theme has undergone a compression in three essential stages (indicated by brackets and italic numbers above example 5–12).

Example 5–13: Third Symphony, III, hypothetical first theme (after Schmidt)

The Trio, beginning in m. 53, has essentially a binary form:

A, mm. 53–61

A, mm. 61–69

B, mm. 69–78

A, mm. 78–86

B + transition, mm. 86–98

The Trio directly addresses two of the larger-scale issues of the Third Symphony. First, it returns to the metrical "problem" posed in the preceding two movements. From the very beginning of the A section, the notated third beat takes on the quality of a downbeat, and the meter appears or sounds to be shifted to the "left" (ex. 5–14). The theme also takes up the pitch conflict exposed in the Allegretto. The first chord, which appears on the notated third beat of m. 53, is enharmonically A♭ minor, which shifts to A♭ major on the downbeat of m. 54. This oscillation, which continues throughout the Trio, echoes the alternation between C minor and major in the surrounding Allegretto.

Example 5–14: Third Symphony, III

Fourth movement: Allegro

In a more fundamental and satisfying sense than in either of the first two symphonies, the finale of the Third serves as the true culmination of the work as a whole. The thematic and harmonic processes set in motion but left unresolved in the preceding movements find a magnificent fulfillment. The structure of the finale represents a modification of sonata form similar to that found in the finale of the First Symphony. There is a complete exposition (main theme group in F minor, mm. 1–52; second theme beginning in C major, mm. 53–75; closing group in C minor, mm. 75–108). The development (mm. 108–71) begins with statements of the main theme in the tonic, and the recapitulation (mm. 172–246) begins not with the first theme but essentially midway through the first group, at the point where the restatement of the first group had left off at the beginning of the development.[9] The all-important coda (mm. 246–309) concludes with the reappearance of the opening theme of the symphony.

The movement begins shrouded in mystery; the first theme is played *sotto voce* and unharmonized, in unison and octaves. (The initial texture, mood, and even motivic neighbor-note figure recall the beginning of the finale of the Second Symphony.) The key is F minor, the complement to the C minor of the preceding Allegretto: together, these two movements make up the half of the symphony that is a kind of "minor" mirror image to "major" first half, which comprises the F-major Allegro and C-major Andante.

Although the notated key is F minor, a root-position tonic is nowhere to be found. The first theme of the finale unfolds on the dominant, the identity of which is strongly reinforced by the prominence of the B♮ neighbor-note or leading tone. By opening on the dominant, Brahms manages to sustain the large-scale dominant tension that has built up across the middle movements of the symphony.

Much as in the preceding movements, the opening theme begins in a metrically stable fashion but is then reinterpreted or destabilized. The theme initially lasts a tidy four measures, divided into 2 + 2 (ex. 5–15a). In its harmonized counterstatement or second presentation (m. 9, ex. 5–15b), the fourth note of the theme, D♭, originally a quarter note, is held out for three full beats, as is its D♭ analogue in the original third measure. The first extension serves to displace onto beat 2 of the second measure the C–D♭ eighth notes that were on beat 4 of the first measure. The theme as a whole now ends in the middle of its fifth measure. The rhythmic-metrical effect is that of a remarkable "stretch" or inner expansion of the basic thematic unit. The harmonic corollary to this stretch is no less important. The sustained melodic D♭s of mm. 9 and 12 are harmonized by D♭ and G♭ triads respectively, chords that play an important role in this movement as ♭VI and the Neapolitan.

At m. 18 Brahms reaches a half cadence on the dominant, after which we might expect the emergence of a theme firmly in the tonic. Instead, the half-cadential pizzicato Cs in the low strings give way to unison/octave E♭s intoned by the trombones, and the "missing" second theme from the Andante move-

Example 5–15: Third Symphony, IV

ment appears on the dominant of D♭ in the form of a solemn chorale (ex. 5–16). This gnomic theme had been absent in the recapitulation of the Andante and replaced by a more stable and lyrical one (m. 108; see above, ex. 5–11). Like the first theme of the finale, this one refuses to settle down into a definite key and hovers harmonically at first in an implied D♭ minor (suggested by the F♭s of m. 21) and then major (suggested by the F♮s of mm. 26–27).

Example 5–16: Third Symphony, IV

The theme closes with a final invocation by the trombones, then vanishes as mysteriously as it came. At m. 30, the orchestra takes up where it left off at the half cadence of m. 18 almost as if unaware of, or choosing to ignore, the preceding parenthesis or detour. The main theme is varied intensively in the manner of a transition or bridge, which in turn leads to the arrival of the second theme in C major at m. 52 (ex. 5–17).

We might assume that, with the arrival at m. 52, sonata-form convention has at last prevailed. In fact, the second theme is anything but stable and

Example 5–17: Third Symphony, IV

confirmatory. Like its predecessors in this movement, this theme appears *only* over its dominant, here G, and never affirms its ostensible key, C major; indeed, it hardly ever touches down on a C-major triad. The theme's nervous triplet rhythms, which evaporate on each succeeding downbeat and then must reconstitute themselves, reinforce its transitory nature. In performance, the second theme is misrepresented when approached by a ritardando and then played as a broad melody.[10]

Despite the momentary stability of C minor, the harmonic language of the closing group (m. 75) is among the most explosive in all of Brahms, who, when he wishes to do so, can be as fully chromatic as his supposed opposite, Wagner. The intense chromaticism of a passage like that shown in ex. 5–18 (mm. 83–87) provides a good example on a small scale of Brahms's technique. The larger goal is a cadence to C minor from the dominant, G. But the dominant is enriched or prolonged by stepwise voice-leading that lifts it well out of the immediate harmonic orbit of C minor. The progression is shocking because of chords so foreign to the context—B♭ minor is about as remote from C as possible—yet the whole is held together by the dominant that serves as the point of departure and return.

Example 5–18: Third Symphony, IV

The larger tonal scheme of this remarkable sonata exposition deserves consideration here, especially as it relates to the symphony as a whole. As we have seen, Brahms moves from an unstable F minor, to a fleeting C major, to a more secure C minor. At first glance, this tonic–dominant progression may seem normal for an exposition. In fact, it is not common for sonata movements in the *minor* mode to move to the dominant (either the major or minor dominant) as a secondary key; a much more conventional goal is the relative major or possibly the minor-mode version of the mediant (as in the first movement of the First Symphony).[11]

In the first movement of the Third Symphony, where we *would* have expected the dominant as the key of the second group, it was noticeably absent: the exposition moved to A major, then A minor. The finale in a sense fulfills the expectation thwarted in the first movement. Yet C major is not the ultimate goal of the finale's exposition, which turns emphatically, almost angrily, to C minor at m. 75. The presence of the dominant *minor* is even more unusual than the dominant major as the secondary key for a minor tonic. The only other example in Brahms is in the G-Minor Rhapsody, op. 79.[12]

Working out the tonal conflict between F major and minor, specifically between the key-defining pitches A♮ and A♭, becomes the principal task of the powerful development section. In m. 149, the chorale theme, which appeared and disappeared so mysteriously in the exposition, reemerges in canon in the winds and brasses. It moves upward tonally in an astonishing series of shifts through the regions of C minor (m. 155), D♭/C♯ minor (m. 159), and E minor (m. 163). At mm. 167–70, as the chorale is wrenched upward one more half step to F major, the A♮ is triumphantly asserted above a $^6_4$ chord.

But the victory of the A♮, and of the tonic major, is short lived. In the next measure the A♮ sinks down to A♭ and the recapitulation gets underway in the tonic minor. The energy and unresolved tension of the development are so strong that they utterly transform the main theme, which begins not *sotto voce* but *fortissimo* at a point formally analogous not to the beginning of the exposition but to the transition of m. 30. The chorale theme is absent from the recapitulation, having already reached its apotheosis in the development section.

It is the task of the magnificent coda, beginning at m. 246, to provide resolution to F major, a process that is combined with references to the Andante and with a gradual return to the opening theme of the first movement. At m. 267, with the final, sustained dominant chord of the "stretched" version of the theme (from the counterstatement of the exposition), the key signature changes to that of F major and Brahms introduces the tempo marking *Un poco sostenuto* (ex. 5–19). This shift should bring back—if a conductor wants to have the material from the first movement emerge at its original tempo—something like the tempo of the first movement, whereby a half note of the coda of the finale will equal a dotted quarter note of the first movement.

As F major emerges, the melodic D♭ is reinterpreted as C♯ and resolves upward to D in the violins of m. 269 and the cellos and basses of m. 272. At this moment comes the first of several epiphanies in this coda: we become aware of the rhythmic relationship between the head motive of the

Example 5–19: (a) Third Symphony, IV; (b) Third Symphony, II

finale, C–B♮–C–D♭, and that of the Andante movement, C–D–B♮–C, which
was similarly singled out and stretched in m. 122 of that movement's coda
(ex. 5–19b). Furthermore, the variant of the finale's head motive given in
the clarinet mm. 271–72 bears a distinct resemblance to the violins' cadential figure in mm. 121–22 of the Andante (as seen in ex. 5–19b).

Just as this thematic association is being made, a second epiphany
occurs: in m. 273, the motto of the first movement enters quietly in the oboes
and is echoed a few measures later by the horns. The motto fits into this context so naturally that we may not at first realize that it is actually being
imported from the first movement. The motto's second note, D♭ in this trans-
position, harmonizes smoothly with the chromatic G♭ of the finale's head
motive (as seen in m. 273 of ex. 5–19a); the two figures share the gesture of
an emphasized or "sore" chromatic note on the third beat. The contrapuntal
combination of these two figures in the coda of the finale, at once breathtak-
ing and logical, is one of the great masterstrokes of this symphony.

At m. 297 the finale's head motive returns and is once again combined
with the motto from the first movement, now in its whole-note form (ex. 5–20).
The sense of return becomes still more powerful as the head motive is harmonized by the chords associated directly with the motto and main theme of

the first movement: F major–D♭–F diminished-seventh. More precisely: the F-major–F-diminished outer harmonies of mm. 297–98 are those of the original motto; and the F–D♭ progression within m. 297, already so familiar from the main theme of the finale in its "stretched" form, is now heard to derive ultimately from the harmonic shift in m. 5 of the first movement.

Example 5–20: Third Symphony, IV

The stage is now set—it could not be set more effectively—for the final revelation, the return of the main theme of the first movement (ex. 5–1). This theme appears in m. 301, in duple meter, dissolved in shimmering string tremolos and free of all its original chromatic paroxysms (ex. 5–21). The F–D♭–F-diminished progression of the preceding measures has been definitively exorcised. Some tension remains, however, as the theme is syncopated across the bar line in mm. 301–04. In the next three measures even that rhythmic-metrical conflict is dissolved: in mm. 305–06 the theme is heard one last time in the violas and cellos, free of any syncopation or displacement.

It can be said that with the coda of the finale of the Third, Brahms achieves the most fully rounded work among his symphonies, perhaps

Example 5–21: Third Symphony, IV

among any of his multimovement instrumental compositions. To be sure, there are other works, including the Third String Quartet, op. 67, the Fourth Symphony, and the Clarinet Quintet, op. 115, that end with a return of material from the opening movement. But nowhere else in Brahms's music do thematic and harmonic associations develop as strong a sense of growing recognition for the listener as in the Third Symphony. Brahms's unerring ability to create or stimulate these connections musically makes this symphony, despite its modest overall dimensions, one of the greatest explorations of instrumental form in the Classic-Romantic era.

Chapter 6

THE FOURTH SYMPHONY, OP. 98

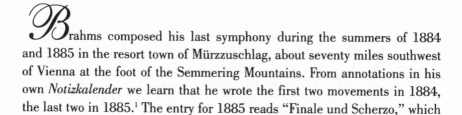

*B*rahms composed his last symphony during the summers of 1884 and 1885 in the resort town of Mürzzuschlag, about seventy miles southwest of Vienna at the foot of the Semmering Mountains. From annotations in his own *Notizkalender* we learn that he wrote the first two movements in 1884, the last two in 1885.[1] The entry for 1885 reads "Finale und Scherzo," which might suggest that the finale actually predated the scherzo in that summer.

Brahms offered the first performance not, as in the case of his two preceding symphonies, to the Vienna Philharmonic but to the court orchestra of Meiningen, whose music director was his good friend Hans von Bülow. In a letter of September 1885 to Bülow, he wrote:

> I have a few entr'actes—which are customarily together referred to as a symphony. On tour with the Meiningen Orchestra I have often pictured to myself the pleasure it would give me to rehearse it with you— and I still think so today, wondering at the same time whether it would get much of an audience. I'm really afraid that it tastes like the climate here. The cherries don't ripen in these parts; you wouldn't eat them![2]

Brahms's concern about the accessibility of the work emerges with some frequency in his comments reported at this time.

His immediate circle in Vienna was at first lukewarm. In early October 1885, an august group assembled informally to hear Brahms and another composer, Ignaz Brüll, play through the two-piano arrangement of the symphony. The page turners were Eduard Hanslick and Hans Richter, respectively the most eminent critic and conductor in Vienna; among the listeners were the surgeon Theodor Billroth, the critic Gustav Dömpke, and the musicologist C. F. Pohl. The scene was described by Brahms's biographer Max Kalbeck:

> After the wonderful Allegro . . . I expected that one of those present would at least break out in a loud "Bravo." I wouldn't allow my humble self to upstage the master's older and more competent friends in that way. Into his blond beard Richter murmured something that from afar could be taken as an expression of approval. Brüll cleared his throat and slid back and forth on his piano stool with diffidence and embarrassment. The others remained persistently quiet, and since Brahms also said nothing, a rather painful silence prevailed. Finally Brahms grumbled, "So, let's go on!" and gave a sign to continue; whereupon Hanslick heaved a sigh and quickly exploded, as if he had to relieve his mind and yet feared speaking up too late: "For the whole movement I had the feeling that I was being given a beating by two incredibly intelligent people." Everyone laughed, and the two players continued.[3]

The rehearsals for the Fourth began at Meiningen in mid-October. Of some historical interest here are the reactions of the young Richard Strauss, who was assistant to Bülow at the time and not yet converted to the Wagnerian cause. He wrote to his father on October 24, 1885, that the Fourth was "beyond all question a gigantic work, with a grandeur in its conception and invention, genius in its treatment of forms, periodic structure, of outstanding vigour and strength, new and original and yet authentic Brahms from A to Z."[4]

Despite all the hemming and hawing among Brahms's initiates, the premiere of the Fourth at Meiningen on October 25, under the composer's direction, was a great success, as were most of its subsequent performances around Austria, Germany, Holland, and England in the winter of 1885–86. But the fact remains that the Fourth is not a work that unlocks its secrets easily; it is not a work, like the Second, whose sensuous beauty beckons listeners inside. In his last symphony, Brahms seems to be writing precisely for the kind of cultivated, musically literate listener whose disappearance at the end of the nineteenth century he sorely regretted.[5]

Like the three preceding symphonies, the Fourth has a special color or quality—analogous to what Verdi referred to in his own operas as a "tinta"—imparted by certain harmonic and thematic features that span all four movements. The most renowned of the unifying devices is the chain of descending thirds (and its inversion, ascending thirds) that forms the skeleton of the opening theme of the first movement, reappears in the scherzo, and then comes to dominate the concluding pages of the finale. These thirds saturate both the thematic and harmonic—or horizontal and vertical—dimensions of the symphony to such a degree that, as Edward T. Cone has suggested, any traditional distinction between the two is broken down: both dimensions are fully "congruent," that is, draw on the same basic intervallic relationships.[6]

A second element that binds the symphony—it is related to the chain of thirds and the idea of congruence—is the sixth scale degree of E minor, C♮, as both a thematic and harmonic force. This note is prominent in the first theme of the first movement. At first it is underpinned (in m. 2) by the sub-dominant or A-minor triad; at the moment of recapitulation (m. 249), the analogous note is supported by a sustained C-major chord. Elsewhere in the movement (for example, m. 16), the C in the bass underpins an augmented sixth chord. C♮ and C major become prominent in the second movement as an inflection within E major. The scherzo is fully in the key of C. And in the finale, despite an apparently restrictive E-minor framework, C major emerges as a key area in the latter part of the movement (variations 26–28); the German sixth chord based upon C becomes a powerful force in the coda.

The symphony is also given a special coloring by a third element, the aug-mented triad, one of the most ambiguous—or, to use Schoenberg's term, *vagrant*—sonorities available in tonal music. (It is ambiguous because it is composed exclusively of major thirds and thus, acoustically, has no inversions and often no clear root.) This distinctive sonority is first heard in m. 4 as a chord of G–B–D♯ over the E pedal (ex. 6–1a). As Louise Litterick has observed, the same augmented triad is embedded in the chain of descending thirds as articulated at several points in the movement (mm. 208–10, for example).[7] As both a vertical and horizontal element, then, this pitch configu-ration shares fully in the integral "congruence" of the symphony. At m. 44 of the first movement, the augmented triad returns as a D–F♯–A♯ chord that func-tions as an altered dominant of G (ex. 6–1b). Two moments in the finale, in variations 21 (mm. 175–76) and 30 (m. 252), bring back the augmented triad.

First movement: Allegro non troppo

The first movement is in a sonata form that is distinctive, among other things, for being the only first movement among the symphonies to lack a repeated exposition. The exposition is articulated into a first group (mm. 1–53), a sub-stantial transition (53–86), a second group (87–106), and a closing group

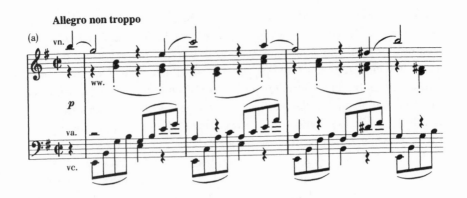

Example 6–1: Fourth Symphony, I

(107–44).[8] The development (mm. 145–246) begins with a return of the first theme in the tonic, the recapitulation (mm. 246–393) with an augmented version of that theme. The coda begins at m. 394.

The Fourth is also the only one of Brahms's symphonies to open straightaway with what is to be the "real" main theme. All three preceding symphonies, as we have seen, begin with some kind of introductory or preliminary gesture: in the First, a full-fledged slow introduction; in the Second, a thematic complex that serves in part as a prelude to the stable melody at m. 44; in the Third, a bold three-note motto that gives way to the theme proper only in the third measure.

In this light, it is striking that Brahms had second—and third—thoughts about the opening of the Fourth. The autograph manuscript of the symphony shows that, after having written out the full score, Brahms added four introductory measures intended to be inserted at the opening of the work.[9] These constitute a broad plagal cadence: two measures of a sustained A-minor harmony over an E pedal, resolving to two measures of E minor, the last of which contains the upbeat to the main theme (ex. 6–2).

As Litterick has suggested, the added measures prefigure a number of significant tonal relationships within the movement.[10] Its 6–5, C–B, melodic

Example 6–2: Fourth Symphony, I, alternative opening by Brahms

motion becomes expanded in the opening theme (as B–C–B), which also, in a sense, reverses the harmonies of the introduction: iv–i becomes i–iv. The 6–5 melodic motion and the exact harmonic pattern of the introduction—iv–i over an E pedal—reappear in the final cadence of the movement, in mm. 439–40.

Brahms's instincts ultimately served him well, however. Unlike the "motto" of the Third Symphony, which is boldly set out as a distinctive motivic-harmonic entity and which will recur throughout the movement at important structural moments, the plagal cadence of Brahms's deleted introduction to the Fourth is a one-time preview of tonal relationships to come. Brahms perhaps came to feel that a projection of these relationships at the opening was unnecessary, especially since they are immediately set out in the main theme, which is in itself rather abstract and "neutral."

The Fourth Symphony, as we know it, begins directly with the theme that for most of this century has been understood as the *locus classicus* of Brahms's fabled intervallic-motivic economy. As early as 1914, the critic Walther Vetter pointed out that the first eight measures of the theme trace a chain of thirds, which descend in the antecedent phrase (mm. 1–4) and ascend in the consequent (5–8).[11] The continuation after the opening period begins on C, the endpoint of the thirds chain, and essentially sits on that note for five measures.

The first period of the theme (mm. 1–8) uses basic triadic harmonies, unfolding over diatonic scale degrees (E–C–G–D–A).[12] In the second period (mm. 9–19), chromaticism emerges strongly as the bass rises in stepwise semitones from the D♯ of m. 9 to the A of m. 15. The consequent of the second period is extended from the normal four measures to seven, and its cadence in m. 19 overlaps with a return of the opening motive.

Beginning in m. 19, the first theme is repeated in varied form, its second period now greatly extended from the original eleven measures to twenty-nine. This expansion is one of the most massive of its kind in Brahms, coming at last to a strong half cadence on V/V in m. 53, from which a new and distinct theme emerges as the transition. This is the fanfarelike figure, introduced marcato by the horns and woodwinds, sharing with first group material an emphasis on 6–5 scale degrees, here D–C♯.

Across the transition, associations with the first group increase as the fanfare figure transmutes into a chain of four descending thirds—outlining a ninth—which now accompany a broad theme sung by the cellos (ex. 6–3). With the resolution to B major in m. 95, the second group can be said to begin—and then collapse mysteriously in m. 107 onto a diminished triad (ex. 6–4). The main rhythmic motive of the fanfare returns in the trumpets; the strings arpeggiate a chord that is the German sixth of B major. That chord resolves to B-major in $^6_4$ position, and the fanfare appears in that key only to dissolve onto another diminished triad, built on E♯, in m. 114.

Example 6–3: Fourth Symphony, I

However a listener chooses to parse the exposition, its shape and process are distinctive among the Brahms symphonies in a way that has not been sufficiently highlighted in previous analyses of the Fourth. In the long transition (mm. 53–94) Brahms is able to maintain a high degree of tension by avoiding any clear harmonic resolution to B. The final cadence of the broad cello theme in m. 73, where we would expect the melodic B to be given the firm support, is thwarted. The harmonic preparation in mm. 71–72 comprises a full dominant seventh of B, but the last beat has a D in the bass, which turns

Example 6–4: Fourth Symphony, I

the final two beats—if we hear them as representing a coherent harmony—into a kind of D augmented chord with seventh and ninth (D–F♯–A♯–C♯–E; ex. 6–5). This prepares what is essentially a deceptive resolution (deceptive from F♯) to G major and the return of the fanfare at m. 73.

Perhaps no moment shows better the genuine congruence of this movement, how deeply the relentless descending thirds affect harmonic syntax and motion. For the D in the bass on the last beat of m. 72 is a result of, or the endpoint of, a chain of descending thirds that plays a large role in the transition (see above, ex. 6–3). Here the series consists of G–E–C♯–A♯–F♯–D. The

Example 6–5: Fourth Symphony, I

middle four notes of the chain constitute, of course, the dominant seventh chord of B. The addition of the first note can also be understood, within that harmonic context, as the ninth. But the D endpoint serves to undermine or make extremely ambiguous the dominant function. D has no easily discernible or explicable role in an F♯ dominant complex. In this way, the pervasive thirds serve (as in another famous instance, the Intermezzo in B Minor, op. 119, no. 1) to muddy conventional harmonic progressions.

A further aspect of the harmonic language of this movement should be noted. We have seen how, in the sonata-form movements of the preceding three symphonies, Brahms employs something of a Schubertian three-key exposition. In the first movement of the Fourth, the arrangement is essentially E minor–B minor–B major, a plan that has obvious points of contact with the preceding symphonies, especially perhaps the finale of the Third, in which a minor-mode exposition also moves to the dominant.

In the Third, Brahms was seeking to provide a dominant that had been noticeably absent in the first-movement exposition and had then emerged across the central movements. In the first movement of the Fourth, Brahms adopts the inverse strategy. The dominant offers a way to avoid the more conventional G major (III), or even C major (VI), as a goal for the second group, and to save the C–G complex for its larger role in the symphony. Brahms directs tonal motion toward B, and more generally toward the "sharp," or dominant, side of E. And to confirm B, Brahms moves as far clockwise around the circle of fifths as G♯ (m. 91), which is V/V/V of B major.

The array of keys around E minor can be depicted as follows:

(flat side) C major–G major–D minor–A minor
E minor
(sharp side) B major–F♯ major–C♯ major–G♯ major

C major lies as far on the flat side of E minor as does G♯ on the sharp side. Brahms is clearly interested in exploring this kind of tonal symmetry in the Fourth Symphony: that much is obvious from the opening theme, whose thirds are unfolded in descending, then ascending, fashion.

The real apotheosis of the C–G complex in the first movement comes at the moment of recapitulation, in mm. 246–58. Here the melodic notes C and B, respectively the fourth and eighth pitches of the original theme, are now each sustained for four measures over C-major and G-major harmonies, respectively (ex. 6–6a, b). In each case, the harmony unfolded by the arpeggios is the familiar, pervasive augmented triad, colored by the flatted sixth.

Example 6–6: Fourth Symphony, I

The opening of the recapitulation draws on an analogous pair of "frozen" moments already discussed in the exposition, at mm. 107–10 (ex. 6–4) and 114–16. There, diminished triads are sustained, the strings have broad arpeggiations, and the head motive of the fanfare sounds in the trumpets. These sonorities informed much of the development section (mm. 184–206) and thus have been reinforced in the listener's ear. As the recapitulation then also freezes in mm. 249 and 255, we are aware to what extent developmental processes can affect all parts of the sonata form.

Second movement: Andante moderato

For the key of the Andante of the Fourth Symphony, Brahms turns to the parallel major of the first movement, a strategy that allows him to expand the range of tonal explorations around E. Indeed, the exposition of the Andante shares numerous features with the preceding one. Its secondary key is the dominant, B major, but throughout there are strong inflections toward the flat-side keys of C major and G major.

Brahms wastes no time in making these associations. Although the key signature announces E major, it is the diatonic scale of C major that forms the basis for the brief fanfarelike introduction that begins the Andante (ex. 6–7).

Like the opening theme of the first movement, but in a different way, this fanfare figure is symmetrically conceived and is based on thirds: it rises a third
above E and sinks a third below.

Like the slow movements of the Second and Third Symphonies, this one
manifests an imaginative adaptation of sonata form in which the development section is either greatly truncated or displaced into the recapitulation.
In the Andante of the Fourth, the recapitulation begins in m. 64 directly after
a brief extension of the close of the exposition in the dominant.

The first group of the exposition unfolds initially almost as a theme (m. 5)
and variations (mm. 13, 22). The sense of variation is imparted to some extent
by the closed nature of the units, each of which leads back to the tonic. The
first dissolves the regular phrase structure of the original theme into a series
of fanfarelike outbursts, which hark back to the unison and octaves in the

Example 6–7: Fourth Symphony, II

woodwinds in the introduction. The second deviates in its consequent phrase (m. 26), which is transformed into a more lyrical melody.

Where in most sonata expositions by Brahms (and other composers) the transition tends to grow directly out of the first group, in this one the transition begins with a theme (m. 36) that is essentially new and, in fact, proves to be the beginning of the second group. The theme set forth in stentorian tones by the woodwinds in B minor (m. 36) becomes transformed into the lyrical cello theme in B major (m. 41). This theme is then given a kind of developmental extension that prolongs the dominant, and the decorated reprise enters—without the four-measure fanfare introduction—in m. 64.

The first variation of the theme begins as expected in m. 74, then explodes outward into a brief but powerful development, where the rugged character of the transition theme is explained, or justified; or it might be said that the theme has been given its appropriate context, following as it does (m. 84) directly upon the developmental expansion of the head motive.

In m. 106, soon after it begins, the coda seems to pause for five measures over a dominant pedal, which supports a diminished triad ($G\sharp$–B–$D\natural$; ex. 6–8). Above the rippling arpeggios and the timpani roll, the woodwinds float fragments of the consequent phrase of the second "variation" from m. 26. This magical moment immediately links up with similar "frozen" moments in the first movement, especially those in the second group (mm. 107ff.; see above, ex. 6–4) and at the recapitulation (mm. 249ff.; see above, ex. 6–6b). The harmony is different, but the figuration in the strings and the general mood are very similar.

At m. 110, the coda resumes its progress and the dominant, which had been suspended in time, now moves purposefully to the tonic. At the moment of resolution in m. 113, the fanfare figure returns in its original instrument, the horn, and is then taken up by the other woodwinds, as in the introduction. As if recalling and wishing to assert its initial pitch level, the fanfare now forces a final, powerful harmonic shift to C (ex. 6–9).

Example 6–8: Fourth Symphony, II

Example 6–9: Fourth Symphony, II

The presence of B♭ in the violins, clarinet, and bassoons in mm. 114–15 suggests that the C harmony might be functioning as a German sixth chord in E. The conventional resolution of this chord, as shown in ex. 6–10 (with a notated A♯), is one that Brahms has distinctly avoided in the Andante and in the preceding Allegro. He has refused thus to rationalize the distant C and C-oriented harmonies. Here again the apparent German sixth fails to resolve; rather it takes on a strikingly different function as an implied dominant of the F-major chord that emerges on the last beat of m. 116 over a tonic pedal (ex. 6–9).

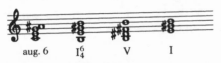

Example 6–10: Standard resolution of "German" sixth chord

Brahms often makes his final cadences work hard, but perhaps nowhere more so than in this movement, in which the conclusion encapsulates the most important tonal processes. The succession C–F–E across the last three measures is a splendid sonic emblem of the harmonic juxtapositions that have colored the entire movement.

Third movement: Allegro giocoso

The Allegro giocoso of the Fourth Symphony is the only third movement among Brahms's larger instrumental works to completely shun the traditional large-scale ternary format. The tone and mood are unmatched by even his sunniest finales or most bumptious scherzi. With its curious pauses, odd accent patterns, ostentatious counterpoint, abrupt harmonic shifts, and jingling triangle, this scherzo might be more at home in the rowdy undergraduate world of the Academic Festival Overture than in the sedate concert hall. (This was, however, the movement that had the greatest success in the symphony's first performances; by popular acclaim, it had to be repeated.) Especially within the Fourth Symphony, which is otherwise elegiac, pensive, or downright grim, the aggressive blast of C major seems anomalous.

Yet the scherzo is an integral part of Brahms's Fourth, looking both forward and backward within the symphony. From the harmonic point of view, its C major serves to bring fully, gloriously into the open the key that has shadowed E minor in the first movement and E major in the second. This key will also play a significant role in the finale.

Thematically, the movement refers back to both preceding movements. The theme that bursts in in Eb to interrupt the first group at m. 10 recalls the descending portion of the main theme of the Andante. This relationship becomes still clearer at the end of the development (Poco meno presto, m. 181), where the theme appears in the remote key of Db. The ubiquitous descending thirds of the first movement appear here as well, at mm. 48–51, just before the entry of the second group.

Perhaps the most important thematic relationship is the foreshadowing ("prehearing," as Alan Walker has called it[13]) of the finale theme that unfolds across the movement, beginning with the lowest dyad of an F-major chord, F–A, attacked *fortissimo sforzando* in m. 5 (ex. 6–11a). When the main theme returns at the start of the development section (m. 93; ex. 6–11b), this somewhat bizarre gesture is expanded to two full measures and is then alternated between sections of the orchestra, with the beginnings of a melodic ascent (A–C–D). In the coda (m. 317; ex. 6–11c), the pattern is further adjusted and expanded to yield, in the top line, the pitches A–B♮–C–D–E♭, which represent—when brought into the same register—the first five notes of the passacaglia theme of the next movement.

The sonata form of the scherzo is of a type we have encountered in the finales of the First and Third Symphonies: the opening theme of the first group appears in the tonic at the start of the development section, and the recapitulation begins at the point in the first group where that theme had

Example 6–11: Fourth Symphony, III, "prehearing" of finale

broken off. As in those movements and all similar ones, this formal device is anything but schematic in Brahms's hands. The larger structure of the scherzo can be represented as follows:

EXPOSITION
    First group, C major, m. 1
    Second group, G major, m. 52

DEVELOPMENT, m. 89

RECAPITULATION
    First group, beginning in E♭, m. 199
    Second group, C major, m. 247

CODA, m. 282

A striking aspect of this plan is the length of the development section in proportion to the exposition and of the coda in proportion to the recapitulation: consisting of 111 measures, the development is nearly 25% as long again as the 88-measure exposition; consisting of 70 measures, the coda is only 15% shorter than the recapitulation. These relative proportions, especially that of the development section, deviate substantially from those described as normative by Webster in his analysis of Brahms's later sonata forms.[14] They suggest that, in this scherzo, Brahms is placing greater emphasis on development and fragmentation than on exposition and variation. Any triolike middle section would have vitiated the developmental momentum of the movement.

It is not only the larger proportions that stress development; the sense of fragmentation permeates even to the level of the individual themes, especially the first group. The first group is remarkable for its surface discontinuity; it has three basic thematic components, each separated by a distinct caesura or hiatus (ex. 6–12). The first unit, *a*, comes to a sudden halt in m. 5 on the low subdominant chord. The second unit, *b*, takes off from this F-major sonority and moves to the dominant in m. 10, when Brahms shifts abruptly over the G bass from G major to E♭ major for idea *c*. Five measures later, G major returns, leading to a restatement of *b* in the tonic. This element, which has been interrupted by *c*, now resumes its course and builds up to a return of *a* in the tonic at m. 35.

Despite the discontinuity, the three elements are thematically linked. Theme *a* consists of two voices moving in contrary motion (the voices are inverted upon the return of the theme in m. 35). The descending contour is taken over and transmuted in *b*, whose initial pitches descend A–G–E–D. In the third unit, *c*, the neighbor figure G–F–G is taken over from *a*. After the interruption of *c*, the first group returns to C major, not with theme *a*, as we might expect, but with *b*, which then becomes a kind of transition or build-up to the return of an inverted *a* at m. 35.

The element of surprise or discontinuity continues in the restatement of the main theme. Instead of *c* and an abrupt shift to E♭, the first group seems

Example 6–12: Fourth Symphony III

to fall apart and regress to the thematic material of the first movement. The descending thirds are murmured in the bass (E♭–C–A) at mm. 44–45, repeated in sequence in mm. 46–47, then extended to a full chain in the woodwinds at 48–51.

The development section works up all three elements of the first theme; near the end, at the Poco meno presto (m. 181), theme c settles in the horns into a gentle, pastoral mood. This represents the kind of thematic or lyrical fulfillment we have seen before in Brahms's development sections. It begins in the remote key of D♭ and by m. 192 has worked its way around to the dominant G.

We expect this G to resolve to C major and usher in a return of the first theme. Instead, at m. 199, the c theme bursts out *forte* in its original form and over its original harmony, E♭; we are suddenly aware that the recapitulation is under way. The juxtaposition of the two forms or moods of c—pastoral and martial—across the moment of recapitulation makes for a splendid effect.

Fourth movement: Allegro energico e passionato

The finale of the Fourth Symphony, perhaps the most extraordinary symphonic movement written in the post-Beethoven and pre-Mahler era, is cast in the form of a theme with thirty variations, plus a coda. The variation structure here draws not on the Classic-Romantic tradition of melodic decoration above a stable bass/harmonic pattern—a type of variation to which Brahms had himself contributed in numerous works—but rather on the Baroque tradition of the passacaglia or chaconne. (There seems no agreement on the distinction between the terms passacaglia and chaconne; Raymond Knapp has suggested that Brahms himself preferred the latter term, which I will use.)[15] A chaconne uses a relatively compact theme of four or eight measures that appears first in the bass and may migrate to other parts of the texture, but which is always present in some form.

By 1884, Brahms was already well versed in chaconne composition. In 1873 he had used the form in masterly fashion for the finale of his Haydn Variations, in which the main theme becomes truncated to a four-measure ostinato. Four years later, Brahms transcribed for piano left-hand Bach's famous Chaconne in D Minor, originally for solo violin.

The most immediate stimulus for the finale of the Fourth Symphony—as well the probable source for the ostinato subject itself—appears to have been the last movement of Bach's Cantata No. 150 (*Nach dir, Herr, verlanget mich*). In early 1882, Brahms is reported to have played it to some friends and asked, "What would you think about a symphony written on this theme some time? But it is too clumsy, too straightforward. One must alter it chromatically in some way."[16] Indeed, as can be seen by comparing Bach's subject (ex. 6–13) with Brahms's (ex. 6–14), the latter is altered chromatically by the addition of the raised fourth degree, or A♯.

Example 6–13: Bach, Cantata 150, chaconne subject

Example 6–14: Fourth Symphony, IV

The "generic background," as Knapp calls it, of Brahms's finale also includes an E-minor Ciacona for organ by Buxtehude, Bach's Passacaglia and Fugue in C Minor, and the finale of Beethoven's *Eroica* Symphony, among other works.[17] The movement represents a unique moment in the history of the nineteenth-century symphony as the most thoroughgoing attempt to synthesize ancient and modern practice. Brahms's finale in turn became the direct model for the finales of Max Reger's Organ Suite in E Minor, op. 16 (1895), and Alexander Zemlinsky's early Symphony in B♭ (1897), for Webern's Passacaglia for Orchestra, op. 1 (1908), and for other works.

Brahms set himself the challenge of creating out of what is by nature an additive form the continuity and forward motion appropriate to a large-scale structure. One device on which he relies is that of grouping variations in pairs or in still larger units. Variations 4–9 (mm. 33–80) form a coherent

unit based on the successive diminution and variation of the violin melody
of variation 4. Pairs of variations include variations 14–15 (mm. 113–28),
based on the same choralelike theme in the trombones; variations 19–20
(mm. 153–68), based on a marcato melody in the violins; variations 22–23
(mm. 177–92), based on a triplet rhythm set against syncopations; and variations 27–28 (mm. 217–32), based on a melody presented in the woodwinds
in doubled thirds.

Another significant element of the large-scale design of the finale is
Brahms's beloved sonata form. It is not the tonal scheme that Brahms
imports from the sonata but its formal-thematic tensions and its balance
between exposition, development, and recapitulation. The sonatalike dimensions of the finale can be characterized as follows:

EXPOSITION (Theme, variations 1–15)

> First theme group: Theme and variations 1–9 (mm. 1–80). Here
> the basic material is set out. Variation 4 introduces a broad melody
> that builds successively in intensity across subsequent variations,
> especially with the rhythmic diminutions of varia-tions 8 and 9.

> Transition/Bridge: Variations 10 and 11 (mm. 81–96). The rhythmic
> momentum comes to a halt; mood changes.

> Second theme group: Variations 12–15 (mm. 97–128). A series of
> slower variations with strong melodic emphasis. Change of meter at
> variation 12 and of mode, to major, at variation 13.

DEVELOPMENT (Variations 16–24 [mm. 129–92])

> Begins, like the developments of the first and third movements,
> with a restatement of the opening theme in its original form (first
> four measures of var. 16), then moves off into less stable, more chro-
> matic music. String tremolos of variations 17 and 18 are distinctly
> developmental in effect. Development ends with dominant pedal in
> mm. 190–92, which serve as retransition.

FREE OR PARTIAL RECAPITULATION (Variations 24–30
[mm. 193–252])

> The return begins with a decisive resolution to the tonic, followed
> by *fortissimo* variations closely resembling those at the opening of
> the movement. Variation 24 recapitulates variation 1, with horns
> and timpani playing strong attacks on the downbeat and strings
> and trombones playing on the second beat. Variation 25 recreates
> variation 2, taking over the same string melody, now with tremolos.

> Variation 26 corresponds closely to variation 3, whose staccato
> melody is transformed into a legato one. After variation 26, the
> "recapitulation" moves toward a still more dramatic return: the
> reappearance in variations 29 and 30 of the descending thirds
> from the first movement.

CODA (mm. 253–311)

It is striking—and surely not coincidental—that Brahms's adaptation of
sonata form in this movement has the same features as the third movement
of the symphony, in which the main theme reappears in the tonic at the start
of the development and the recapitulation begins at that point in the first
group where the theme has broken off at the start of the development. Here
the ostinato returns literally for the first four measures of variation 16, and
the recapitulation begins at variation 24 with a reworking of variation 1. The
variation form, made up of smaller, independent units, adapts itself ideally
to this kind of structure.

The fact that the "theme" of this movement is not precisely a melody, a
bass line, or a fixed harmonic pattern allows Brahms—or, we should say, by
his choice of the chaconne form, Brahms allows himself—enormous flexi-
bility within the apparently restrictive eight-measure limit of the chaconne.
The almost miraculous tonal subtleties of the movement have received too
little attention in the critical literature: they reveal the finale of the Fourth
as a fully late Romantic work, as "modern" in its way as the supposedly
more advanced music of Wagner, Bruckner, Wolf—and even the early
Strauss and Mahler.

Always working with the chaconne subject, Brahms adapts the harmonic
structure of each variation, or group of variations, to reflect larger formal
principles. Among the results he achieves: the creation of dominant tension
or preparation to lead into the next variation; the avoidance of such tension
by suppressing the dominant and stressing instead the subdominant; and the
initiation of modulations to other keys, especially C major.

Most of the tensions of the movement are already present in the ostinato
subject itself (ex. 6–14). It begins and ends on the note E; the final E is preceded by two measures of B. A conventional harmonization would begin on
E minor and end there with a well-prepared dominant cadence. But from the
start, Brahms has other ideas. He begins on A minor, and despite the presence of three E triads in the theme, its harmonic structure can be said to be
oriented largely around or toward the subdominant.

Reckoning E minor as tonic, we could analyze the harmonic progression of the chaconne theme as:

$iv^6-ii^6-i-iv^6-V/V-i-$French sixth$-I$

The French sixth identified as the penultimate chord, however, has no real function within E minor. Resolving to E major, it behaves instead as a dominant preparation in A minor.[18] The A-minor chord at the start of variation 1 seems to confirm this function.

The initial harmonization of the chaconne subject in mm. 1–8 could thus equally well be analyzed in A minor:

$i^6-vi^6-v-i^6-V/V/V-v^6-ii_3^{4+}$ [French sixth]$-V$

The advantage of this analysis is that it shows a logical progression across the theme from i to V. The disadvantage is the distinct presence of minor v chords (tonic minor chords in our first analysis), which have no diatonic function or force in A minor.

The ambiguity is, of course, intentional: there is no correct way to "read" the harmonized chaconne subject. Overall, it is the E-minor reading that makes the most sense, especially because of the entrance of the timpani (and trumpets) on E in m. 5, moving to B in m. 7, then back to E in m. 8 (as shown in ex. 6–14); this pattern seems to reinforce a hearing of E as tonic. But the strong presence of A minor in the theme as something more than a mere subdominant is a feature Brahms will exploit throughout the movement.

Having adumbrated the tonic/subdominant ambiguity in the theme and variation 1, Brahms seeks across variations 2 and 3 to set up and confirm the "real" tonic, E minor, by intensifying its own dominant, B major, which has been entirely absent heretofore. In m. 23 (var. 2), the French sixth analogous to that of mm. 7 and 15 is gone; it is replaced on the last beat by a conventional dominant of E. Variation 3 is oriented still more toward the dominant, which now appears in the second and seventh measure (mm. 26, 31).

With the start of variation 4, Brahms has confirmed the tonic. As if to mark the significance of this moment, he introduces the finale's first real melody (apart from the chaconne subject itself). Indeed, in the sonatalike analogy suggested above, one might consider variation 4 as the real beginning of the "exposition" and what has preceded as a kind of introduction. The new melody surges forward passionately in the first violins, as the chaconne subject retreats for the first time into the bass, a position it retains throughout the "first group," variations 4–9.

In the paired variations 8 and 9, Brahms alters the cadential B–E of the final two measures of the subject to E–A (ex. 6–15), effectively transposing the pattern down a fifth (or up a fourth) and bringing these variations to a close on A minor. This cadence revives the subdominant tendencies of the original theme, and it serves to indicate that the "first group" of variations 4–9 is drawing to a close.

The subdominant emphasis and the concomitant suppression of the tonic E are sustained across the two "transitional" variations, 10 and 11. At the start of both variations, the first note of the chaconne subject supports an E⁷ chord, an implied dominant seventh of A minor. Variation 10 moves toward E minor, but it ends (in mm. 87–88) with a deceptive cadence in which the bass of the dominant seventh chord of E resolves properly while the upper parts form a subdominant triad. In order to avoid premature closure onto the tonic and to prepare the subsequent tonic more firmly, Brahms employs in m. 96 (the last measure of variation 11) a dominant chord with a B in the bass, which resolves definitively onto E minor at the start of variation 12 (ex. 6–16).

Example 6–15: Fourth Symphony, IV

Example 6–16: Fourth Symphony, IV

The introduction of the dominant at the end of variation 11, though it may appear a modest alteration, is truly remarkable. In the original chaconne subject, m. 8 is one of *resolution*, in which the Bs of mm. 6–7 cadence to E. (This is especially apparent in the harmonization of variation 2, with its emphatic i_4^6–V–i final cadence in mm. 22–24.) But in variation 11, the final measure is utterly transformed in function in order to continue or prolong the dominant tension. Brahms achieves this effect by redefining the final note of the subject, E, as a dissonance, a melodic suspension to the D♯.

The "second group" of the movement, the magnificent slow variations 12–15, is among Brahms's most expressive portraits in tone color. Where the "first group" of the movement tended to be dominated by bold melodies in the strings, the second group features the brasses and woodwinds: flute in variation 12, clarinet and oboe in variation 13, horns and trombones in variation 14, and the combined woodwind-brass choirs in variation 15.

Across variations 14 and 15 Brahms again subverts the harmonic structure to create continuity (ex. 6–17). In variation 14, the original B–B–E cadence of mm. 6–8 of the subject (mm. 118–20) is recast as B–D♯–E; the B and D♯ support the dominant of E major/minor, but with the arrival on E in m. 120 comes a remarkable deceptive resolution to a ii⁷ sonority (F♯–A–C–E) over an E pedal, leading to the tonic major at the start of variation 15. A similar pattern occurs at the end of variation 15, where, however, a C♮ substitutes entirely for the bass E (as shown in the example).

This adjustment in the harmony has a different effect in each of the two variations. The tonic is reached only with the beginning of variation 15 (mm. 121) as a *plagal* resolution of the preceding ii⁷ chord. At the end of variation 15 the chord is more purely a subdominant; the F♯ appears only in the descending flute melody. The subdominant is sustained because the return of the chaconne subject in its original form brings with it the first measure harmonized with A minor, now in root position (m. 129, ex. 6–17; cf. m. 1, ex.

Example 6–17: Fourth Symphony, IV

6–14). At the moment of return in variation 16, we realize that A minor has been employed in the final measures of the preceding variation specifically to prepare this moment.

In the "retransition" of variation 23, the chaconne subject returns in the horns—only the first six notes are distinct—as a way of announcing the "recapitulation" in variation 24 (ex. 6–18). As he has done in variation 11, which had similarly preceded an important arrival on the tonic, Brahms reinterprets the last three measures of the subject to put the B in the bass

Example 6–18: Fourth Symphony, IV

and thus create dominant tension across all three measures, leading to the E that appears on the downbeat of m. 193. The effect is even more powerful here—appropriately so—than before the "second group."

After the recapitulatory variations 24 and 25, which confirm E minor, Brahms makes the final, and the most remarkable, tonal excursion of the movement, to C major. This key, which has been touched upon but then abandoned in variation 3, comes into its own when that variation is recapitulated and transformed as variation 26. A C pedal point is sustained for five measures, and the variation actually ends with a dominant of C, which then resolves to C major at the opening of variation 27 (ex. 6–19). The strong presence of C major in variations 26–28 harks back to the scherzo move-

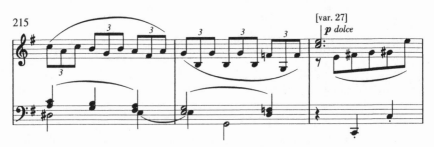

Example 6–19: Fourth Symphony, IV

ment and the memorable C-major moments in the first and second movements. The C major also reinforces the role played by the sixth scale degree of E minor in the symphony as a whole.

If the C major of variations 26–28 serves as a *harmonic* reference to preceding movements, what follow in the final pair of variations, 29 and 30, are still more powerful *thematic-motivic* allusions. Brahms forges from the first

Example 6–20: Fourth Symphony, IV, descending thirds and chaconne subject

four notes of the chaconne subject a chain of descending thirds that brings us directly back to the material of the opening theme of the symphony (ex. 6–1). In one of those epiphanies that Brahms is so good at creating, we recognize all at once the relationship between the first theme and the chaconne subject: when every fourth note from a chain of descending thirds is abstracted or given metrical stress, the result is a rising stepwise line— hence, the first four notes of the chaconne (as shown in ex. 6–20).

In the coda, beginning at m. 253, the original subject gets "stuck" on its fifth note, A♯, which is enharmonically respelled as B♭. It is harmonized first by G minor, then with a C⁷ or (in E) German sixth chord, which brings the pitch C forcefully back to center stage in the symphony (ex. 6–21a). The effect of this "freezing" on the German sixth is to send the subject into a kind of contrapuntal-harmonic warp instead of toward the normal closure

Example 6–21: Fourth Symphony, IV

with the B–B–E cadential figure. The B♮, which indeed appears in m. 261, now behaves like the fifth note of the theme, as if usurping that role from the A♯/B♭. It rises one further half step, to the all-powerful C.

As the coda moves into its final exhilarating segment, Brahms at last rationalizes the German-sixth sonority to lead toward the dominant of E. In mm. 289–91 (ex. 6–21b), the rising line again gets stuck on B♭ in the woodwinds; but the rest of the orchestra grabs hold of the note, redefines it as A♯, and resolves it emphatically and repeatedly upward to the dominant B. When the melodic A♯ appears again in mm. 295–96 (ex. 6–21c), it is no longer harmonized by the German sixth but by V⁷/V, whose root is F♯. The "sharp" identity of A♯ is now confirmed, and C♮ disappears for good as a harmonic force.

The struggle in the coda between the "flat" and "sharp" interpretation of the pitch located between A and B, and the concomitant redefinition of the flatted sixth, C, make for a splendid summary of the harmonic tensions that have governed the symphony as a whole. Each of the movements has dealt in some way with the axis around E, laid out horizontally in the chains of ascending and descending thirds at the opening of the symphony. In each movement the flat-side C major was a powerful counterforce to the traditional sharp-side dominant.

Anyone who analyzes closely the finale of the Fourth Symphony will, or should, come away with a sense of astonishment at the range of Brahms's compositional powers. Nowhere in his music are formal, thematic, and harmonic techniques brought into better coordination. Nowhere does it display such congruence on all levels. Nowhere are the principles for which we value this composer most in greater evidence.

Chapter 7

PATTERNS OF RECEPTION

$\mathcal{B}$roadly defined, the history of reception studies how, where, when, and why works of art have been understood, performed, and appreciated. We can distinguish between contemporary reception, which deals with works in their own day, and posthumous reception, which focuses on the period after a composer's death. Each of these very grossly drawn categories can—and must—be further broken down. For it is clear that reception of individual works will vary within a composer's life.

In an absolute sense, reception can be said to include every human response to a work outside of the work itself. Indeed, for those who claim that the work itself has no meaningful identity apart from its "receiver," reception is the fundamental, inescapable condition of an artwork. This is the position argued by Carl Dahlhaus and Leo Treitler, who see each listener's dialogue with a musical work as the defining aspect of its history.[1]

There are many different kinds of sources for what is generally understood by the term *reception*. An important one for music historians dealing with music after about 1700 is journalistic criticism, which has been drawn upon in chapter 1 of the present volume. Other barometers of reception are performance statistics and the response to works or composers outside the music-critical sphere, for example in the other arts. The kind of influence a composer has upon his contemporaries and upon those who follow also represents a significant kind of reception. It will not be possible within the scope of this chapter to treat all these aspects of reception of the Brahms symphonies. My goal will be rather to give an overview of some of the major issues or themes involved in the way these works have been understood.

All four of Brahms's symphonies appeared within a single decade, between 1876 and 1885, and the emergence of each one affected the reception or perception of those that had preceded it. The appearance of the Second in 1877 had an immediate impact on the understanding of the First, which had been premiered in the previous year. The two symphonies were often compared in reviews and in critical accounts of Brahms's works, and one was often judged by the standards of the other. By 1886, when all four symphonies of Brahms were in circulation throughout the performing world, reviewers, commentators, analysts, and historians tended frequently to refer to them as a group.

THE SYMPHONIES IN THE CONCERT HALL

Among the bluntest but nonetheless informative indicators of reception are performance statistics. Although there have been a few dips and peaks along the way, the four symphonies of Brahms entered the standard concert repertory soon after their premieres and have remained strong presences ever since. From the journal *Musikalisches Wochenblatt*, Siegfried Kross has gathered statistics for performances of the symphonies in Europe and America from the years 1890 to 1902—thus a period stretching somewhat before and somewhat after Brahms's death in 1897.[2] These figures suggest a respectable, steady stream of hearings, with the following overall totals for performances:

Second Symphony	207
Third Symphony	176
First Symphony	154
Fourth Symphony	123

What may surprise somewhat in these figures is the ranking. For in statistics gathered from specific orchestras over a longer period of time, the First tends to dominate and the Third to be the least performed. The statistics cited by Kross confirm that the First, despite its enormous popularity in the twentieth century, took some time to become established in the repertory. This much is also clear from concert reviews over the last quarter of the nineteenth century, which frequently indicate a lack of enthusiasm—although plenty of respect—for the First Symphony.[3] As for the Third: because of its quiet, contemplative ending, it has not in modern times been as popular on concert programs as the other three. Conductors and those who plan programs are normally reluctant to end either half of a symphony concert with the Third.[4]

To turn to individual orchestras: in the repertory of the New York Philharmonic, the Brahms symphonies have been performed virtually without interruption for almost a century. Between 1898 and 1995, only five years (1900, 1905, 1908, 1911, 1973) have passed without one of the Brahms symphonies on the Philharmonic's concerts.[5] The total number of times each symphony has been played at all types of concerts by the New York Philharmonic between 1877 and 1995 is:

First Symphony	338
Second Symphony	334
Third Symphony	163
Fourth Symphony	263

The roster of conductors who have led the Philharmonic in the First reads like a "Who's Who of Maestros." Theodore Thomas performed the First in December 1877—having lost by only a week a race with Leopold Damrosch over who was to give the American premiere. Over the years the Philharmonic played the First under the batons of Mahler, Mengelberg, Furtwängler, Toscanini, Walter, Klemperer, Barbirolli, Stokowski, Mitropoulos, Cantelli, Solti, Bernstein, Giulini, Leinsdorf, Kubelik, Levine, Mehta, and Masur, among others (many of these figures were music directors of the orchestra).

Statistics for the Vienna Philharmonic, the orchestra which gave premieres of two of Brahms's symphonies, have been analyzed in a comprehensive fashion by Desmond Mark to show patterns of performance—what he calls *Lebenszyklen*, or life cycles—for some of the major composers between 1842 and 1974.[6] By 1890, when all four of Brahms's symphonies were in circulation, his orchestral works comprised eleven percent of the Philharmonic's repertory, more than any composer except Beethoven, whose works comprised twenty percent. At this time Bruckner's works constituted only four percent.[7] The curve of Brahms's popularity with the orchestra varied over the course of the twentieth century, averaging around ten percent of the repertory.

It is worthy of note, but not of censure, that the Brahms orchestral works attained their highest percentage of the Vienna Philharmonic's repertory, fourteen percent, during the later Nazi period, 1941–45. As an *echt deutsch* composer, Brahms was eminently playable at this time.[8] But he was nevertheless far below the *echt Wiener* Bruckner, whose symphonies spiked up from eight percent of Vienna's repertory in 1936 to twenty-two percent in the

years 1941–45 (and then dropped down sharply to thirteen percent immediately after the war). At the height of the war, Bruckner even surpassed
Beethoven in the Philharmonic's repertory.

In terms of numbers of performances by the Vienna Philharmonic in the
period 1842–1974 (the period studied by Mark), the Brahms symphonies
are second only to the last seven of Beethoven and Schubert's Ninth, the
"Great" C-Major. The number of times individual Brahms symphonies were
programmed from 1842 to 1974 was as follows:[9]

First Symphony	33
Second Symphony	33
Third Symphony	26
Fourth Symphony	33

By way of comparison: Beethoven's Fifth Symphony, the most frequently performed work, was played fifty-two times in the same 132-year period. The
apparent gap between Beethoven and Brahms narrows somewhat if one allows
for the fact that when the Vienna Philharmonic was founded in 1842, all of
Beethoven's symphonies were already long since available—and popular—
while Brahms's began to appear in 1876 and were all in circulation only by
1885. Throughout the period 1878–1942 in the repertory of the Vienna
Philharmonic, Brahms's First, Second, and Fourth Symphonies ran well ahead
of the individual symphonies of Mozart (the "Jupiter": 28 performances),
Schumann (the Fourth: 29 performances), Bruckner (the Seventh: 21 performances), and Mendelssohn (the Third, "Scottish": 19 performances).

The Berlin Philharmonic is another orchestra that, since its founding in
1882, has been closely associated with the Brahms symphonies. In the century extending from 1882 to 1982, the works were programmed as follows on
regular subscription concerts:[10]

First Symphony	54
Second Symphony	53
Third Symphony	43
Fourth Symphony	49

These figures are fairly consistent in proportion to those of the other major
orchestras: the First and Second Symphonies remain the most popular on
programs, with the Fourth running just behind, and the Third lagging somewhat more.

THE BEETHOVEN PROBLEM

One aspect of Brahms's symphonies that has engaged commentators over the past century and a quarter is the works' relationship to the symphonies of Beethoven. This "Beethoven problem," as we may call it, is especially apparent in assessments of Brahms's First; but it affects the reception of other symphonies as well. Many standard music history textbooks begin an account of Brahms's symphonies with a discussion of their indebtedness to Beethoven or their place within the Beethoven symphonic tradition.[11]

Brahms is not alone in this respect, for, as we saw in chapter 1, virtually no composer of symphonies after Beethoven, at least within the Austro-German sphere, escaped being measured by the master. The fact that the finale of Brahms's First seemed to allude directly to the "Ode to Joy" theme of Beethoven's Ninth—a feature remarked upon by many critics—made a comparison with Beethoven only more inevitable. Ingrid Fuchs, who has examined critical responses to the Viennese premiere of the First Symphony on December 17, 1876, observes that the relationship to Beethoven is taken up by at least two-thirds of the reviewers. Angelika Horstmann, who surveyed eighty-five different newspaper reviews of the First Symphony, notes that while many critics make reference to Beethoven, they differ as to whether Brahms is the genuine heir to—or a weak follower of—Beethoven's symphonic achievement. According to Fuchs, about a third of the reviewers of the Viennese premiere tarred the First as the work of an epigone. Thus, the anonymous critic of the *Wiener Morgen-Post* wrote: "With his newest work Brahms has confirmed the old saying that Beethoven wrote the *last* symphony."[12] The anonymous critic for the *Wiener Abendpost* elaborated on Brahms's epigonal status. He suggested that in much of the debate about Brahms's First

> the principal issue remains unexamined: whether a further development of Beethoven's symphonic form is possible or—if it were possible— desirable. By itself Brahms's symphony surely does not represent this development; indeed, if we understand it correctly, Brahms by no means wishes it to do so. It in no way reaches beyond Beethoven, in the sense of seeking either to go back before him or go on ahead of him. Rather the symphony cleaves directly to Beethoven, grasps his symphonic form by the arm and remains earnestly at its side, step by step, just as a younger, weaker sibling goes beside the larger, more powerful one.[13]

Other critics sought to address the Beethoven-Brahms relationship more sensitively and sensibly. Richard Pohl, after making the obligatory mention of the First Symphony's allusions to Beethoven's Ninth, commented:

> It was foreordained that in the area of the symphony Brahms would tend sympathetically to follow Beethoven, which he had already done most decisively in general. But where he will now go with his Second Symphony, which surely must follow—that is what we wait expectantly to see after the impressions that the First has made upon us.[14]

A report on the First Symphony from the distinguished scholar and friend of Brahms, Friedrich Chrysander, in the *Allgemeine musikalische Zeitung* of 1878, is worth citing at some length for its perspicacity:

> The symphony by Brahms will soon be evaluated at greater length; for now let us note only that it belongs to those musical works that are significant not only through their specific musical content, but also through the position they occupy in the development of music. The reference to Beethoven, the linkage to the last or Ninth Symphony of that master, is so obvious that with an artist like Brahms we must presume it to be not feeble, unproductive imitation, but conscious intention. And it is precisely this intention, this artistic will, that gives the work its historical significance.
>
> What is involved here is the problem of how to create an antitype [*Gegenbild*] to the last portions of the Ninth Symphony, an antitype that can, without the aid of the human voice, match the manner and strength of the Ninth. And insofar as this attempt has succeeded, it signifies an attempt to lead back [*Zurückführung*] from the symphony that comprises instruments and voice to the purely instrumental symphony. At the same time it signifies an expansion of those effects that can be created through purely instrumental means.[15]

Chrysander shows a genuine appreciation of the difficulty Brahms faced in approaching the symphony and of the nature of Brahms's achievement in relation to Beethoven. He understands that while taking account of Beethoven's Ninth, Brahms is nonetheless seeking a means of restoring the purely instrumental symphony to its proper status.

Brahms was by no means the only prominent symphonist of his day who was measured by the Beethovenian yardstick. A parallel example is offered by the response to Bruckner, especially to the Third and Ninth Symphonies, premiered in 1877 and 1903 respectively, both in D minor. Many critics were made uncomfortable by the similarities to Beethoven's Ninth.[16] But others saw the echoes as logical, such as the writer who noted: "It's not at all necessary to clear Bruckner of the suspicion that he sought to imitate Beethoven's Ninth. It is not unworthy of a great man to strive after another great man and imitate his example."[17] The same could be said of Brahms.

SYMPHONY AS CHAMBER MUSIC

In 1918 writer Paul Bekker developed an elaborate metaphor of space—large, public room vs. small, private chamber—to characterize the difference between Beethoven and his immediate successors in the area of the symphony:

> If we, coming from Beethoven's Ninth Symphony, cast a glance over the entire symphonic output of a Mendelssohn, Schumann, and Brahms—I name here intentionally only the greatest and really typical representatives of this group—then we must truly be terrified at the almost imponderable *narrowing* of the range of vision and feeling that at first strikes us. It is as if we move suddenly from a large *ballroom* with views that extend far into the distance over a heroic landscape, to a bourgeois parlor with a view of roofs and alleys. To be sure, this parlor makes us feel pleasantly cosy; it is fitted out with much care, with a refined taste for the unassuming and genuine. We find nothing false, no rhetorical elegance, no ostentation, only that which is fundamentally justified in this space, and this is executed with learned skill. But it nevertheless gradually becomes rather narrow and oppressive.[18]

Bekker's remarks reveal quite clearly the relationship between the Beethoven problem and another important aspect of the reception of Brahms's symphonies: the charge, frequently encountered, that they are really large-scale chamber music. A Brahms symphony appeals more to the connoisseur ("refined taste") and is characterized by modest scale ("bourgeois parlor"), intricate, finely worked textures, and complex motivic processes ("learned skill"). These features contrasted with the broader dimensions, bolder melodies, and more direct appeal of the symphony, or what was called the "symphonic style" in chapter 1.

The generic and aesthetic issue of symphonic identity seems to have become particularly acute with the reception of the Brahms, in part perhaps because as a symphonist Brahms emerged before the public late in his career. This was a public that through much of the 1860s and 1870s had come to view, and admire, Brahms as a composer of chamber music who had breathed new life into the genre with a magisterial set of works stretching from the Piano Trio, op. 8, to the String Quartets, op. 51.

From the very first, even within Brahms's own circle, there was a tendency to feel that his symphonies were not adequately symphonic. The middle movements of the First Symphony were judged by some to be too slight for their context. Hermann Levi, the conductor and Brahms's friend, wrote to Clara Schumann in November 1876 that "the last movement is certainly the greatest thing that he [Brahms] has composed up to now in the realm of instrumental music; after that, for me, comes the first movement. But in regard to the two middle movements, I have my doubts. As beautiful as they are, they seem to me to fit better in a serenade or suite than in a symphony that is otherwise so broadly laid out."[19]

Critics questioned the symphonic credentials of the First. In a review in the *Neue Zeitschrift für Musik* in 1877, Hermann Zöpff remarked that the first movement was "unquestionably the most symphonic," implying that the others were somehow less so.[20] A Dresden critic addressed the composer directly in a review of the Second Symphony: "Why don't you restrict yourself to chamber music, in which you have created such competent things?"[21]

Perhaps the most prominent contemporary to tar Brahms with the chamber-music brush was Richard Wagner, in an article, "On the Application of Music to Drama," published in 1879. Wagner mentions no works or composers by name, but it is clear that his targets are the first two symphonies of Brahms. His comments are worth citing at some length because, as the excerpt cited from Bekker reveals, they echo down through the decades into the twentieth century:

> The said symphonic compositions of our newest school—let us call it the Romantic-classical—are distinguished from the wild-stock of our so-called Programme music not only by the regretted absence of a program, but in especial by a certain clammy [*zähe*, literally "sinewy," "chewy"] cast of melody which its creators have transplanted from their heretofore retiring "Chamber-music." To the "Chamber," in fact, one had withdrawn. Alas! not to the homely room where Beethoven once poured into the ears of few and breathless friends all that Unutterable he

kept for understanding here alone, instead of in the ample hall-space, where he spoke in none but plastic masses to the Folk, to all mankind: in this hallowed "chamber" silence long had reigned; for now one must hear the master's so-called "last" Quartets and Sonatas either badly, as men played them, or not at all—till the way at last was shewn by certain outlawed renegades, and one learnt what that chamber-music really said. No, those had already moved *their* chamber to the concert-hall: what had previously been dressed as Quintets and the like, was now served up as Symphony: little chips of melody [*Melodien-Häcksel*, literally melodies of "chaff" or "bits of straw"], like an infusion of hay and old tea-leaves, with nothing to tell you what you are swallowing but the label "Best" [*Ächt*, literally "genuine," "authentic"]; and all for the acquired taste of World-ache [*Weltschmerz*].[22]

Wagner here suggests that Beethoven had a profound understanding of what kinds of works were appropriate for the "chamber" and what for the concert hall. Brahms fails to understand these distinctions: he simply moves his chamber to the concert hall and "serves up" as symphonies what is really overblown chamber music.

Wagner seems also to make a more technical or compositional argument: that a more finely worked kind of melody (characterized negatively as being "clammy" and made up of "little chips"), perhaps more at home in the realm of chamber music, is inappropriately transferred by Brahms and his like into the realm of symphonic music, which should by implication feature a different kind of melodic style.

The distinctions made in Wagner's article are taken up in numerous subsequent commentaries on Brahms's symphonies. In an important article, Margaret Notley has shown how the commentaries of Wagner and other contemporaries have sociopolitical overtones that were particularly resonant in late-nineteenth-century Vienna.[23] The notions of symphony-as-democratic and chamber-music-as-elitist, and the selection of Brahms as a target for criticism, reflect the powerful tug of values between the newer right-wing, populist, radical movement and the older bourgeois establishment of Austrian Liberalism, the so-called *Bildungsbürgertum* (educated middle classes). Brahms allied himself clearly with the latter group, from which most of his friends and acquaintances came, including several prominent Jewish families.[24] It was this segment of society that was opposed by the Catholic, anti-Semitic, Pan-German extremists who eventually came to power in Vienna with the election of Karl Lueger as mayor in 1897, the year of Brahms's death. Carl Schorske has described this dramatic historical shift—the death of traditional liberalism—as "politics in a new key."[25]

Musical politics modulated accordingly. The anti-Liberals tended to view chamber music with suspicion as an intellectual, exclusionary genre; they championed the symphony as practiced by a figure like Bruckner, a darling of the Catholic right wing. Theodor Helm compared Brahms's Clarinet Quintet, op. 115, and Bruckner's Eighth Symphony, both premiered in 1892:

> What does even the most beautiful "chamber piece" signify—a genre that is effective only in a small space and therefore addresses itself to narrow circles—in comparison with a symphony like the latest by Bruckner, whose thrillingly all-powerful tonal language . . . is capable of inspiring thousands upon thousands who have ears to hear and a heart to feel what is heard![26]

For Helm, as for Wagner, Brahms's symphonies were generically misbegotten: Brahms was a composer of chamber music who had no business—or at least would have no success—in the public arena of the symphony.

It is striking how this sociopolitical dimension of Brahms's work continued to influence twentieth-century criticism. Bekker's reference to Brahms's proper space as a "bourgeois parlor" puts the composer squarely in the context of late-nineteenth-century middle-class Austro-German Liberalism. Later in his book, Bekker expands upon the implied sociological distinctions between chamber music and symphony:

> The most characteristic element of the symphonic artwork is that its conception is borne by the idea of the *large community*, to which it directs itself; it is thus *received* as monumental by the soul of the musician. This is precisely what does not happen in Brahms's symphonies. Insofar as they are not to be reckoned in their present form as chamber music for orchestra, as occurs in many of the middle movements, they reveal themselves as attempts to monumentalize chamber music. As efforts to reinvent and renew the symphonic style they certainly are worthy of the greatest attention. But they can never reach their goal, because the symphonic style does not arise out of an intensification of the chamber-music style, but grows from an entirely different, unique root.[27]

Two important later commentators who have taken up Bekker's views, though not the negative slant on Brahms, are the philosopher Theodor Adorno and the music historian Carl Dahlhaus.[28] Dahlhaus analyzes the "chamber music tendencies" of the Third Symphony, which include developing variation, motivic concentration, and thematically conceived textures.[29] In Dahlhaus's arguments we can a see link back to—and a kind of redemption of—Wagner's diatribe against the Brahms symphonies. Developing variation and "logical" (as opposed to "architectonic") form are positive ways of describing what Wagner pilloried as the attempt to build larger structures out of little chips of melody.

Dahlhaus offers a distinctive interpretation of the sociological dimension of the symphony-as-chamber-music phenomenon. Brahms's symphonies are aimed not at a class of connoisseurs, nor at any collective group,

> but primarily at the individual listener, at the "subject" immersed in his feelings and thoughts, and are thus perceived, by aesthetic criteria, as though they were chamber music. . . . A Brahms symphony is virtually a musical attestation of the fact that each member of a crowd, though fully aware of the surrounding crowd, is nevertheless entirely on his own.[30]

Brahms might have been puzzled by such a metaphysically oriented description of his audience. But he would have agreed with Leon Botstein's slightly different characterization of Brahms's "public" as one whose level of musical education and literacy had declined across the latter half of the nineteenth century.[31] In his symphonies, Brahms refused to write down to this group. As Botstein says, "Brahms's ideal audience . . . were the individuals who could either play or follow him and, in [Rudolf] Louis's words, 'uncover the hidden soul of Brahms's world of sound.'"[32]

The twentieth-century composer who took very seriously the notion of monumentalizing Brahms's chamber music was the one who similarly refused to concede anything to the general public and who in this regard considered himself Brahms's heir: Arnold Schoenberg. In the works composed after 1908, Schoenberg's densely motivic style carried the notion of little chips of melody—of creating forms from small thematic units—to a level well beyond, and yet with clear origins in, Brahms's music.

In 1936 Schoenberg set himself the task of scoring for full orchestra Brahms's Piano Quartet in G Minor, op. 25. Strictly speaking, this extraordinary feat does not belong to the reception history of the Brahms symphonies. But in the act of scoring the piano quartet, Schoenberg acknowledges an intimate relation in Brahms between chamber and symphonic music. His orchestration reveals, and in some cases creates, the motivically significant inner parts and the rich textures that are latent in Brahms's piano quartet and are characteristic of Brahms's real symphonies.[33]

HEART VS. BRAIN

Implicit in much of the discussion about the chamberlike nature of the Brahms symphonies is the notion that his music is directed too much toward the intellect and is not enough concerned with expression and sensuous appeal. Chamber music is seen as the more appropriate locus of the densely worked thematic and contrapuntal techniques with which Brahms packs his symphonies.

From the first, the reception history of the Brahms symphonies was indelibly colored by this line of argument, expressed either as praise or condemnation. Even Brahms's friends and partisans were wary of the intellectual dimension of his symphonic works. In an often-cited review of the First Symphony, Eduard Hanslick observed:

> The new symphony is so earnest and complex, so utterly unconcerned with common effects, that it hardly lends itself to quick understanding. . . . Brahms seems to favour too one-sidedly the great and the serious, the difficult and the complex, and at the expense of sensuous beauty. We would often give the finest contrapuntal device (and they lie bedded away in the symphony by the dozen) for a moment of warm, heart-quickening sunshine.[34]

Peter Gay has shown how contemporary critics in England and France used terms like *abstruse, dry pedantry,* and *calculating intellectuality* to describe Brahms's symphonies. A reviewer of the Third Symphony in Manchester observed that "the symphony gave us all the mental occupation we could desire."[35] Perhaps the only symphony that escaped this kind of criticism entirely—or almost entirely—was the Second.

In the case of the Fourth Symphony, which because of its finale was deemed the brainiest of the symphonies, some critics could hear beyond the formidably learned surface. In 1886 a writer for the Leipzig journal *Musikalisches Wochenblatt* said of the last movement: "Despite the stupendous contrapuntal art, which in this movement inspires especially the professional musician to astonishment and wonder, the effect of the whole is nonetheless of a continuous improvisation, the equal of which has never been heard in the area of the symphony."[36] Likewise Hanslick, who had criticized the First Symphony for academicism, found a redemption of the intellect in the finale of the Fourth, which was characterized by "an astonishing harmonic and contrapuntal art never conspicuous as such and never an exercise of mere musical erudition." Like the Leipzig critic, Hanslick noted, and did not fault, the appeal of the movement to the professional: "For the musician, there is not another modern piece so productive as a subject for study. It is like a dark well; the longer we look into it, the more brightly the stars shine back."[37]

These reactions to the Fourth were presaged most remarkably by Brahms's friend Elisabet von Herzogenberg, to whom the composer sent the just-completed manuscript of the Fourth Symphony in the late summer of 1885. After analyzing some of the first movement's intricate structural features, she confessed in a letter of September 8, "I have the feeling that this work of your brain is designed too much with a view to microscopic inspection, just as if its beauties were not there for every simple music-lover to see." The symphony is too cerebral, Elisabet said; it makes the listener or score reader work too hard: "We feel we should like to fold our hands and shut our eyes and be stupid for once, leaning on the composer to rest instead of his driving us so relentlessly afield."[38]

Elisabet, however, held back this letter—it remained a fragment—and a few weeks later sent another in which she enclosed the earlier one and apologized:

How glad I am now that I did not air my half-formed impressions. . . . [The first movement] has become an old acquaintance to which many of the remarks I made the other day seem quite inapplicable. . . . I can now trace the hills and valleys so clearly that I have lost the impression of its being a complicated movement; or rather I no longer look upon the complication I read into it as detrimental to its effect in any way.[39]

The shift in attitude is significant, showing how even among Brahms's initiates, familiarity with a work was necessary to breed admiration. What Elisabet's second thoughts suggest is that the distinction between heart and brain, between feeling and intellect, between inspiration and pedantry— there are many ways of describing this dialectic—is ultimately a false one. The more one gets to know a work intellectually and technically—or, as

Hanslick said, the longer we gaze into the dark well—the more one responds to it through feeling or emotion, the brighter the stars shine back.

Nowhere in the tradition of responses to Brahms is the attempt to break down the distinction between heart and brain more powerful than in the commentaries of Schoenberg. In his essay "Heart and Brain in Music" of 1946, Schoenberg acknowledged that "counterpoint, contrapuntal style, is definitely attributed to the brain. It is honoured by the highest appreciation but tolerated only if it does not destroy the warmth of the dreams into which the charm of the beautiful has led the listener."[40] Brahms is the only major composer, apart from himself, whom Schoenberg invokes in this context, before concluding:

> It is not the heart alone which creates all that is beautiful, emotional, pathetic, affectionate, and charming; nor is it the brain alone which is able to produce the well-constructed, the soundly organized, the logical, and the complicated. First, everything of supreme value in art must show heart as well as brain. Second, the real creative genius has no difficulty in controlling his feelings mentally; nor must the brain produce only the dry and unappealing while concentrating on correctness and logic.[41]

In the famous essay of 1947, "Brahms the Progressive," Schoenberg again singled out Brahms as a composer in whom inspiration and intellect could not be separated. Like many critics before him, Schoenberg turned to the Fourth Symphony, in which he analyzed admiringly the return of the opening descent by thirds in the last variations of the finale. "It would look like a high accomplishment of intellectual gymnastics if all this had been 'constructed' prior to inspired composing," he remarks. But in fact in a composer like Brahms the "power of inspiration . . . can produce combinations no one can foresee."[42]

HERMENEUTIC TRADITIONS

Although Brahms's symphonies have endured the charge of intellectualism for over a century, they have also been subject to many kinds of poetic, narrative, and otherwise extramusical interpretations. As such, the symphonies fall into traditions of musical understanding that, as suggested in chapter 1, have their roots deep in the nineteenth century and may be said to lie between or beyond the simple distinction of program vs. absolute music.

Some critics of Brahms's day were only too eager to read programs or narratives into the symphonies. Richard Pohl, a card-carrying New German, was very much aware of the plot archetype of the First Symphony. Listeners will have the feeling, he said in 1876,

> that a distinct, logical sequence of thoughts underlies the work, that poetic content here attains musical expression. Although the first three movements can certainly be explained without resorting to a program of ideas [eines idealen Programms], the continuous fourth and fifth movements [i.e., the slow introduction and finale proper] cannot. Here the style is in places so dramatic, the musical language so full of life, that we feel involuntarily directed toward a specific meaning, one which, however, only the composer himself could provide with complete certainty. But—he has remained completely silent about it.[43]

Writing of the Fourth Symphony in 1886, the Viennese critic Ludwig Speidel suggested that the work "absolutely cried out for a program" and said that the finale had been referred to by "someone" as depicting a soldier's burial.[44]

This kind of response to Brahms's music began to merge in the latter part of the century with the desire on the part of critics—and their public—to explain works of music in words. There emerged a rash of concert guides, program notes, pamphlets, and handbooks to the musical repertory. Botstein, who has written incisively on this trend, observes: "Here was an opportunity to prepare the listener for a musical experience by describing it in a text whose mixture of musical and metaphoric terms assumed the character of a prose of journalistic narrative."[45]

The most prominent of such vade mecums to the standard repertory was the multivolume Führer durch den Concertsaal (Guide to the Concert Hall) by Hermann Kretschmar (1848–1924), which appeared first in 1886 and went through many, ever enlarged editions into the late 1930s, well after the author's death.[46] Kretschmar saw his goal as that of developing what he called a "musical hermeneutics," consisting of analysis and interpretation. In the Führer he sought, in his own words,

> to spark the reader's interest, to penetrate into the interior and intimate world of the work itself and the soul of its composer, and wherever possible to reveal what connects the work to its own time, to the musical context in which it came about, and to the spiritual trends from which it arose.[47]

Into the same general category as Kretschmar's writings fall the commentaries by Philip Goepp in the United States, Max Kalbeck in Vienna, and Julius Harrison—and even Donald F. Tovey—in England. These writers, and numerous commentators and program annotators like them, use brief musical examples in the text and thus assume a certain basic level of musical literacy in their readers. But, as Botstein points out, the examples are not intended to recreate the experience of score reading and thus to approximate the real temporal experience of listening or playing; rather, they are mnemonic signposts in a word-based narrative.[48]

Each of the critics mentioned above tackled Brahms's First Symphony, one of the warhorses of the symphonic repertory. It seems appropriate here to give a brief comparison of their accounts of the finale and its slow introduction, the portion of the symphony that, as Pohl suggested, seemed most to demand some kind of narrative clarification. (In the citations below, I have replaced the musical examples used by the authors with square brackets containing the relevant measure numbers.)

Given the ambitiousness of his stated goals, Kretschmar's analysis (1886) is relatively modest in scope and restrained in its use of metaphor and imagery. He traces a minidrama in musical terms, in which the individual instruments or the entire orchestra are the main protagonists that steer the mood from melancholy to joy:

The introductory Adagio commences with melancholy strains [mm. 1–5]. The violins try energetically and desperately to distract from the path of melancholy, in a phrase that is very sharply characterized by *pizzicato* and *stringendo* and that reappears at critical points in the Allegro. In vain! The imagination strays agitatedly in a dark circle; at the motive [woodwinds, m. 22] the orchestra reaches a state of open revolt. The timpani give out a terrifying roll. Then the French horn appears, like a peaceful messenger from heaven, with the following melody [horn, mm. 30–38]. We are in the Andante, the second part of the introduction. The mood softens, becomes more elevated, and prepares for the mighty, joyful hymn with which the principal section of the finale, the Allegro, begins [mm. 62–65].

A long and folk-like melody develops out of this first section. This melody serves as the primary bearer of representation in this movement.[49]

Philip Goepp's commentary (1902) is more elaborate than Kretschmar's, but similar in tone and technique. He too traces an evolution from darkness

to light in the slow introduction and beginning of the finale. His language
and syntax, with omitted articles and twisted word order, are, to say the least,
idiosyncratic:

> *Adagio* begins a dim passing of chords like clouds across the tonal hori-
> zon, all in the spirit of the first thought of the symphony. But now the
> harmonies of the woodwind are topped by a clear melodic idea in the
> high strings [mm. 1–2] that marks a new token. No reminiscent phrase
> is here that harks back to earlier prophecy; the outcome is at hand, the
> bright result and reward of the groping and striving. . . .
>
> Finally come mere pelting accents (still of an ancient motive) [wood-
> winds, m. 27] against basses marching steadily up the chromatic line.
> There is an overpowering mass of heaped and strained expectation. As the
> answer sings 'mid softest hum of light wood and lowest brass and strings,
> in clear and passionate notes of the horn, here is one of the most over-
> whelming moments of sublime beauty in all poetry [mm. 30–32]. . . .
>
> Slowly a madrigal of responsive voices is reared. In the midst is a sin-
> gle strain of pure hymn, in low brass and wind, in strict choral steps,—a
> passing touch, in still higher empyrean, as of pure religious truth. Even
> the hum of strings has ceased. There is somehow a more human ring as
> the clarion message bursts out again, more joyously, with new echo in
> companion horn. The pace, though faster than the first *Adagio*, is still a
> serenely slow Andante swing. As it moves, now with almost feverish glow,
> we feel dimly that it is itself mere herald for the new song that breaks
> forth in firm array of martial tones and step [mm. 62–65].[50]

Max Kalbeck's narrative of this passage, from his Brahms biography
(1910), is still more vivid and makes much greater use of extramusical
imagery. Not mere melancholy, but terrifying madness and chaos reign in the
first part of the slow introduction. To suggest the redemption that comes with
the Alphorn, Kalbeck outfits the melody with words of hope and suggests an
analogy to the medieval romance *The Song of Roland:*

> It is like a first, weak ray of light that the sun sends forth into the gray
> dawn of morning. The rubato-pizzicato of the strings, an effect that has
> become famous, flutters up in agitation, like a frightened night-bird that
> shudders at the daylight. . . . The dawning day has also affected us pow-
> erfully; caught up, we stare down into the turbulent, chaotic night, into
> a dark abyss of madness, where objects change place, where thoughts

change their order, where everything whirls around in crazy anguish—shreds of spiritual connections that have been torn apart, ruins of systems that have collapsed and fragments of beloved idols! . . .

All at once we hear, like a call from above, the melody of the first horn speaking in tones [mm. 30–38]. It is a strong voice, a "voice of the Lord". . . . Pious spirits even like to place under the melody the words: "Fürchte dich nicht, spricht der Herr, sei getrost, ich bin bei dir!" [Do not fear, saith the Lord, be of good hope, I am with thee!] And when we recall "Mynheer Dominus," as the twenty-one-year-old Brahms used to call his fatherly friend Schumann, who showed him the "new paths" and set him his future task, then we discern the same meaning. We also enjoy reminding ourselves of the dying Roland and his good horn Oliphant—as well as many another hero or genius of humanity, who from Ronceval, the earthly vale of stones, thorns, and tears, has entered in glory the paradise of eternal day. The trombones [mm. 47–50] blow not to the dead, but to him arisen in a new existence, him to whom, with the entrance of the splendid C-major theme [mm. 62–78], flowing forth broadly in full sonorities, appears the sun of victory, nevermore to set.[51]

In 1939, the English composer and conductor Julius Harrison published a full-scale account of the Brahms symphonies that is clearly part of the "guide" genre. His discussion of the finale of the First Symphony is once again a blend of musical and metaphoric language:

The note C, that central orb of the music, is the quintessential feature of the *Adagio* introduction. What themes cluster round it, and they are many, but serve to demonstrate its omnipotence. Whatever modulations occur are short-lived, the music being drawn back to the C as if by some centripetal force. . . .

Ghosts of the past stalk around in barely recognizable shapes. . . . [At m. 24] the Violins break out into rapid figurations which, taken with their context, form a remarkable epitome of all the black despairing moods that have haunted the Symphony from its very first C. . . .

And in this instant Brahms makes us understand that these last convulsive efforts are not so much the death-pangs of evil spirits as the struggle of positive forces breaking through darkness to the refulgence of a never-ending day. . . .

A long conflict is ended at the Horn theme with the appearance of the C major chord [m. 30], to which the solemn hymn [mm. 47–51] acts

as a natural and mystical corollary. From this music arises a great song
of jubilation [mm. 62–78], one that might well express the joy of a man
whose soul is loosed from bondage.[52]

Harrison's commentary, like virtually all those cited up to this point, is
based on a plot line in which something triumphs over or dominates some
"Other." In this case, the power that enables the victory is embodied in the
"refulgent" note/chord of C major, which banishes the "ghosts" and the
"black despairing moods." This kind of analysis draws on aspects of the
music that more recent critics have sought to unmask as narratives of power
based largely on gender and sexuality. It is, in fact, a relatively small step
hermeneutically from Harrison's commentary to the exploration of "narrative
agendas" that Susan McClary has undertaken in Brahms's Third Symphony.

McClary argues that all Classic-Romantic instrumental music employs
"two interlocking narrative schemata," those of tonality and sonata form,
both of which rely on difference, on identifying and eventually subduing an
Other.[53] Tonality in the common practice period implies a central key from
which the composition departs and to which it returns. Sonata form is based
on the same oppositions, which for almost two hundred years have been cast
by critics or theorists in gendered terms: the "masculine" first theme vs. the
"feminine" second theme. In this narrative, as in that of tonality, the masculine dominates. Thus Classic-Romantic "absolute" music plays out "the
most fundamental ideological tensions available within Western culture: the
story of a hero who ventures forth, encounters an Other, fights it out, and
finally reestablishes secure identity."[54]

For McClary, the first movement of Brahms's Third engages this narrative
in an especially complex fashion. The initial motto is heroic—and masculine—in the Beethovenian sense; but its prominent A♭, creating a cross-rela-
tion with the initial A♮, is an "anomaly" that proceeds to derail traditional
tonal—and gender—relationships. The second theme appears not in the
dominant, but in the key of the problematized third, A major (m. 36). This
grazioso theme "already occupies a position on the 'feminine' side of nineteenth-century cultural semiotics," McClary observes.[55] She points out that
Kretschmar clearly responded to this aspect with his image of the A-major
theme as a "seductive . . . Delilah-figure" that "seeks to lull the powerful
elements of the composition to sleep."[56]

The "feminine" theme "is less a threat in and of itself than it is a projection of the hero's own ambivalence."[57] The principal tension in the movement is not between the first and second themes, but "between a first theme

that is dissonant with respect to the conventions that sustain its narrative procedures and those conventions themselves."[58] Thus Brahms reshapes the traditional narrative into one that reflects his own internal conflicts about the tonal procedures and formal conventions he inherited. McClary's view accords well with the analysis of the Third Symphony presented in chapter 5, in which it was suggested that Brahms avoids the conventional dominant relationships at places where we might expect them, but employs them on a larger scale across the symphony.

The idea of an inner conflict within the composer also lies at the core of another gender-oriented study of Brahms's symphonies, an attempt by Robert Fink to develop what he calls a "sexual hermeneutic" for music.[59] Fink takes as his starting point McClary's ideas of the basic sexual narratives embedded in tonality and sonata form, which he then augments by Freud's theory of repression to shape an interpretation of Brahms's First Symphony. Fink argues that the first theme group of the first movement, normally a masculine one within the sonata archetype, contains two conflicting thematic ideas: a rising chromatic figure (our motive x in chapter 3) that represents "disruptive sexual desire," and a triadic figure (z) representing the "opposed ability to control and transcend that desire."[60] Fink historicizes the analysis by suggesting that the chromatic x bears a distinct resemblance to the most famous musical image of sexual desire, the "Longing" motive of rising semitones from Wagner's *Tristan*, a work that Brahms may have known as early as 1862, when he completed work on the first movement of the First Symphony.

Since both x and z are part of the first group, Fink argues, we have "a struggle for sexual control not between male and female, but within one male psyche, divided against itself."[61] The cadence that begins the Allegro in mm. 38–42 constitutes an act of denial or repression in the Freudian sense of keeping something out of consciousness: Brahms tries to deny or reject the chromatic passion of the slow introduction.

Fink buttresses his interpretation with close musical analysis of passages from the symphony and a brief exploration of aspects of Brahms's biography, especially the composer's relationships with and attitudes toward women. As Fink suggests, his own reading essentially represents a recasting in Freudian terms of issues that other commentators, including Kalbeck and Musgrave, have long seen as central to the First Symphony, especially Brahms's feelings about Clara and Robert Schumann.

Despite somewhat differing perspectives and methods, both McClary and Fink are arguing that Brahms's symphonic music, however absolute it may seem, carries within it the traces—traces that are recoverable in the musical language itself—of social and sexual conflicts basic to modern Western culture. Because they are endemic to that culture, these issues presumably show up in the works of *all* composers writing within it. (This is the essentialist aspect of the McClary-Fink position that disturbs many critics.) What makes Brahms's symphonies different or more interesting than others, for these authors, is the way in which he modifies the traditional musical forms to communicate his own ambivalence or inner struggles.

Skeptical readers and listeners may argue that these methodologies yield little that cannot be found in more conventional tonal analysis. Do we need a sexual hermeneutic to explain the A♭–A♮ conflict of the Third Symphony or the chromatic-triadic dichotomy of the First? To ask such questions is, however, to miss the point. For McClary—and before her, Adorno—there is neither any such thing as "pure" music, nor the possibility of a purely technical description that is meaningful. By its very nature music reflects society; society is built upon certain constructions of sexuality and gender, which the critic is obliged to investigate.

Whatever story is told by the writers examined here, the fact that a hermeneutic tradition continues actively up to the present day is, above all, an indication of the strength and appeal of the Brahms symphonies themselves. The symphonies will outlast any individual analysis; what is encouraging is that they continue to stimulate new ones.

Chapter 8

TRADITIONS OF PERFORMANCE

At the beginning of the last chapter it was observed that the symphonies of Brahms have remained a more-or-less constant presence in the concert hall since the end of the nineteenth century. Yet over time their sonorous identity, as determined by the ways in which they are realized in performance, has unquestionably changed. Much of the early history of this aspect of the symphonies is unrecoverable or unverifiable. Brahms's symphonies came into being at the dawn of the age of recorded sound. We know that Brahms took a lively, even participatory interest in recording technology.[1] But neither he nor any of the conductors who led early performances of his symphonies—Otto Dessoff, Hans Richter, or Hans von Bülow—ever made recordings. Thus the question of how a Brahms symphony might have sounded to his own ears is tantalizingly just out of reach.

There is nonetheless considerable information that can help us approach Brahms's sound world. Why should we want to do so? Such questions and the attempts to answer them touch on the categories of performance practice and early music, both of which in recent years have begun to encompass repertory as late as Brahms.[2] In conducting research in this area, we can learn much about the works but should never assume that we are getting close to some absolute truth or "authenticity."[3] Aware of these important caveats, we can embark on a brief exploration of the traditions of performance of the Brahms symphonies over the last century.

ORCHESTRAL SIZE AND ARRANGEMENT

Although orchestras tended to grow in size across the nineteenth century, their individual dimensions varied greatly according to function, locale, and available resources. As Daniel Koury notes in his valuable study, "One should not take for granted any unanimity in the romantic orchestra as far as size is concerned."[4] In the latter half of the century, the small end of the scale in Austria and Germany was represented by a private court orchestra like that at Meiningen, which gave the premiere of Brahms's Fourth Symphony; the large end was represented by the urban-based Vienna Philharmonic, which gave the premieres of both the Second and Third Symphonies. In 1884 Eduard Hanslick described Meiningen under Bülow as having forty-eight players as compared to his "home town" orchestra in Vienna, which had ninety.[5] In 1885, the year of Brahms's Fourth, Bülow himself referred to Meiningen as having forty-nine players, with only eight first violins. It was in this remarkably "lean and mean" sound world that the Fourth Symphony was first brought to life. Brahms was apparently quite content; he argued against supplementing the strings for a richer sonority.[6]

A characteristic size for most municipal orchestras of the period is probably that of the Leipzig Gewandhaus, which performed all the Brahms symphonies in their initial seasons. In 1881 a seating plan for Leipzig showed a total of seventy-two players, about midway between Meiningen and Vienna, in the following proportions:[7] 12 first violins, 10 second violins, 8 violas, 8 cellos, 6 double basses; 2 flutes, 1 piccolo, 1 oboe, 1 English horn, 3 clarinets, 1 bass clarinet, 3 bassoons, 1 contrabassoon; 5 horns, 3 trumpets, 3 trombones; 1 timpani, 1 harp.

These figures, inferred from visual seating plans, must not be taken as firm. Although there is a general pattern of growth for an orchestra like the Gewandhaus, there is also considerable fluctuation. Thus, a seating plan for 1890 suggests a total of ninety-eight players, one for 1896 a total of eighty-six.

Many different seating placements were adopted across the nineteenth century.[8] Brahms himself expressed a preference for an arrangement proposed by his friend George Henschel, the first director of the Boston Symphony in 1881 (fig. 8–1), in which the violins, cellos, and double basses are all divided across the stage at various depths and the violas are grouped in the middle.[9]

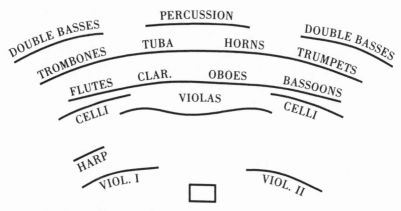

Figure 8–1: Orchestral seating plan after George Henschel

ORCHESTRAL TECHNIQUE

The sound of many instruments—and hence of many orchestras—was different in Brahms's day than it is today. The upper strings of stringed instruments were made of gut rather than today's steel wire; the result was a richer, more vivid sound, one in which the higher overtones were more prominent.[10] Performing technique was also different. As Jon Finson and Robert Philip have shown, the use of string vibrato was much more restrained in the late nineteenth and early twentieth centuries than it usually is today. Portamento, or gliding between nonadjacent notes, presents the opposite picture: it was used more frequently as an expressive device, by both soloists and entire orchestra sections, than it is today.[11]

In the European recordings of the Brahms symphonies made in the first half of this century, one can indeed hear a much greater use of string portamento than in present-day ones. One notable example is the 1936 recording of the Third Symphony by Bruno Walter and the Vienna Philharmonic (Koch 3–7120–2 H1), in which most of the nonadjacent notes of the Allegretto melody are connected by gliding: for example, the connection from E♭ to G across mm. 1–2, and that from E♭ to B♭ across mm. 3–4, and all the leaps in mm. 9–10. In the recording made of the Fourth Symphony by Hermann Abendroth and the London Symphony Orchestra in 1927 (Victor M31), the first violins apply substantial portamento in the opening theme of the first movement.

A still clearer example, because it involves a solo instrument, occurs in the famous passage for violin near the end of the Andante of the First

Symphony, in the recording Otto Klemperer made with the Berlin State Opera Orchestra in 1928 (Koch 3–7053–2 HI). This rendering, beginning at m. 91, is full of swooping portamenti played between both adjacent and non-adjacent notes. Although the use of portamento persisted in some locations, it appears to have diminished considerably after the 1930s, even in passages like this one that seem particularly prone to such interpretation.[12]

INTERPRETATION: THE RICHTER-BÜLOW DICHOTOMY

There is, of course, no "authentic" way of performing the Brahms symphonies. As Christopher Dyment has observed, "Interpretive approaches among conductors at the beginning of the century were so various and sharply differentiated that it is impossible with confidence to assert that any one could be singled out as the standard bearer of a Brahms 'tradition.'"[13] Yet among the conductors most closely associated with Brahms's works, there emerge two interpretive "schools," or ends of a spectrum, roughly the strict and the free. These extremes are embodied in Richter and Bülow, who were, in the words of Charles Villiers Stanford, "the archetypes from whom modern conducting has descended."[14]

Richter's performances were never marked by excesses. Economical in his gestures, generally steady in his tempi, he aimed to project the larger dimensions of a work rather than fine detail. Ernest Newman, who observed Richter often in England, said that "the great thing was not the inner life of the line but the general breadth of the page."[15] One violinist who worked under Richter noted in 1927: "The great difference between Richter and most (not all) present-day conductors is that Richter was a plain, blunt musician, without any frills or pretentiousness, but a man who knew his job from A–Z."[16]

What many such commentators admired as straightforward professionalism in Richter, others, including Brahms, vilified as dullness and lack of inspiration. Stanford recalled in 1922 that when Richter led a performance of the slow movement of the First Symphony at the Gesellschaft der Musikfreunde (no date is given), "so metronomic was it that Brahms, who was listening in a box with a friend, suddenly seized him by the shoulder and said, 'Heraus!', hurrying him away."[17] The second Viennese performance of the First, given by Richter and the Philharmonic in December 1878, was characterized by Brahms as "recht mise," or truly awful.[18]

In December 1895, when Richter again performed the First with the Vienna Philharmonic, Richard Heuberger noted in his Brahms memoirs that the piece was "underplayed miserably, without understanding or poetry."[19] In his review of this same concert, published in the *Wiener Tagblatt* on December 12, Heuberger was minimally more diplomatic. He remarked that Brahms's C-Minor Symphony "is one of those pieces that appear quite alien to Herr Hans Richter. One cannot approach this masterwork from the standpoint of color, and from the thematic standpoint it has perhaps not yet been sufficiently investigated."[20]

Apparently anticipating this kind of performance, Brahms avoided the concert and went for a walk. Later, when Heuberger described the performance to him, the composer said, "Well, if my symphony were really such a dull thing, so grey and mezzoforte, like Richter plays it to people today, then they would be right to speak of the 'brooding [*grüblerisch*] Brahms.' That's how completely misunderstood everything was!"[21]

Bülow, mercurial and unpredictable on the podium, was considered the antipode of Richter. He conducted with the freedom of a solo pianist, as Hanslick reported in 1884:

> Bülow conducts the [Meiningen] orchestra as if it were a little bell in his hand. The most admirable discipline has transformed it into an instrument upon which he plays with utter freedom and from which he produces nuances possible only with a discipline to which larger orchestras would not ordinarily submit. Since he can achieve these nuances securely, it is understandable that he applies them at those places where they would seem appropriate to him if he were playing the same piece at the piano. I would be unjust to call these tempo changes 'liberties,' since conscientious adherence to the score is a primary and inviolable rule with Bülow.[22]

Hanslick goes on to discuss certain aspects of Bülow's performance (of Beethoven, in this case) as "unmotivated," "affected," and "mannered." But these "interpretive peculiarities" did not, in his view, disrupt "the spirit of the compositions."[23]

Brahms favored and himself employed considerable elasticity of tempo, as well as freedom in rhythm and phrasing.[24] Yet he seems at times to have been bothered by Bülow's more extreme idiosyncrasies. In 1887, after the relationship between the two men had soured somewhat, he remarked:

> Bülow's conducting is always calculated for effect. Immediately a new phrase begins, he makes a small pause, and likes also to change the tempo a little. I have deliberately denied myself this in my symphonies; if I had wanted it, I would have written it in.[25]

This rather harsh judgment contrasts with what Bülow himself reported
Brahms as saying: "Bülow, you can play my things just as you wish."[26]

Indeed, Brahms approved of Bülow's basic musical values; he certainly
preferred them to Richter's. The composer contrasted these two conductors
vividly in a remark of 1892, when told by Heuberger that the Vienna
Philharmonic was going to program his Fourth Symphony:

> Yes, it would be splendid if such a piece could for once be rehearsed in
> a methodical manner with the people [Leuten, presumably the players].
> Clearly this must be done by a Kapellmeister who knows the things!
> The last movement of the Fourth Symphony, when it is methodically
> rehearsed—how it explodes [kracht]! But it will once again be lamely
> underplayed. No one knows his stuff, least of all Richter. And then we'd
> hear again: it is poorly orchestrated, etc., in short, Brahms is at fault!
> But how Bülow rehearses such a piece![27]

Reported timings of their performances provide a bit more information
about Bülow and Richter as interpreters of Brahms. In October 1884, before
he was to bring his orchestra to Vienna, Bülow corresponded about possible
programs with the leading concert agent, Albert Gutmann. Bülow suggested
placing all three Brahms symphonies—the Fourth had not yet been written—on a single concert in the order 3, 1, 2. "The sequence has been care-
fully considered," he noted, suggesting that the Second made for the climax.
Gutmann apparently balked at this idea—his letter does not survive—perhaps suggesting, among other things, that the concert would be too long.
Bülow responded, seeking to persuade:

> If you knew what kind of absolutely unalloyed pleasure you forego
> through your rejection of the Brahms trilogy! I recently tried the exper-
> iment: the First lasts thirty-seven minutes; the Second, thirty-eight
> minutes; the Third, thirty-four minutes. (To be sure, I omit the repeat of
> the exposition of the first movement in the First and Second, which the
> master himself has moreover authorized!)[28]

It is of interest to note that in the two "older" symphonies, the First and
Second, Bülow omits the repeats of the first-movement exposition, while in
the newer Third he retains it.

Individual timings for Richter's premiere of the Second Symphony in
December 1877, as given in table 8–1, were provided by C. F. Pohl, the friend

of Brahms and archivist of the Gesellschaft der Musikfreunde, in a letter to Brahms's publisher Simrock.[29] If one corrects or compensates for the repeat of the exposition, which I have done based on the proportions in modern recorded performances, the timing of Richter's first movement would come to about fourteen minutes. This adjustment would bring the total duration of Richter's rendering of Brahms's Second, without repeat, to thirty-eight minutes—precisely the same as Bülow's! Of course, we must take as approximate timings reported in an era well before digital stopwatches. Bülow's, moreover, are presented in a polemical spirit; he wanted to prove how all three symphonies could be played in a single evening. The coincidence of the overall duration between Richter and Bülow is nonetheless striking.

In table 8–1, I have presented these timings in the context of others ranging from the earliest recorded performances of the Brahms symphonies to some of the later twentieth century. In the case of the Second Symphony, we see that the Bülow-Richter durations fall somewhere in the middle of a range that extends from a brisk thirty-three minutes by Felix Weingartner to a glacial forty-three by Leonard Bernstein (as rounded to the nearest full minute).

Overall, the timings given in table 8–1 suggest that, in general, performances have slowed down since the late nineteenth or early twentieth centuries. But they also make us aware that when conductors as temperamentally different as Bülow and Richter clock in at the same time, we learn little that is really meaningful about traditions of performance and interpretation.

Some aspect of the Bülow approach—or at least of what Walter Blume called an authentically "Meiningen tradition"—can perhaps be glimpsed from the markings and comments in scores of the Brahms symphonies made by Fritz Steinbach. Steinbach (1855–1916) succeeded Bülow at Meiningen in 1886, the year after the premiere of Brahms's Fourth by that orchestra. Kalbeck reports that Steinbach actually took Brahms himself as his "model" (*Vorbild*) for conducting and that his performances were highly regarded by the composer.[30]

In 1933 Blume, who had been a pupil of Steinbach's in 1914–15, transcribed and published the markings from Steinbach's scores.[31] Blume claimed that in the 1930s performances of the Classic-Romantic repertory had become faster, more motoric, and less nuanced, a phenomenon for which he felt jazz was partly to blame. (There is more than a whiff of an attack on cultural degeneracy in Blume's comments.)

In the Meiningen tradition, Blume maintained, rhythmic precision was allied with flexible and frequent modification of tempo. In general, the Steinbach markings, as reported by Blume, bear out this claim. Take, for

(*text continued on page 173*)

TABLE 8-1

Comparative Timings

	Symphony No. 1				
CONDUCTOR/ORCHESTRA/DATE	MOVEMENT				
	I	II	III	IV	
Dessoff, Karlsruhe Orchestra, 1876[1]	14:00* 11:30†	9:00	4:00	16:00	[total† 40:30]
Bülow, Meiningen Orchestra, 1884[2]					[total 37:00]
Fried, Berlin State Opera, 1923 (DGG 66304–08)	12:13	9:06	4:27	14:40	[total 40:26]
Weingartner, London Symphony, 1923–24 (Columbia M9 [67042–6D])	11:41	7:07	3:52	14:32	[total 37:12]
Stokowski, Philadelphia Orchestra, April 25–27, 1927 (Biddulph WHL 017–18)	12:36	8:25	4:17	15:14	[total 40:32]
Klemperer, Berlin State Opera, February 1928 (Koch 3-7053-2 HI)	12:58	9:46	4:12	14:48	[total 41:44]
Weingartner, London Symphony, February 18, 1939 (EMI CHS 7 64256 2)	11:35	8:57	4:17	14:29	[total 39:18]
Toscanini, NBC Symphony, March/May/December 1941 (RCA 60277-2-RG)	12:03	8:35	4:21	16:24	[total 41:13]
Furtwängler, Lucerne Festival, August 27, 1947 (Music & Arts CD-804)	14:56	10:25	5:08	16:59	[total 47:28]
Walter, Columbia Symphony, 1960 (Columbia M4S 615)	14:00	8:23	4:41	17:20	[total 44:24]
Karajan, Berlin Philharmonic, 1964 (DGG 2740 242)	13:38	9:04	4:50	17:45	[total 45:17]
Böhm, Vienna Philharmonic, 1976 (DGG 2563 587)	13:54	10:34	4:54	17:49	[total 47:11]
Solti, Chicago Symphony, January 1979 (London D 225335)	16:40* 13:28†	9:45	4:38	17:28	[total† 45:19]
Bernstein, Vienna Philharmonic, 1982 (DGG 410 081-2)	17:29* 14:06†	10:52	5:34	17:54	[total† 48:26]
Norrington, London Classical Players, November 1990 (EMI CDC 7 54286 2)	14:32* 11:52†	7:53	4:20	15:15	[total† 39:20]

Symphony No. 2

CONDUCTOR/ORCHESTRA/DATE	MOVEMENT				
	I	II	III	IV	
Richter, Vienna Philharmonic, December 1877[3]	19:00* 14:00†	11:00	5:00	8:00	[total† 38:00]
Bülow, Meiningen Orchestra, 1884[4]					[total 38:00]
Stokowski, Philadelphia Orchestra, April 29–30, 1929 (Biddulph WHL 017–18)	14:34	10:30	6:10	9:54	[total 41:08]
Fiedler, Berlin Philharmonic, 1931 (Biddulph WHL 003–4)	14:54	9:25	5:05	8:58	[total 38:22]
Weingartner, London Symphony, February 26, 1940 (EMI CHS 7 64256 2)	13:49	8:15	5:02	7:48	[total: 32:54]
Furtwängler, Vienna Philharmonic, January 28, 1945 (Music & Arts CD-804)	14:14	10:09	5:47	8:28	[total 38:38]
Toscanini, NBC Symphony, February 11, 1952 (RCA 60258-2-RG)	14:33	8:27	5:23	8:53	[total 37:16]
Karajan, Berlin Philharmonic, 1964 (DGG 2740 242)	15:18	10:42	5:11	8:53	[total 40:04]
Böhm, Vienna Philharmonic, 1976 (DGG 2563 588)	15:31	11:44	5:35	9:51	[total 42:41]
Solti, Chicago Symphony, January 1979 (London D 225335)	20:38* 15:11†	10:28	5:25	8:40	[total† 39:44]
Bernstein, Vienna Philharmonic, 1982 (DGG 410-082-2)	20:40* 15:22†	11:57	5:31	10:05	[total† 42:55]
Norrington, London Classical Players, September 1992 (EMI CDC 7 54875 2)	19:28* 14:28†	8:40	4:45	8:34	[total† 36:27]

Symphony No. 3

CONDUCTOR/ORCHESTRA/DATE	MOVEMENT				
	I	II	III	IV	
Bülow, Meiningen Orchestra, 1884[5]					[total 34:00* 31:00†]
Stokowski, Philadelphia Orchestra, September 25–26, 1928 (Biddulph WHL 017–18)	9:43	10:24	5:49	9:18	[total 34:14]

Walter, Vienna Philharmonic, May 18–19, 1936 (Koch 3-7120-2 H1)	8:42	7:23	5:31	7:50	[total 29:26]
Weingartner, London Philharmonic, October 6, 1938 (EMI CHS 7 64256 2)	8:38	7:29	5:38	7:57	[total 29:42]
Furtwängler, Berlin Philharmonic, December 18, 1949 (Virtuoso 2699072)	13:12* 10:06†	9:32	6:20	9:12	[total† 35:10]
Toscanini, NBC Symphony, November 4, 1952 (RCA 60259-2-RG)	13:38* 10:24†	9:32	6:52	8:51	[total† 35:39]
Karajan, Berlin Philharmonic, 1964 (DGG 2740 242)	9:35	7:31	6:45	8:45	[total 32:36]
Böhm, Vienna Philharmonic, 1976 (DGG 2563 589)	10:54	10:22	6:34	8:40	[total 36:30]
Solti, Chicago Symphony, May 1978 (London D 225335)	13:45* 10:25†	9:20	6:23	8:43	[total† 34:51]
Bernstein, Vienna Philharmonic, 1982 (DGG 410 083-2)	15:33* 11:55†	9:41	7:04	9:33	[total† 37:43]

Symphony No. 4

CONDUCTOR/ORCHESTRA/DATE	MOVEMENT				
	I	II	III	IV	
Fiedler, Berlin State Opera, 1930 (Biddulph WHL 003–4)	12:29	11:59	6:16	10:55	[total 41:39]
Stokowski, Philadelphia Orchestra, March 4, April 29, 1933 (Biddulph WHL 017–18)	11:16	11:33	5:59	9:27	[total 38:15]
Walter, BBC Symphony Orchestra, May 18–19, 1933 (Koch 3-7120-2 H1)	11:46	11:58	5:29	9:58	[total 39:11]
Weingartner, London Symphony Orchestra, February 14, 1938 (EMI CHS 7 64256 2)	11:23	9:24	6:34	9:40	[total 37:01]
Furtwängler, Berlin Philharmonic, December 15, 1943 (Music & Arts CD-804)	12:02	12:15	6:13	9:12	[total 39:42]
Toscanini, NBC Symphony, December 3, 1951 (RCA 60260-2-RG)	10:51	10:15	6:04	9:00	[total 36:10]
Karajan, Berlin Philharmonic, 1964 (DGG 2740 242)	13:04	11:38	6:10	10:15	[total 41:07]
Böhm, Vienna Philharmonic, 1976 (DGG 2563 590)	13:07	11:56	6:36	10:09	[total 41:48]

Solti, Chicago Symphony, May 1978 (London D 225335)	12:30	12:48	6:09	10:13	[total 41:40]
Bernstein, Vienna Philharmonic, 1982 (DGG 410 084-2)	13:18	12:42	6:12	11:36	[total 43:48]

Recordings listed as CDs when available in that format; otherwise LP or 78 numbers are provided.

*Played with repeat of exposition.

†With first-time exposition and first ending subtracted, to allow for comparisons.

[1] As reported by Richard Pohl, *Musikalisches Wochenblatt* 7 (1876): 658.

[2] Hans von Bülow, *Briefe und Schriften*, ed. Marie von Bülow (Leipzig: Breitkopf & Härtel, 1908), vol. 7, p. 305.

[3] As reported by C. F. Pohl, *Johannes Brahms Briefwechsel*, rev. eds. (Berlin: Deutsche Brahms-Gesellschaft, 1912–22), X, 66.

[4] Hans von Bülow, *Briefe und Schriften*, ed. Marie von Bülow (Leipzig: Breitkopf & Härtel, 1908), vol. 7, p. 305.

[5] Hans von Bülow, *Briefe und Schriften*, ed. Marie von Bülow (Leipzig: Breitkopf & Härtel, 1908), vol. 7, p. 305.

example, the powerful climax of the coda of the first movement of the First Symphony (mm. 470–74) and the subsequent falling away (mm. 475ff.). Brahms himself indicates no tempo modification here. But the Steinbach score suggests, according to Blume:

> About five measures before **P** [m. 470] . . . the Tempo is driven rather strongly until **P** [m. 475]. The pizzicato [m. 475] has to arrive in the original tempo [of the Allegro], such that a noticeable jolt [*Ruck*] occurs. To achieve this jolt and the precision of the pizzicato, one should beat the last three eighth notes before **P** in the subsequent tempo.[32]

It would be thrilling to hear a performance like this. Yet if the Meiningen tradition is lost to us today, other early performing styles survive on recordings.

The Coda of the First Movement of the First Symphony: A Comparison

The coda in which the passage just examined is embedded provides a small but intriguing case study. The continuous repetition, from m. 475, of the same rhythmic figure (in eighth-note beats: 6–1, 2–3, 6–1, and so forth) suggests a performance with a steady pulse, even though, as Norman del Mar observes, "the full drive of the impetuous Allegro becomes ever less appropriate."[33] Brahms himself applies the brakes when, immediately prior to the Meno Allegro, he changes the eighth-note rhythm to quarter note duplets (mm. 492–94).

Modern conductors tend to maintain a relatively steady tempo coming out of the recapitulation into the coda. Solti emerges, for example, at $\downarrow$ = 108, a tempo he reduces somewhat with the arrival at m. 478 of the lyrical violin theme derived from what we have called motive x in chapter 3. Norrington's tempi are brisker but comparable. His recapitulation ends at about 116; at the violin theme he slows a bit to 108. The big shift for Solti and Norrington, as for most modern conductors, comes at the Meno Allegro itself (m. 495). Solti slows down to less than half the previous tempo ($\downarrow$ = ca. 50), Norrington to about 66.

Several recordings of the Brahms First from earlier in the century reveal a very different approach to the final pages of the first movement—and, indeed, to the movement as a whole. The principle here seems to be to make the big ritardando much earlier, at the violin melody of m. 478, and then to slow up still further at the Meno Allegro of m. 495.

The earliest available recording of the symphony is one made by Oskar Fried (1871–1941) and the Berlin State Opera Orchestra in 1923 (DGG 66304–08). Best known as a strong advocate of Mahler's symphonies—he made the first recording of the Second—Fried conducted the Romantic repertory with a wide range of tempo fluctuations. His Brahms First, very different from virtually any performance we would hear today, is a fascinating study in sudden shifts of mood and tempo.[34] At the passage in question, Fried emerges from the recapitulation very briskly, at about $\downarrow$ = 120. Then, at the violin theme of m. 478, he slows dramatically to 76, a tempo he maintains more or less until the Meno Allegro, when he drops down to about 60. Proportionally the largest shift has come at m. 478.

A strikingly similar approach to the coda is found in the recording of the First Symphony by Hermann Abendroth and the London Symphony Orchestra, which was made in 1928 (HMV D1454–58).[35] Abendroth (1883–1956), a prominent figure in Germany earlier in this century, served as a conductor in Cologne in the 1910s and 20s, after which he became conductor of the Leipzig Gewandhaus Orchestra until 1945. He also worked in Bayreuth during World War II.

Abendroth conducts Brahms with extreme fluctuations of tempo, although his shifts appear to be more structurally determined than those of Fried. In the first movement, for example, he slows down dramatically—far more than any present-day conductor would do—at m. 156, just before the closing group of the exposition. Similarly, at m. 294, the still center of the development, Abendroth brings the music virtually to a halt before beginning a slow climb to the climactic retransition.[36] He approaches the end of the recapitulation almost as fast as Fried, at ♩. = 116. Then, at the violin theme of m. 478, he similarly slows down almost by half, to 60. At the Meno Allegro of m. 495, he drops still further, to 40. Like Fried, he has made the most extreme change of tempo not at the Meno Allegro but at the earlier violin theme.

Otto Klemperer's recording of the First with the same orchestra, Berlin State Opera, also made in 1928 (Koch 3-7053-2), similarly makes the largest shift of tempo at m. 478. Like Abendroth, Klemperer begins the coda at 116, then at m. 478 drops down almost fifty notches, to 70. The Meno Allegro begins at ♩. = 57, only minimally "meno" than what has immediately preceded.

Two of Wilhelm Furtwängler's recordings of the First, those from August 1947 (Music & Arts CD-804) and February 1952 (Virtuoso 269072), also make a very large ritardando at m. 478, with a further adjustment at the Meno Allegro. Weingartner's 1939 recording (EMI CHS 7 64256 2) is much less extreme, as one might expect. Like most conductors of today he reserves the greatest shift for the Meno Allegro. Yet even he makes a significant ritardando at the violin melody of m. 478, slowing from 120 to 108.

The early recordings raise, even if they do not answer, important questions about the legacy of performance styles. Do the approaches of Fried, Abendroth, Klemperer, and Furtwängler—and to a lesser extent, Weingartner—to the coda of the first movement, all of which are remarkably consistent, represent a particular tradition dating perhaps from Brahms's own day? Might the extreme ritardando that these conductors make at m. 478, a shift one would not intuit from the score alone, be one of the kinds of nuances for which Bülow was known or which Brahms might have recognized as legitimate, but which have essentially been lost to us today? (This particular ritardando does not seem to be part of the "Meiningen tradition" discussed above. Steinbach gives no indication of any slowing up at m. 478. His principal shift—and this only a return to the movement's main tempo—comes with the "jolt" at m. 475.)

It is clear that Brahms himself vacillated over the question of proper tempo in the coda of the first movement in ways that are suggestive, but hardly definitive, for the study of performance practice. In the first edition of the symphony, the passage at m. 495 is marked not Meno Allegro but Poco sostenuto, like the opening of the movement. The Poco sostenuto marking imparts to the end of the coda a sense of symmetry by returning to the tempo and mood of the beginning. In a letter to his publisher Simrock of December 1878 Brahms asked for the indication to be changed:

> A stupid error has struck me. At the end of the first movement it should not say *Poco sostenuto*. People misunderstand that and take the same tempo as in the introduction. *Meno allegro* is what should be there.[37]

Brahms implies that over the first two years of performances of the First Symphony conductors tended to slow up too much at the Poco sostenuto of the coda. Interpreting Brahms's remarks and his alteration, Robert Pascall observes that, by changing the indication to Meno Allegro, Brahms "brought the coda into closer relationship with the main body of the movement rather than keeping a relationship with the slow introduction—which, incidentally, he had not spotted before publication."[38] Del Mar argues that Brahms realized the inappropriateness of resuming the original tempo at the end of the coda: "The change indicates that Brahms decided against too great a loss of momentum such as could result in an over-protestation of deep tragedy rather than melancholy." For a conductor, Del Mar explains, "there is thus no question now of going back into 6, although an appreciably slower dotted crotchet [quarter-note] pulse of 56 will have been reached [at the Meno Allegro] by the very gradual dissipation of the movement's energy."[39] In other words, the music will already have slowed by this point, and one should not exaggerate further by resuming the original tempo, or beating pattern, of the opening Poco sostenuto.

In fact, however much they slow down at the end of the movement, from the violin melody of m. 478 onward, none of the historic conductors on record approaches the slow tempo of the introduction. All remain at least several notches faster than the opening Poco sostenuto:

CONDUCTOR/DATE	POCO SOSTENUTO	MENO ALLEGRO
	(m. 1)	(m. 495)
Fried 1923	♩. = 36	♩. = 46
Klemperer 1928	♩. = 29	♩. = 57
Abendroth 1928	♩. = 33	♩. = 40
Weingartner 1939	♩. = 35	♩. = 48
Furtwängler 1947	♩. = 25	♩. = 35

I would offer a different and more speculative interpretation of Brahms's comments and actions than either Pascall or Del Mar. Neither author gives the composer quite enough credit for knowing his own composition and observing the practice of conductors. That Brahms "had not spotted" the identity between the Poco sostenuto markings of the coda and slow introduction, as Pascall claims, seems highly unlikely despite the composer's admitting to being "struck" by a "stupid error." More probable is that Brahms planned the symmetry and the sense of return much as he did in other places in his music. An example somewhat analogous to the first movement, though not identical in effect, occurs in the finale of the same symphony, where the choralelike theme from the slow introduction (mm. 47–51) reappears in the coda (mm. 407–16) with its note values doubled, thus—when the effect is understood by conductors—bringing it back to its original tempo.[40]

In the case of the first movement, a somewhat complicated chain of inferences is necessary to suggest why Brahms may have created, and then eliminated, the introduction-coda symmetry of tempo. It is generally believed— based on evidence from a letter by Clara Schumann—that Brahms added the slow introduction after the body of the first movement was completed.[41] If this is true, then at first the Poco sostenuto of the coda stood alone, with its solemn timpani pedals and slowly moving chromatic lines. When, at some point in the fourteen-year evolution of the symphony, Brahms added the slow introduction, he set up, de facto, a relationship between the two ends of the movement. And I think it very possible that he intended, in his mind's ear, that they would share a tempo, even as they share thematic and timbral features.[42]

When the symphony was first performed in the fall of 1876, I suggest, conductors tended to take the introduction very slowly, so slowly that Brahms came to realize that no real symmetry or return was possible without the coda turning to musical putty. There was little he could, or would, do about the introduction itself; he refused to add metronome markings. But by deciding two years, and many performances, later to change the final Poco sostenuto to Meno Allegro, Brahms could at least discourage conductors from slowing too much at the end. With this decision he sacrificed for good the possibility of temporal symmetry between introduction and coda.

WEINGARTNER AND BRAHMS

Among early or historic recordings of the Brahms symphonies, those by Weingartner are among the most significant, in part because there is a direct link to the composer. Weingartner (1863–1942), who first conducted the

Berlin Philharmonic in 1891 and whose performances became known to Brahms during the last years of the composer's life, saw himself more in the Richter than in the Bülow line. In his writings, especially the well-known pamphlet *Über das Dirigieren* ("On Conducting") of 1895, he was highly critical of what he took as the extreme freedom of interpretation, the "mania for nuance," and the exaggerations of Bülow's style. Weingartner himself stressed fidelity to the score, but at the same time he deplored "wretched literalists."

Weingartner was ambivalent toward the music of Brahms. In his little book, *The Symphony since Beethoven*, published in German in 1898, he characterized the symphonies, especially the Third and Fourth, as often lifeless and unexpressive, as "scientific music."[43] But there seems little question that he approached Brahms with the same professional attitude that he displayed toward the other scores with which he became associated in his long career.

And his approach met with the composer's highest approval. In April 1895 the Berlin Philharmonic came to Vienna for a series of three concerts conducted, respectively, by Richard Strauss, Weingartner, and Felix Mottl. Brahms, who seems to have attended all the performances, was especially impressed with the young Weingartner, who conducted the Second Symphony. The composer wrote to his publisher Simrock:

> By far the most enjoyable and finest was the second evening under Weingartner, whose healthy, fresh personality was uncommonly sympathetic. It began with my symphony, which he conducted from memory really splendidly. Right after the first movement the whole orchestra had at last to rise to acknowledge the response. The third movement had to be repeated. The performance was truly wonderful.[44]

Later that year Weingartner again conducted Brahms's Second with the Berlin Philharmonic, this time in Hamburg. A local critic, Rudolf Philipp, described the performance, which also included Beethoven's Eighth Symphony and *Leonore* Overture No. 3, in terms that seem to corroborate Brahms's impressions of Weingartner's style. Philipp admired the way Weingartner restrained the "bravura" element "so that the classical beauty of these masterworks lost nothing of its proper nobility." All the pieces were distinguished by "overpowering sweep, fiery enthusiasm, spirited presentation that never fragments the whole, and the clearest possible diction."[45]

That Brahms himself could at the same time approve of Weingartner's interpretation and show respect for Bülow's more highly nuanced style—the composer is not likely to have described a Bülow performance of the Second as "healthy" and "fresh"—suggests that he had no fixed image of how his music should sound. Like most composers, he was open and responsive to compelling interpretations of different kinds.

Weingartner recorded the Second Symphony with the London Symphony in 1940.[46] This period was, of course, almost half a century after the performances with the Berlin Philharmonic described above. Weingartner was now almost eighty and near the end of his life. Moreover, he was in a recording studio, with all its restrictions, including the need to stop the music every four minutes or so to change disks. Yet most accounts suggest that Weingartner's interpretations of music changed very little over the course of his career, and in the recorded Second, as in the other symphonies, one can still hear—and admire—something of the clarity and "health" to which Brahms and contemporary critics referred.

Weingartner's Second, clocking in at 32:54, has, in fact, the shortest overall duration of any recording of the work listed in table 8–1 and is probably the fastest on record. The timings bring Weingartner in well below the Richter or Bülow duration of thirty-eight minutes and even below the 36:27 of Norrington's prevailingly brisk, historically informed recording. Yet with the possible exception of the finale, the performance never seems rushed or breathless. What Weingartner displays above all—and one can well imagine Brahms responding positively to this—is the ability to project a rhythmic trajectory through an entire movement. This aspect of Weingartner's performances has been addressed most articulately by Peter Rabinowitz:

> What is most important about rhythm in Weingartner's performances . . .
> is not its steadiness or subtlety, but its rhetorical function. . . . Wein-
> gartner conceived of rhythm as a source of progression rather than a
> means for emphasis, a way to link details rather than highlight them. To
> put it in other terms, rhythm (which Weingartner saw in terms of artic-
> ulation and phrasing as well as tempo) was the key to formal structure,
> the key to the relation between parts and whole.[47]

None of this is to imply that Weingartner's rendering of the Second Symphony is without considerable nuance. Indeed, anyone trying to calibrate his performance with a metronome will be extremely frustrated. Within a movement, Weingartner will employ a restricted range of tempi. In the first movement of the Second, he never goes below ♩ = 88 or above 126, a span narrower than many conductors past and present. But within these limits Weingartner moves flexibly, giving the impression of suppleness without exaggeration.

TABLE 8-2
Comparative Tempi in Recordings of Second Symphony, I

CONDUCTOR	EXPOSITION				DEVELOPMENT			CODA		
	m. 1	44	82	136	183	212	298	455	477	497
Stokowski 1929	♩ = 100	100	100	116	100	120	116	100	88	104
Fiedler 1931	♩ = 100	112	96	116	96	138	100	92	84	104
Weingartner 1940	♩ = 96	112	104	112	104	126	96	104	88	108
Furtwängler 1945	♩ = 108	100	116	120	100	138	104	112	84	112
Solti 1979	♩ = 104	108	108	112	96	126	108	96	76	96
Norrington 1992	♩ = 100	108	108	120	108	132	108	100	84	100

THE FIRST MOVEMENT OF THE
SECOND SYMPHONY: A COMPARISON

Rather than consider Weingartner in isolation, we can compare his rendering of the first movement of the Second Symphony to other historical accounts, including those of Leopold Stokowski, Max Fiedler, and Wilhelm Furtwängler, and to the more recent performance on original instruments by Roger Norrington. The performance by Georg Solti, a respectable one, can serve as representative of a more modern and mainstream control group. Table 8–2 compares the tempi that each of these conductors takes at certain important structural moments in the first movement of the Second Symphony:

m. 1:	the opening theme
m. 44:	the broad violin theme
m. 82:	the start of the second group
m. 136:	the canonic development within the second group
m. 183:	the horn solo at the beginning of the development section
m. 212:	near the climax of the fugato in the development section
m. 298:	the descending scale in the retransition at the very end of the development section
m. 455:	the beginning of the horn solo in the coda
m. 477:	the violins' melody based on the opening theme
m. 497:	the scherzando segment of the coda

It must immediately be pointed out that metronome markings like those in table 8–2 are not easily arrived at. For even the steadiest of these conductors, a tempo at any given moment will represent no more than a point on a continuum on the way to or from other tempi. Representations like table 8–2 must therefore be consulted in conjunction with the actual recordings: there is no substitute for listening to get a sense of a conductor's sense of time and rhythm.

Stokowski's 1929 pressing of the Second Symphony with the Philadelphia Orchestra has undoubted historical value as probably the earliest Second on record. As can be inferred from table 8–2, his range of tempi is relatively restricted and tends to fluctuate even less than Weingartner's. Stokowski's is a performance of neither stark contrasts nor great ideas. It is nicely shaped, and the Philadelphia Orchestra plays very beautifully indeed; but there is little that is compelling about the interpretation.

The absolute antipode to the more classical interpretations of Weingartner and Stokowski is the heavily nuanced recording made by Max
Fiedler and the Berlin Philharmonic in 1931. Fiedler (1859–1939) worked
from 1882 until 1908 principally in the city of Brahms's birth, Hamburg. He
made his debut with the Berlin Philharmonic in 1897, the year of Brahms's
death, and thereafter conducted it often. In 1908 Fiedler (no relation to
Arthur) came to the United States to assume directorship of the Boston
Symphony Orchestra, which he held until 1912, when he returned to
Germany and took up a post in Essen. He continued to be active well into
the years of the Third Reich.

Dyment has suggested that Fiedler's recorded Brahms is "flabby" and
represents that of "a man advanced in years." He quotes the commentator
Richard Aldrich, who already in 1908 criticized Fiedler for "a tendency to
an exaggerated modification of tempo, to retardation and acceleration and to
the excessive modeling of the phrase, which destroy the repose, the continuity of line and disrupt the larger symmetry of outline without the projection
of the deeply felt or emotional effect that is intended."[48] Yet, as late as 1933
a German critic could write, when reviewing a Brahms evening of the Berlin
Philharmonic led by Fiedler, "For decades Fiedler has had the reputation as
one of the most important Brahms interpreters, which he most impressively
justified."[49]

Fiedler's Brahms, at least as represented by his recording of the Second
Symphony in 1931, is indeed one of enormous extremes of tempo. Where
Weingartner's range in the first movement covers only about 30 degrees on
the metronome, Fiedler's extends almost one hundred, from $\bemol = 44$ at the end
of the horn solo in the coda to 138 at the height of the fugato in the development section. At times continuity is broken entirely as Fiedler comes almost
to a complete halt. To be sure, many conductors make this kind of shift at
such moments as the passage for trombone and timpani in the first group and
again just before the second group. But Fiedler's Second has a large share of
such gestures, often coming at unexpected moments, as in the brief imitative
passage between brasses and woodwinds in mm. 224–26. Fiedler slows down
dramatically here, making a large Luftpause immediately before the downbeat
of m. 227 (and again in the analogous spot before m. 233). His tempi are not
easy to calibrate, for he has a tendency to begin a phrase or melody under
tempo and to reach the desired or prevailing tempo at the end of the first measure or first few notes.

The overall impression one takes away from the Fiedler is not that of "flabby" performance but of one with a very different sense of time and rhythm from
Weingartner. Whether the kinds of nuances and ritards in Fiedler bear any

similarity to those "mannerisms" deemed characteristic of Bülow's style cannot be determined. But if, as Stanford suggested, Bülow and Richter form the late nineteenth-century antipodes of conducting style, then Fiedler and Weingartner stand in an analogous relationship in the next generation.

Between these two extremes emerges Furtwängler, who recorded each of the Brahms symphonies numerous times between 1932 and 1954.[50] In the opinion of this listener, Furtwängler emerges as the finest Brahms conductor of his generation, perhaps of all time. Furtwängler is perhaps most readily associated with the more rugged "outer" Brahms symphonies, the First and Fourth. But his glorious 1945 recording of the Second with the Vienna Philharmonic displays many of the same qualities that have made him a legend in this repertory, and the performance of the first movement offers several convenient points of comparison with those already discussed.[51]

Furtwängler displays at once a greater attention to detail and to Brahms's markings than his contemporaries and at the same time a larger sense of rhythmic-temporal flow that is never deflected by the individual nuances. He has an extraordinary ability not only to respect, but to make musical sense of, dynamic markings and the indications of crescendo and diminuendo. A few places in the first movement where this happens—and the examples could be multiplied throughout Furtwängler's recorded legacy— are the diminuendo in mm. 20–23, the *sforzando* on the last beat of m. 58, the swell and diminuendo in mm. 78–81, the *pianissimo* at m. 171, the swell and diminuendo at mm. 275–77, the *sforzando* at m. 298, the crescendo into mm. 450–51 and subsequent diminuendo.

Three of these moments merit some consideration. Measures 20–23 are in the large introductory portion of the first group of the exposition. In the score, Brahms marks a gradual swell and decrease for the woodwinds in mm. 17–23. The climax (merely *piano*) comes at the last beat of m. 19 and in m. 20, where the violins, who have entered on the last beat of m. 17, move to their high E. The hairpins are placed by Brahms only in the woodwind parts, but Furtwängler quite sensibly, and beautifully, has the violins and violas participate in the diminuendo as they spiral downward. Weingartner pays no real attention to this moment, or perhaps he is too literalist in assuming the strings do not partake in the diminuendo: they remain at the same dynamic level throughout. Fiedler may be said to over- or misinterpret this spot. He has the strings play a *subito piano* at the high E on the last beat of m. 19; they then remain at the same dynamic level throughout the subsequent phrase.

At the approach to the second group in mm. 78–81, Furtwängler reads the hairpins very expressively but without exaggeration. Like virtually all conductors, he slows down, but he does so only near the climax of the phrase, at the

E of m. 80. Weingartner's reading of this phrase is far less compelling. He makes a crescendo, but one that is not followed by any real diminuendo. Weingartner slows down here more than Furtwängler but to less effect, largely because the former begins his ritard in m. 79, considerably earlier in the phrase and thus robs the transition of much of its urgency and forward-leaning qualities. Fiedler reads this phrase much more successfully than Weingartner and really on a par with Furtwängler. Fiedler creates an elegant, true crescendo and diminuendo across mm. 78–81, and he makes his ritard very effectively, even later than Furtwängler, at the height of the phrase in m. 81. But Fiedler then loses much of the intensity by bringing in the second group itself (at m. 82) with a slow tempo ($\downarrow$ = 96). Furtwängler's brisker $\downarrow$ = 116 for the start of the second group seems more responsive to the spirit of the theme and its relation to what has gone before. The transition phrase has been characterized by a hemiola, which by its very nature slows the overall metric-rhythmic flow. Unlike Fiedler, Furtwängler senses that in order to counter or rectify that hemiola, the second group should not begin at too slow a tempo.

The third moment for comparison comes at the beginning of the coda, at the lead-in to the lengthy horn solo. Here words almost fail to account adequately for the difference between Furtwängler and the others. Furtwängler begins at m. 447 with a genuine *piano*, then makes a dramatic, intense crescendo, which culminates on the downbeat of m. 451 with a *forte* that is full, rich, but not harsh. Furtwängler actually begins a diminuendo in the very same measure, before Brahms's own notated one in m. 452. But the effect is exactly right and makes a splendid preparation for the emergence of the solo horn in m. 455. Weingartner's reading pales by comparison. He begins the coda at m. 447, not with a true *piano*, but with something approaching *mezzoforte*. Unlike Furtwängler, he fails to compensate for the fact that the full orchestra is entering here after two measures of only strings. Thus, although the individual instruments may be playing, or think they are playing, *piano*, the whole effect is much louder. Weingartner remains at this dynamic level throughout the phrase; there is no real crescendo as with Furtwängler, and the *forte* downbeat of m. 450 sounds much shallower or hollower than Furtwängler's.

Fiedler is closer to Furtwängler in spirit and technique, but also falls well short of the latter's magic touch. Fiedler creates a diminuendo in m. 446, the last measure of the strings, although this is not in the Brahms score; the purpose is to have the full orchestra emerge in the next measure as a dynamic contrast. Yet there is no real *piano* as in Furtwängler. Fiedler's crescendo in the subsequent measures, leading up to the *forte* in m. 450, is a flaccid thing, lacking the intensity and conviction of Furtwängler's. Furtwängler is the only one of the three conductors to really understand the *molto* of Brahms's *crescendo molto*. He not only understands it but breathes life into it, makes music out of it. This is true of almost every detail of dynamics or phrasing that he observes in the movement.

What comes through amply in the Furtwängler Second of 1945, as in his other performances, is the rare combination of a conductor who understands both sound and structure. Several younger conductors who have closely studied Furtwängler's recordings have commented on the beauty of tone, which never, however, takes precedence over expression. Vladimir Ashkenazy's remarks could certainly apply to the various *sforzandi* or other accented or louder passages mentioned above, which are never harsh. Ashkenazy observes that the Furtwängler sound

is never rough. It's very weighty but at the same time it is never heavy. In his *fortissimo* you always feel every voice. . . . It is quite unique. I have never heard so beautiful a *fortissimo* in an orchestra.[52]

The remarks of Daniel Barenboim, another Furtwängler admirer and emulator, strike a similar note:

Technically speaking, with regard to sonority, [Furtwängler] had a subtlety of tone color that was extremely rare. His sound was always "rounded," and incomparably more interesting than that of the great German conductors of his generation.[53]

The first movement of the Second Symphony from 1945 fully bears out these opinions. It also gives credence to the comments made by Otto Strasser, a violinist who played in the Vienna Philharmonic from 1922 to 1967. Strasser remarks on the impact made on the players by Furtwängler, whose long association with the orchestra began the same year Strasser joined: "While Weingartner, as we only now realized, had conducted Brahms in a somewhat objective manner, Furtwängler devoted himself with every fibre of his being to this music, which he fashioned in a manner at once romantic and ecstatic."[54]

NORRINGTON'S BRAHMS

The most intriguing recordings of Brahms symphonies in recent years are those of the First and Second by Roger Norrington and the London Classical

Players.[55] These constitute the first modern attempt at an historically aware rendering. Among the most significant aspects of Norrington's recordings are:

> An orchestra of about sixty players that seeks a more even balance between the strings and the winds and brasses than is normal in modern orchestras. Norrington seeks to achieve the "equal choirs" that he believes Brahms and other contemporary composers had in mind, with an average of nine players for each of the string groups, nine winds, and nine brasses.[56]
>
> An arrangement of the orchestra that involves seating the first and second violins (and, in this case, horns and trumpets) on opposite sides of the stage, a practice that was common throughout the nineteenth century. Norrington also divides the double basses, as was suggested in the seating approved by Brahms (fig. 8–1).
>
> Stringed instruments strung with gut and wound-gut strings, played nearly always without vibrato.
>
> Pitch at A = 435.
>
> Tempi that are generally brisk and do not fluctuate widely.

Norrington's recordings merit careful listening and study. They rarely achieve the power of Furtwängler, the poetry of Walter, or the rhythmic continuity of Weingartner, but their sheer sound is appealingly, and illuminatingly, different. Although the tempi are prevailingly quick, they are by no means uniform or unvaried. Indeed, as table 8–2 shows, Norrington's range of tempi in the first movement of the Second Symphony is almost as wide as that of the "extremist" Fiedler.

One is struck in particular in Norrington's recordings by the even balances between the strings and the winds and brasses. In the slow introduction to the finale of the First Symphony, for example, the horn and flute solos (at mm. 30 and 38, and again at m. 114) stand out cleanly without needing to be forced or blown too hard. As the background to the canon unfolding in the second group of the first movement of the Second Symphony (mm. 134ff.), the syncopated horns and clarinets sound wonderfully taut and crisp. Another bracing aspect is provided by the timpanist's use of leather-covered sticks, which give welcome definition and presence to the normally fuzzy pedal points at the opening of the First Symphony and to the rolls in the finale, as well as to those near the beginning of the Second Symphony. Furthermore, the gut strings, played in a vibrato-free manner, impart a sound that is at once warm and mellow, expressive and restrained. The lyrical F♯-minor theme of the first movement of the Second Symphony (m. 82) is articulated cleanly; it emerges as a lilting dance rather than—as in so many renderings—a throbbing, passionate melody. Performed in this way, it becomes truly a transitional phenomenon on the way to the strong dominant-oriented themes that follow.

There are other moments like these, when the clarity of texture and phrasing in Norrington's recordings brings out, whether intentionally or not, structural aspects of the music that are not normally heard in other performances. At m. 186 of the finale of the First Symphony, for example, when the main Allegro theme returns to initiate the development section, it is punctuated on the weak beats by chords in the woodwinds and brasses. The distinctive sonority of these chords and their strong presence in Norrington's recording reinforce how different this moment is from the first appearance of the theme at m. 62.

Some commentators have suggested that the restatement of the theme in m. 186 presages a rondo- or sonatalike structure. Tovey notes that when the "great tune" reappears, it is "as if the movement were, in spite of its elaboration, to be a rondo."[57] But with Norrington's orchestra, the theme sounds fundamentally different than at the opening of the Allegro, and there can be no mistaking it for a rondolike return. The punctuation of the theme by the brass and woodwinds evokes a serenadelike texture that is distinctly lighter than the serious, hymnlike utterance of the strings and horns in m. 61. The theme as presented in m. 186 thus creates an entirely different trajectory for the development section, which now proceeds to become very serious indeed by the time the Alphorn theme returns over a diminished chord in m. 285.

The stichomythic exchanges between the first and second violins in mm. 24–25 of the slow introduction to the finale emerge with particular clarity in Norrington's interpretation. In both modern and historic recordings, where first and second violins are normally placed on the same side of the orchestra, the downward scales of mm. 24–25 sound like continuous runs. Norrington's placement of the first and seconds on opposite sides of the conductor allows Brahms's intended effect to be heard.

And it is an important effect. The three-note downward motive (E♭–D–C and its transpositions) that emerges in the first violins when they are separated from the seconds is the one that surges toward an intense climax in mm. 27–28 and then, transposed to major, forms the beginning of the Alphorn theme moments later in m. 30. Only when this motive is isolated in the violin runs of mm. 24–25, as occurs in the Norrington, is its evolution made clear. The motive does not, as in many performances, emerge as if new in m. 27; it has been prepared in mm. 25–26.

In Norrington's recording of the First Symphony, it is the seating and arrangement of the orchestra that brings out an important aspect of structure. In the recordings of Furtwängler, it is phrasing, dynamics, and attention to voicing and sonority. In those of Weingartner, it is rhythmic flow and organization. In those of Abendroth, it is large-scale shifts of tempo. In each case, the relationship between music as performed and music as heard and understood is very close, indeed inseparable. Anyone who admires the Brahms symphonies will know that no matter how familiar the works are to a listener, a performance can—and should—stimulate new analytical or critical insights. As this chapter has tried to suggest, both the nature of performance and, consequently, the nature of our understanding of these works have been evolving for over one hundred years and will continue to evolve. With compositions as durable as the Brahms symphonies, traditions of performance and understanding never stand still; they redefine the music for each generation.

Appendix I

A Chronology of the Brahms Symphonies

The First Symphony, op. 68

June 1862: Brahms shows first movement to Albert Dietrich and Clara Schumann.

1862–66: Brahms's friends inquire often about progress on the symphony.

September 1868: Brahms sends Clara "Alphorn" theme used in finale.

1870–74: Brahms encouraged by friends to complete the symphony.

September 1876: Brahms completes and dates the autograph manuscript of the symphony.

October 1876: Brahms makes revisions in the Andante and Allegretto.

November 4, 1876: Premiere of symphony at Karlsruhe under Otto Dessoff.

December 17, 1876: First performance in Vienna, with Brahms conducting orchestra of Gesellschaft der Musikfreunde.

Nov. 1876–April 1877: Performances in Mannheim, Munich, Leipzig, Breslau, Cambridge, and London.

Spring 1877: Brahms extensively revises the Andante in preparation for publication.

May 31, 1877: Brahms sends score and parts to his publisher Simrock.

June 24, 1877: Brahms completes autograph of four-hand version of the symphony and sends it to Simrock.

October 1877: Publication of score, parts, and four-hand version.

The Second Symphony, op. 73

June 1877:	Brahms begins work on the symphony.
Mid-October 1977:	The symphony is completed.
November 1877:	Brahms completes the four-hand arrangement of the symphony.
Early December 1877:	Brahms and Ignaz Brüll play four-hand arrangement in private performance in Vienna.
December 30, 1877:	Premiere of the symphony by the Vienna Philharmonic under Hans Richter.
January–June 1878:	Performances of the symphony in Leipzig, Munich, Amsterdam, The Hague, Dresden, and Düsseldorf.
March 1878:	Score and parts sent to the publisher Simrock.
April 3, 1878:	Four-hand arrangement sent to Simrock.
August 1878:	Publication of score, parts, and four-hand arrangement.

The Third Symphony, op. 90

Summer 1883:	Brahms composes the symphony and begins to arrange for its premiere.
Fall 1883:	Brahms completes two-piano, four-hand arrangement of the symphony.
November 8, 1883:	Brahms sends string parts to his publisher, Simrock, for engraving (for Brahms's own private use).
November 9 and 22:	Brahms and Ignaz Brüll play two-piano, four-hand arrangement in private performance.
December 2, 1883:	Premiere of symphony by the Vienna Philharmonic under Hans Richter.
January–April 1884:	Performances in Berlin, Wiesbaden, Meiningen, Leipzig, Cologne, Düsseldorf, Barmen, Elberfeld, Amsterdam, Dresden, Frankfurt, and Budapest.
December 1883 (?):	Brahms probably sends copy of score to Simrock for engraving.
March–April 1884:	Publication of two-piano, four-hand arrangement.
May 1884:	Publication of score and parts.

The Fourth Symphony, op. 98

Summer 1884:	Brahms composes the first two movements.
Summer 1885:	Brahms completes the symphony.
October 8, 1885:	Brahms and Ignaz Brüll play four-hand, two-piano version in a private performance in Vienna.
October 25, 1885:	Premiere of the symphony in Meiningen, with the Court Orchestra under Brahms.
Nov. 1885–May 1886:	Performances in Meiningen, Frankfurt, Essen, Wuppertal, Utrecht, Amsterdam, The Hague, Krefeld, Cologne, Wiesbaden, Vienna, Berlin, Mannheim, Leipzig, Dresden, Breslau, Hamburg, Hannover, and London.
February 1886:	Joseph Joachim suggests some revisions of the opening to Brahms, who provisionally incorporates introductory measures into the autograph but then deletes them.
May 1886:	Four-hand, two-piano arrangement published.
October 1886:	Score and parts published.
January 1887:	Four-hand, one-piano arrangement published.

Appendix II

Sources and Editions

AUTOGRAPH SOURCES

Full-score autograph manuscripts survive for fifteen of the sixteen movements of the Brahms symphonies: only the first movement of the First Symphony is no longer accounted for. Of Brahms's own arrangements for four hands (on either one or two pianos), there survive complete sources for the first three symphonies but none for the Fourth. The following summarizes the autograph sources for the symphonies:[1]

FIRST SYMPHONY

Score, movements 2–4. Signed and dated at end of last movement, "J. Brahms / Lichtenthal Sept: 76." J. Pierpont Morgan Library, New York (Mary Flagler Cary Music Collection). Facsimile ed. New York: Dover, 1986.

Arrangement for piano four-hands. Signed and dated at end of last movement, "Pörtschach Juni 77. / J. Br." Library of Congress, Washington D.C. (Whittall Foundation).

SECOND SYMPHONY

Score. Entitled in Brahms's hand on p. 1 verso, "Symphonie. J. Brahms." J. Pierpont Morgan Library, New York (Robert Owen Lehman Collection).

Arrangement for piano four-hands. Entitled in Brahms's hand on p. 1 recto, "Symphonie. J. Brahms." Music Collection of the Stadt- und Landesbibliothek, Vienna.

THIRD SYMPHONY

Score. Signed and dated with date of gift to Hans von Bülow, "Symphonie. F dur." / "Seinem herzlich geliebten Hans v. Bülow / in treuer Freundschaft. Johs. Brahms." "Wien, 8 Januar 1890." Library of Congress, Washington D.C. (Whittall Foundation). Facsimile ed. New York: Robert Owen Lehman Foundation, 1967.

Arrangement for two pianos, four-hands. Library of Congress, Washington, D.C. (Whittall Foundation).

FOURTH SYMPHONY

Score. Zentralbibliothek, Zurich (on deposit from Allgemeine Musikgesellschaft). Facsimile ed. Adliswil-Zurich: Eulenberg, 1974.

PRINTED EDITIONS

Brahms was not one to rush into print with a new large-scale work. Each of the symphonies was given its premiere in the fall or early winter of a given concert season (in Karlsruhe, Vienna, Vienna again, and Meiningen, respectively) and across the subsequent months was played in other cities in Germany, Austria, Hungary, the Netherlands, and England. Although in some cases Brahms sent off score and parts to Simrock, his publisher, before the end of the season, he always waited until after the entire run of what Margit McCorkle has called "trial performances" to authorize the printing.[2]

Along the way Brahms would make many adjustments and corrections. Most were relatively minor. However, in some cases he undertook more significant changes, as in the revision of the Andante of the First Symphony and the provisional addition of four introductory measures to the first movement of the Fourth Symphony.

Brahms thus took an active role in the preparation and dissemination of his symphonies. But this does not mean that first or subsequent editions were error-free. Indeed, the research of Robert Pascall and George Bozarth reveals that copyists employed by Brahms or his publisher made numerous errors, mostly in details of phrasing, articulation, dynamics, and the like. Moreover, Brahms could be quite an indifferent proofreader.[3] The most unfortunate first edition of a symphony was that of the Third, which was so full of errors that in September 1884, only four months after its appearance, Simrock rushed to issue a set of the most important corrections, which were prefaced by an apology.

Despite the relatively extensive control exerted by Brahms and those delegated by him, there is really no such thing as a "definitive text" for any of the

Brahms symphonies, although none of the currently available editions is disastrous. The editions that have the most authority today are those prepared for the Brahms *Sämtliche Werke* (Complete Works) by Hans Gál (Wiesbaden: Breitkopf & Härtel, 1926; reprint, New York: Dover, 1974). Yet these editions are flawed. Gál tended to ignore the autographs even when they were available to him. He used as his primary sources the first editions as amended by Brahms. Brahms's annotated set of so-called *Handexemplare*—his personal copies of the first printings—has been housed since his death in the library of the Gesellschaft der Musikfreunde in Vienna.

Gál took the markings made by Brahms in these scores to represent what German scholars call *die Fassung letzter Hand* (literally "the version of the final hand"). As Pascall has shown, however, the markings in the *Handexemplare* are rather variable in source and intention. Some were not made by Brahms at all and have no authority. Of those that are in Brahms's hand, some constitute what Pascall calls "experimental readings," in which the "personal copy becomes a sketch-book." Others are "private improvements," which were not included by Brahms in any later alterations of the plates in his lifetime.[4] It requires considerable (and probably unachievable) editorial ingenuity to determine which of these might have been intended by Brahms to represent the final word.

Pocket scores of the symphonies were published around 1900 by the firm of Ernst Eulenberg (London, Zurich, Mainz, New York) under license from Simrock. These scores, based exclusively on Simrock's first editions, appeared as nos. 25–28 in Eulenberg's Symphony series. In the 1920s, with the expiration of Simrock's copyright, which allowed Breitkopf to proceed with the *Sämtliche Werke*, Eulenberg prepared new editions (now numbered 425–28) under the supervision of Wilhelm Altmann, who also wrote introductions. These editions form the basis of most pocket scores on the market today, including those prepared by Karl Geiringer for Philharmonia (Nos. 130–33).

The Philharmonia scores served, in turn, as the basis for the pocket editions issued between 1980 and 1984 by the music firm B. Schott in conjunction with the publishers Piper (First Symphony) and Wilhelm Goldmann (Second, Third, and Fourth Symphonies). These extremely useful editions—all but the First are now out of print—have corrections and commentary by German scholars: Giselher Schubert, for the First Symphony; Constantin Floros, for the Second; and Christian Martin Schmidt, for the Third and Fourth.

A new Complete Edition of Brahms's works is in progress in Germany, published by G. Henle Verlag of Munich under the general editorship of Friedhelm Krummacher. The First and Second Symphonies, edited by Robert Pascall, appeared in 1996 and 2001, respectively.

Notes

—————————————— ✀ ——————————————

CHAPTER 1

1. A. B. Marx, *General Musical Instruction,* trans. George Macirone (London: Novello, 1854; original German ed., 1839), p. 91.

2. Cited in Carl Dahlhaus, *The Idea of Absolute Music,* trans. Roger Lustig (Chicago: University of Chicago Press, 1989), p. 11.

3. See the useful survey by F. E. Kirby, "The Germanic Symphony of the Nineteenth Century: Genre, Form, Instrumentation, Expression," *Journal of Musicological Research* 14 (1995): 193–221.

4. *Allgemeine musikalische Zeitung* [hereafter *AMZ*] 15 (1813): col. 457. Cited in Kirby, "The Germanic Symphony," p. 194.

5. Gottfried Wilhelm Fink, "Symphonie," in *Encyclopädie der gesammten musikalischen Wissenschaften der Tonkunst,* ed. Gustav Schilling (Stuttgart: Köhler, 1838), VI, 546.

6. Fink, "Symphonie," pp. 546–47. The translation is mine, as are all translations in this volume, unless otherwise noted.

7. Fink, "Symphonie," p. 548.

8. Fink, "Symphonie," p. 548.

9. Carl Dahlhaus, "Symphonie und symphonischer Stil um 1850," in *Jahrbuch des staatlichen Instituts für Musikforschung* 1983–84, pp. 34–58; see p. 47.

10. Kirby, "The Germanic Symphony," p. 197.

11. Robert Schumann, *On Music and Musicians,* ed. Konrad Wolff, trans. Paul Rosenfeld (New York: Norton, 1969), p. 61. This translation is an abridgement of the review in the original German, from Schumann, *Gesammelte Schriften über Musik und Musiker* (Leipzig: Breitkopf & Härtel, 1854; reprint, Wiesbaden: Breitkopf & Härtel, 1985), III, 133–44. See also the translation and discussion in Jon W. Finson, *Robert Schumann and the Study of Orchestral Composition* (Oxford: Clarendon Press, 1989), p. 19.

12. Schumann, *On Music and Musicians,* p. 62.

13. Robert Schumann, *Gesammelte Schriften,* III, 144. This passage is omitted from the abridged translation in *On Music and Musicians.*

14. Finson, *Schumann,* pp. 20–26.

15.   See Robert Schumann, *Sinfonie Nr. 3: Es-Dur, op. 97 "Rheinische,"* ed. with an introduction and analysis by Reinhard Kapp (Mainz: Goldmann-Schott, 1981), p. 170.

16.   For a comprehensive discussion of the G-minor symphony, see Finson, *Schumann*, pp. 2–17; and Akio Mayeda, *Robert Schumanns Weg zur Symphonie* (Zurich and Mainz: Atlantis and Schott, 1992), pp. 163–209.

17.   Anthony Newcomb has suggested that over the course of the 1830s Schumann's piano music became progressively less conventional and marketable—in an age of salon music—and that with the turn to symphonic composition Schumann sought greater financial security and public recognition. See Newcomb, "Schumann and the Marketplace," in *Nineteenth-Century Piano Music*, ed. R. Larry Todd (New York: Schirmer, 1990), pp. 267–69.

18.   On the origins of the First Symphony and the attendant struggles with the symphonic medium, see Finson, *Schumann*.

19.   On this aspect of the Second Symphony, see especially Anthony Newcomb, "Once More 'Between Absolute and Program Music': Schumann's Second Symphony," *19th-Century Music* 8 (1984): 233–50.

20.   Kirby, "The Germanic Symphony," p. 197.

21.   *Konversations-Lexicon*, ed. Hermann Mendel (Leipzig: List & Francke, 1890), s.v. "Symphonia," vol. 10, pp. 36–46.

22.   Carl Dahlhaus, *Nineteenth-Century Music*, trans. J. Bradford Robinson (Berkeley and Los Angeles: University of California Press, 1989), p. 265. See also Dahlhaus, "Symphonie und symphonischer Stil," pp. 34–58. For an astute critique of Dahlhaus's historiography of the symphony, see Sanna Pederson, "On the Task of the Music Historian: The Myth of the Symphony after Beethoven," *repercussions* 2 (1993): 5–30.

23.   Siegfried Kross, "Das 'Zweite Zeitalter der Sinfonie'—Ideologie und Realität," in *Probleme der symphonischen Tradition im 19. Jahrhundert*, ed. Siegfried Kross (Tutzing: Hans Schneider, 1990), p. 16.

24.   Kirby, "The Germanic Symphony," p. 197.

25.   This important point is made by Dahlhaus, *Nineteenth-Century Music*, p. 24.

26.   Anonymous review of Heinrich Esser, Symphony in D Minor, op. 44, in *Neue Zeitschrift für Musik* [hereafter *NZfM*] 42 (1955): 273.

27.   Anonymous review of Carl Reinthaler, Symphony in D Major, op. 12, in *AMZ* 1 (1863): cols. 401–2.

28.   Review of Robert Volkmann, Second Symphony in B♭, op. 53, in *[Leipziger] AMZ* 2 (1867): 81.

29.   Hermann Deiters, review of Albert Dietrich, Symphony in D Minor, op. 20, *AMZ* 6 (1871): col. 257.

30.   Richard Wagner, "On Liszt's Symphonic Poems," in *Richard Wagner's Prose Works*, trans. W. Ashton Ellis (London: Paul, Trench, Trübner, 1897), III, 235–54. Wagner takes Berlioz to task for trying in *Roméo et Juliette* to recreate too closely in music the plot of the love scene. See also Carl Dahlhaus, *Esthetics of Music*, trans.

William Austin (Cambridge: Cambridge University Press, 1982), p. 59, where it is stressed that in a work like Liszt's *Faust* Symphony, the literary source is not the "content," but only the "subject."

31. See the excellent summary of this ideology in Carl Dahlhaus, *Esthetics*, chapter 10 ("Program Music"). See also "Aporien der Programmusik," in Dahlhaus, *Klassische und romantische Musikästhetik* (Laaber: Laaber Verlag, 1988), chapter 6.

32. Peter Cornelius, review of Richard Wüerst, Prize Symphony in F Major, op. 21, in *NZfM* 41 (1854): 258–59. In the literature and bibliographic sources of the time, the composer's name appears variously as "Würst," "Wuerst," or "Wüerst." Despite the apparent redundancy of the umlaut followed by "e," the latter form seems the correct one.

33. Cornelius, p. 259.

34. Eduard Hanslick, *Vom Musikalisch-Schönen*, excerpted and translated in *Music in European Thought, 1851–1912*, ed. Bojan Bujić (Cambridge: Cambridge University Press, 1988), p. 19.

35. Hanslick, p. 25.

36. Walter Wiora, "Zwischen absoluter und Programmusik," in *Festschrift Friedrich Blume* (Kassel: Bärenreiter, 1963), pp. 381–88; Ludwig Finscher, "'Zwischen absoluter und Programmusik': Zur Interpretation der deutschen romantischen Symphonie," in *Über Symphonien: Festschrift Walter Wiora*, ed. Christoph-Helmut Mahling (Tutzing: Hans Schneider, 1979), pp. 103–5; and Newcomb, "'Once More.'" See also Dahlhaus, *Esthetics*, p. 60.

37. See the fascinating composition and reception history sketched by Kapp in Schumann, *Sinfonie Nr. 3*, pp. 170–206. This and the following citations are from this source.

38. See the excerpts reprinted in *Wagner on Music and Drama*, ed. Albert Goldman and Evert Sprinchorn (New York: Da Capo, 1964), pp. 155–60.

39. Carl Dahlhaus, "Symphonie und symphonischer Stil." Also see Dahlhaus, *Ludwig van Beethoven: Approaches to His Music*, trans. Mary Whittall (Oxford: Clarendon Press, 1991), chapter 4, "The Symphonic Style."

40. Levi's response is in a letter to Clara Schumann in *Clara Schumann: Ein Künstlerleben*, ed. Berthold Litzmann (Leipzig: Breitkopf & Härtel, 1927), III, 343. Dessoff's correspondence with Brahms about the symphony is in *Johannes Brahms Briefwechsel*, rev. eds. (Berlin: Deutsche-Brahms Gesellschaft, 1912–22; reprint, Tutzing: Hans Schneider, 1974), XVI, 142–56. The Dresden critic is cited in Angelika Horstmann, *Untersuchungen zur Brahms-Rezeption der Jahre 1860–1880* (Hamburg: Karl Dieter Wagner, 1986), p. 262.

41. Dahlhaus, "Symphonie und symphonischer Stil," p. 47; idem, *Beethoven*, pp. 76–80.

42. E. T. A. Hoffmann, Review of Beethoven's Fifth Symphony, in Beethoven, *Symphony No. 5 in C Minor*, ed. Elliot Forbes, Norton Critical Scores (New York: Norton, 1971), p. 156.

43. Hoffmann, p. 163.

44. Review of Carl Reinecke, Symphony in A Major, op. 79, in *AMZ* 2 (1864): col. 789.

45. Selmar Bagge, review of Julius Zellner, Symphony in F Major, op. 7, *AMZ* 6 (1871): col. 725.

46. Carl Dahlhaus, *Between Romanticism and Modernism*, trans. Mary Whittall (Berkeley and Los Angeles: University of California Press, 1980), p. 42.

47. Dahlhaus, "Symphonie und Symphonischer Stil," p. 44.

48. William Weber, "Wagner, Wagnerism and Musical Idealism," in *Wagnerism in European Culture and Politics*, ed. William Weber and David Large (Ithaca: Cornell University Press, 1984), p. 38.

49. The standard comprehensive account of Viennese concert life in the first two thirds of the nineteenth century is Eduard Hanslick, *Geschichte des Concertwesens in Wien* (Vienna: Braumüller, 1869–70; reprint, Hildesheim: Olms, 1970).

50. Alexander Ringer, "The Rise of Urban Musical Life Between the Revolutions, 1789–1848," in *The Early Romantic Era*, ed. Alexander Ringer (Englewood Cliffs: Prentice Hall, 1991), p. 10.

51. For a spirited and incisive account of the concert-hall-as-museum phenomenon, see J. Peter Burkholder, "Museum Pieces: The Historicist Mainstream of the Last Hundred Years," *Journal of Musicology* 2 (1983): 115–34.

52. Christoph-Hellmut Mahling, "Berlin: 'Music in the Air,'" in *The Early Romantic Period*, ed. Ringer, p. 136.

53. Hanslick, *Geschichte des Concertwesens*, I, 292.

54. Hanslick, *Geschichte des Concertwesens*, II, 40.

55. See Hanslick, *Geschichte des Concertwesens*, II, table of contents, pp. v–x.

56. Review of works by Lassen, *AMZ* 5 (1870): 49. The review is unsigned, but as the lead article it was almost certainly written by the editor, Friedrich Chrysander.

57. A recent and thorough account of Bruch is Christopher Fifield's *Max Bruch: His Life and Works* (London: Gollancz, 1988).

58. *Brahms Briefwechsel*, III, 87–111.

59. *Brahms Briefwechsel*, III, 93.

60. Fifield, *Max Bruch*, p. 238.

61. *Brahms Briefwechsel*, III, 97.

62. *Brahms Briefwechsel*, III, 99.

63. A splendid recording of the three symphonies is that by Kurt Masur and the Leipzig Gewandhaus Orchestra on Philips CD 420 932-2.

64. Emanuel Klitsch, review of Bruch, Symphony in E♭, op. 28, in *NZfM* 66 (1870): 282.

65. To be fair to Bruch, the development section and retransition are more successful. One might expect that tension would build across the development and retransition, culminating in a climactic return of the head motive on the tonic, or that, as in Brahms's Second, the horn theme would emerge quietly after a "cool

down" at the end of the development. Bruch's solution is neither of these. The head motive is made the climax of the development section as part of a long modulatory group; the tonic returns only with the banal theme from m. 31. In this movement, then, there is no single moment of recapitulation: by the time we reach the tonic, the main theme has already been "recapitulated" within the retransition.

66. Friedrich Chrysander, review of Max Bruch, Symphony in E♭, op. 28, *AMZ* 4 (1869): 67.

67. The quarter-note triplets in the third measure of Bruch's theme also bear a certain resemblance to those in the second theme of the finale of Brahms's Third (mm. 52ff.).

68. For a helpful, though now somewhat outdated, guide through the morass of editions and versions of Bruckner's symphonies, see Deryck Cooke, "The Bruckner Problem Simplified," in his *Vindications: Essays on Romantic Music* (Cambridge: Cambridge University Press, 1982), pp. 43–71.

69. For an extended and thoughtful account of the Brahms-Bruckner relationship, with further bibliographic references, see Constantin Floros, *Brahms und Bruckner: Studien zur musikalischen Exegetik* (Wiesbaden: Breitkopf & Härtel, 1980).

70. See *Ernst Kurth: Selected Writings*, ed. and trans. Lee Rothfarb (Cambridge: Cambridge University Press, 1991), chapters 6 and 7.

CHAPTER 2

1. The article appeared in the *Neue Zeitschrift für Musik* 39 (1853): 185–86. It has been translated numerous times; one of the most colorful is "New Roads," in Robert Schumann, *On Music and Musicians*, ed. Konrad Wolff, trans. Paul Rosenfeld (New York: Norton, 1946), pp. 252–54.

2. A lengthy and shrewd contemporary assessment of the piano sonatas, written by Adolf Schubring in the *Neue Zeitschrift* in 1862, stresses the ambitiousness of their formal and thematic techniques. See Adolf Schubring, "Five Early Works By Brahms," trans. Walter Frisch, in *Brahms and His World*, ed. Walter Frisch (Princeton: Princeton University Press, 1990), pp. 106–16.

3. *Johannes Brahms Briefwechsel*, rev. eds. (Berlin: Deutsche Brahms-Gesellschaft, 1912–22; reprint, Tutzing: Hans Schneider, 1974), V, 47.

4. In July he is writing to Joachim about details of the score. See *Brahms Briefwechsel*, V, 55–56.

5. The chronology and genesis of—and the relationship among—the sonata, symphony, and concerto are by no means clear or easily unraveled. For a summary of different views, see George S. Bozarth, "Brahms's First Piano Concerto, op. 15: Genesis and Meaning," in *Beiträge zur Geschichte des Konzerts: Festschrift Siegfried Kross zum 60. Geburtstag*, ed. Reinmar Emans and Matthias Wendt (Bonn: Gudrun Schröder, 1990), pp. 211–47.

6. Christopher Reynolds, "A Choral Symphony by Brahms?" *19th-Century Music* 9 (1985): 3–25.

7. The letter in which Brahms proposes this transformation is, like many of those in the early Brahms-Joachim correspondence, undated. The editor for the *Brahms Briefwechsel*, Andreas Moser, provides a date of December 1858 (*Briefwechsel* V, 226), which seems illogical. I am grateful to David Brodbeck for suggesting that the context and content of the letter point to December 1859.

8. On the complicated and chronologically intertwined evolutions of the First Serenade, op. 11, and First Concerto, op. 15, see Margit McCorkle, "The Role of Trial Performances for Brahms's Orchestral and Large Choral Works: Sources and Circumstances," in *Brahms Studies: Analytical and Historical Perspectives*, ed. George S. Bozarth (Oxford: Clarendon Press, 1990), pp. 297–305.

9. *Letters to and from Joseph Joachim*, selected and trans. Nora Bickley (New York: Macmillan, 1914; reprint, New York, 1972), pp. 253–54.

10. Donald F. Tovey, "Brahms's Chamber Music," in his *Essays and Lectures on Music* (London: Oxford University Press, 1949), p. 243. Tovey's assessments in that classic essay were taken up and expanded by James Webster in "Schubert's Sonata Forms and Brahms's First Maturity," *19th-Century Music* 2 (1978): 8–35; and 3 (1979): 52–71.

11. For a more detailed analysis of these motivic-harmonic relationships in the Piano Quintet, see my *Brahms and the Principle of Developing Variation* (Berkeley and Los Angeles: University of California Press, 1984), pp. 83–86.

12. Compositional techniques like these are not unique to Brahms's instrumental music; prominent examples can be found in both Beethoven and Schubert, to name only two important musical forebears. Beethoven's *Appassionata* Sonata, op. 57, in the same key of F minor, makes strikingly similar use of the D♭–C relationship and may have served as a model for Brahms. (See my *Brahms and the Principle*, pp. 40–42.) Whatever the ultimate source, the important point is that these procedures, so intensively exploited and developed by Brahms in his chamber works of the mid-1860s, came to shape his symphonies over a decade later.

13. *Letters of Clara Schumann and Johannes Brahms, 1853–1896*, ed. Berthold Litzmann (New York: Longmans, 1927), I, 231.

14. On the early reception of the German Requiem, see Klaus Blum, *Hundert Jahre ein Deutsches Requiem von Johannes Brahms* (Tutzing: Hans Schneider, 1971); and Angelika Horstmann, *Untersuchungen zur Brahms-Rezeption der Jahre 1860–1880* (Hamburg: Wagner, 1986), pp. 130–79.

15. Schumann, *On Music and Musicians*, pp. 253–54.

16. Paul Bekker, *Die Sinfonie von Beethoven bis Mahler* (Berlin: Schuster & Löffler, 1918), p. 17; Theodor Adorno, *Einleitung in die Musiksoziologie* (Frankfurt: Suhrkamp, 1962), p. 104. Adorno uses the term *gemeinschaftsbildend*, "community-forming," which is similar in intent and meaning to *gesellschaftsbildend*.

17. Bekker, *Sinfonie*, p. 18.

18. *Brahms Briefwechsel*, III, 12.

19. See Alfred Orel, "Ein eigenhändiges Werkverzeichnis von Johannes Brahms: Ein wichtiger Beitrag zur Brahms Forschung," *Die Musik* 29/2 (1937): 538. For further information on the compositional history of the C-minor quartet, as well as a more detailed analysis, see my *Brahms and the Principle*, pp. 109–16. See also the three studies in *Brahms 2: Biographical, Documentary, and Analytical Studies*, ed. Michael Musgrave (Cambridge: Cambridge University Press, 1987), pp. 137–96.

20. On the compositional history and critical reception of the Haydn Variations, see Johannes Brahms, *Variations on a Theme of Haydn, Opp. 56a and 56b*, ed. Donald M. McCorkle, Norton Critical Score (New York: Norton, 1976).

21. Walter Niemann, *Brahms*, trans. Catherine A. Phillips (New York: Tudor, 1937), p. 324.

22. Donald McCorkle, in Brahms, *Haydn Variations*, p. 6.

23. Niemann, *Brahms*, p. 327.

24. Niemann, *Brahms*, p. 327.

25. On the issues surrounding the dating and early shape of this work, see James Webster, "The C sharp minor Version of Brahms's Op. 60," *Musical Times* 121 (1980): 89–93.

CHAPTER 3

1. Anthony Newcomb, "Once More 'Between Absolute and Program Music': Schumann's Second Symphony," *19th-Century Music* 7 (1984): 234.

2. For a reconstruction of the slow movement as heard in the original performances of the work during the 1876–77 season, based on partially surviving orchestral parts in the Gesellschaft der Musikfreunde in Vienna, see Robert Pascall, "Brahms's First Symphony Andante—the Initial Performing Version," Papers in Musicology No. 2, Department of Music, University of Nottingham, 1992. Pascall first reported his conclusions in "Brahms's First Symphony Slow Movement: the Initial Performing Version," *Musical Times* 122 (1981): 664–67. For a somewhat different reconstruction of the slow movement, based also on the Vienna parts, see Fritjof Haas, "Die Erstfassung des langsamen Satzes der ersten Sinfonie von Johannes Brahms," *Musikforschung* 36 (1983): 200–211. A CD recording based on Haas's version has been made by the Badische Staatskapelle Karlsruhe, conducted by Günter Neuhold, EBS Records 6081.

3. See Arnold Schoenberg, *Style and Idea*, ed. Leonard Stein (New York: St. Martin's Press, 1975), p. 415.

4. Tovey remarks that Brahms "kept the first three movements by him for ten years before attacking the finale" (*Essays in Musical Analysis*, Vol. I: Symphonies [London: Oxford University Press, 1935], p. 84). As usual, Tovey gives no source for his information, and it cannot be corroborated in any of the standard Brahms sources; but Tovey may well have gotten this information through his relationship with figures in the Brahms circle, especially Joseph Joachim.

5. Tovey, *Essays in Musical Analysis*, I, 91.

6. Johannes Brahms, *1. Sinfonie c-Moll, op. 68*. Einführung und Analyse von Giselher Schubert mit Partitur (Munich and Mainz: Piper/Schott, 1981), p. 69.

7. Brahms, *1. Sinfonie*, ed. Schubert, p. 69.

8. For further discussion of the thematic coherence of the First Symphony as a whole, see Michael Musgrave, "Brahms's First Symphony: Thematic Coherence and Its Secret Origin," *Music Analysis* 2 (1983): 117–33; and Brahms, *1. Sinfonie*, ed. Schubert, pp. 52–74.

9. Robert Pascall has argued that there are twelve movements in Brahms's instrumental oeuvre, including the finale of the First, that show similar types of modification of sonata form; three others fall within the symphonies: the finale of the Third, and the two inner movements of the Fourth. See Pascall, "Some Special Uses of Sonata Form by Brahms," *Soundings* 4 (1974): 58–63.

10. For a discussion of this aspect of the C-Minor String Quartet, see my *Brahms and the Principle of Developing Variation* (Berkeley and Los Angeles: University of California Press, 1984), pp. 110–11.

11. Reinhold Brinkmann, *Late Idyll: The Second Symphony of Johannes Brahms*, trans. Peter Palmer (Cambridge, Mass.: Harvard University Press, 1995), p. 40.

12. Brinkmann, *Late Idyll*, p. 45.

13. Tovey, *Essays in Musical Analysis*, p. 91.

14. Brinkmann, *Late Idyll*, p. 226.

CHAPTER 4

1. Cited in Reinhold Brinkmann, *Late Idyll: The Second Symphony of Johannes Brahms*, trans. Peter Palmer (Cambridge, Mass.: Harvard University Press, 1995), p. 11. The source for the quotation, Brahms's biographer Max Kalbeck, gives no date for the letter.

2. Diary entry cited in Brinkmann, *Late Idyll*, p. 12.

3. See, for example, Johannes Brahms, *Sinfonie Nr. 2, D-Dur, op. 73*. Einführung und Analyse von Constantin Floros (Munich and Mainz: Goldmann/Schott, 1984), pp. 163–64.

4. Brinkmann, *Late Idyll*, p. 21.

5. See his remarks cited by Floros in Brahms, *Sinfonie Nr. 2*, pp. 164, 176.

6. See Brahms, *Sinfonie Nr. 2*, ed. Floros, p. 167.

7. Brinkmann, *Late Idyll*, p. 63.

8. The best detailed analysis of aspects of phrase structure, meter, and tonality in the first forty-three measures of this movement remains Carl Schachter's "The First Movement of Brahms's Second Symphony: The Opening Theme and Its Consequences," *Music Analysis* 2 (1983): 55–68. See also the analysis in David Epstein, *Beyond Orpheus* (Cambridge, Mass.: MIT Press, 1979), pp. 162–75.

9. This exchange of letters is brought to light and treated in detail by Brinkmann in *Late Idyll*, pp. 125–44.

10. For a discussion of the Schubertian design and its resonance in early Brahms, see James Webster, "Schubert's Sonata Form and Brahms's First Maturity," *19th-Century Music* 2 (1978): 18–35; and 3 (1979): 52–71.

11. Schachter, "The First Movement of Brahms's Second Symphony," pp. 62–67.

12. See Epstein, *Beyond Orpheus*, pp. 166–67.

13. The term *secondary development* is Charles Rosen's; see his *Sonata Forms* (New York: Norton, 1980), pp. 104–8, 276–80.

14. Donald F. Tovey, *Essays in Musical Analysis*. Vol I: Symphonies (London: Oxford University Press, 1935), p. 100.

15. For a musical example that sets out the proportional changes in this passage and in the other transitions in this movement, see David Epstein, "Brahms and the Mechanism of Motion," in *Brahms Studies*, ed. George S. Bozarth (Clarendon Press: Oxford, 1990), p. 208.

16. Tovey, *Essays in Musical Analysis*, p. 106.

17. Brinkmann, *Late Idyll*, p. 196.

CHAPTER 5

1. Johannes Brahms, *Sinfonie Nr. 3 F-Dur, op. 90*. Einführung und Analyse von Christian Martin Schmidt (Munich and Mainz: Goldmann/Schott, 1980), p. 157. On other biographical and musical circumstances surrounding the origins of the Third Symphony, see also David Brodbeck, "Brahms, the Third Symphony, and the New German School," in *Brahms and His World*, ed. Walter Frisch (Princeton: Princeton University Press, 1990), pp. 65–67.

2. In Weingartner's recordings of the four symphonies with the London Symphony and Philharmonic (EMI CHS 7 64256 2), for example, the Third clocks in at 29:51, as compared with 39:41 for the First, 35:81 for the Second, and 37:13 for the Fourth.

3. Many commentators since Brahms's first biographer, Max Kalbeck, have interpreted this figure as a musical rendering of the phrase *Frei aber froh* ("Free but happy"), which was supposedly Brahms's counterpart to his friend Joachim's motto, *Frei aber einsam* ("Free but lonely"). Michael Musgrave has persuasively discounted the veracity of the F–A–F association. See Musgrave, *"Frei aber Froh*: A Reconsideration," *19th-Century Music* 3 (1980): 251–58.

4. At m. 31, the actual entrance of the second theme is delayed by what is generally acknowledged to be reference, or allusion, to a theme from the "Venusberg" music of Wagner's *Tannhäuser*, perhaps made as an *hommage* to the composer, who had died in Venice during the winter preceding the composition of the Third Symphony. On the Wagner allusions, see Robert Bailey, "Musical Language and Structure in the Third Symphony," in *Brahms Studies: Analytical and Historical Perspectives*, ed. George Bozarth (Oxford: Clarendon Press, 1990), p. 405; and David Brodbeck, "Brahms, the Third Symphony," pp. 67–69.

5. Arnold Schoenberg, *Theory of Harmony*, trans. Roy E. Carter (Berkeley and Los Angeles: University of California Press, 1978), p. 164.

6. Among editions of the score, there is a revealing notational discrepancy here. In many modern editions of the symphony, including that published in the Brahms *Sämtliche Werke* in 1926, the measure-long notes of the motto throughout mm. 1–6 (and elsewhere in the movement) are printed as dotted whole notes. But Brahms's intention seems to have been to acknowledge visually the motto's inherent duple meter: in the autograph of the symphony, as well as in the first edition of the score, the sustained notes are printed as two tied dotted halves (as in ex. 5–1).

7. David Lewin, "Vocal Meter in Schoenberg's Atonal Music, with a Note on a Serial Hauptstimme," *In Theory Only* 6 (1982): 25.

8. Brahms, *Sinfonie Nr. 3*, ed. Schmidt, p. 209.

9. See Robert Pascall, "Some Special Uses of Sonata Form by Brahms," *Soundings* 4 (1974): 58–63, for discussion of this kind of movement, which Pascall calls "sonata form with conflated response." Pascall's analyses are useful in a general taxonomic way, but I disagree with his basic premise that, in the finale of the Third and in most of the other eleven Brahms movements he identifies, the recapitulation begins directly after the exposition. Pascall suggests that this design reinforces the binary origins of sonata form. To my ears, the reappearance of the first theme after the close of the exposition does not signify the start of the recapitulation any more than it does in the first movement of Mozart's G-Minor Symphony (K. 550) or numerous other works. Beginning a development section with the first theme appearing in the tonic is a conventional device within the sonata-form era. Moreover, in the finale of the Third Symphony, the timbre and mood of main theme are so greatly modified in the two statements at the start of the development (mm. 108, 120) that there is little impression of a genuine recapitulation. While it is true that after the development the first group often resumes at the point where it left off, it does not make musical sense to deny this moment as the actual start of the recapitulation.

10. The recorded performance that best captures the transitory, on-the-move essence of the second theme at m. 52 is that of Furtwängler and the Berlin Philharmonic, made on December 18, 1949 (Virtuoso CD 2699072). Furtwängler, as so often sensitive to musical structure, pushes through this passage to arrive at the big C-minor cadence in m. 75.

11. Some of the relatively rare nineteenth-century examples of minor-mode expositions moving to the major dominant include the first movements of Brahms's Piano Quartet in G Minor, op. 25; Schubert's Piano Sonata in A Minor, D. 784; and Mendelssohn's Piano Trio in D Minor, op. 49.

12. Charles Rosen comments on the unusualness of the tonal relationship in the Rhapsody in G Minor, and he points to only two other instances in the nineteenth century of the use of the dominant minor as a secondary key: Mendelssohn's String Quartet in A Minor, op. 13, and his "Scottish" Symphony, op. 56. See Rosen, "Brahms the Subversive," in *Brahms Studies*, ed. Bozarth, p. 105.

CHAPTER 6

1. See Max Kalbeck, *Johannes Brahms*, rev. eds. (Berlin: Deutsche Brahms-Gesellschaft, 1912–21), III, 445; and *Johannes Brahms: Thematisch-Bibliographisches Werkverzeichnis*, ed. Margit McCorkle (Munich: Henle, 1984), p. 402.

2. Kalbeck, *Brahms*, III, 447.

3. Kalbeck, *Brahms*, III, 451–53.

4. Cited from Willi Schuh, *Richard Strauss: A Chronicle of the Early Years*, trans. Mary Whittall (Cambridge: Cambridge University Press, 1982), p. 98.

5. On the decline of listening and musical abilities in this period, see the fine study by Leon Botstein, "Listening through Reading: Musical Literacy and the Concert Audience," *19th-Century Music* 16 (1992): 129–45. On Brahms's specific relationship to this trend, see Botstein, "Time and Memory: Concert Life, Science, and Music in Brahms's Vienna," in *Brahms and His World*, ed. Walter Frisch (Princeton: Princeton University Press, 1990), especially pp. 4–9.

6. Edward T. Cone, "Harmonic Congruence in Brahms," in *Brahms Studies: Analytical and Historical Perspectives*, ed. George S. Bozarth (Oxford: Clarendon Press, 1990), pp. 185–87.

7. Louise Litterick, "Brahms the Indecisive," in *Brahms 2: Biographical, Documentary, and Analytical Studies*, ed. Michael Musgrave (Cambridge: Cambridge University Press, 1987), p. 231.

8. This parsing of the exposition differs from that of James Webster and Christian M. Schmidt, both of whom seem to view the second group as beginning at m. 53. The starting point for Webster can be inferred from the percentages he provides in "The General and the Particular in Brahms's Later Sonata Forms," in *Brahms Studies: Analytical and Historical Perspectives*, ed. George Bozarth (Oxford: Clarendon Press, 1990), p. 52; for Schmidt's analysis, see Johannes Brahms, *Sinfonie Nr. 4, e-moll, op. 98*. Einführung und Analyse von Christian Martin Schmidt (Munich and Mainz: Goldmann/Schott, 1980), p. 226.

9. A facsimile edition of the autograph manuscript is available as *Johannes Brahms: 4. Symphonie in E-moll Op. 98: Faksimile des autographen Manuskripts aus dem Besitz der Allgemeinen Musikgesellschaft Zürich* (Adliswil-Zurich: Eulenberg, 1974). The first and last pages of the first movement, showing the proposed revision, are reproduced in Litterick, "Brahms the Indecisive," p. 224.

10. Litterick, "Brahms the Indecisive."

11. Walther Vetter, "Der erste Satz von Brahms' e-moll Symphonie: ein Beitrag zur Erkenntnis moderner Symphonik," *Die Musik* 13/3 (1913–14): 3–15, 83–92, 131–45. A very different hearing of the opening of the symphony is proposed by the Schenkerian analyst John Rothgeb in his review of my *Brahms and the Principle of Developing Variation* in *Music Theory Spectrum* 9 (1987): 210. For Rothgeb, the chain of thirds is merely a surface element; the real melodic motion is the more middleground 5–6–5 profile of the theme. Rothgeb's analysis of the opening theme,

though framed in a way overtly hostile to motivic analysis, does highlight the importance of C, the sixth degree of E minor, which plays such a large role in the symphony as a whole. For a more moderated Schenkerian perspective on the first movement of the Fourth Symphony, see Peter Smith, "Liquidation, Augmentation, and Brahms's Recapitulatory Overlaps," *19th-Century Music* 17 (1994): 253–59.

12. By *period*, I adopt Schoenberg's term for an eight-measure unit that divides symmetrically into two phrases. See Arnold Schoenberg, *Fundamentals of Musical Composition*, ed. Gerald Strang and Leonard Stein (New York: St. Martin's, 1967), pp. 24–57.

13. See Alan Walker, *A Study in Musical Analysis* (London: Barrie and Rockliff, 1962), pp. 76–77.

14. Webster, "The General and the Particular," p. 59.

15. Raymond Knapp, "Brahms and the Problem of the Symphony: Romantic Image, Generic Conception, and Compositional Challenge" (Ph.D. dissertation, Duke University, 1987), pp. 575–78.

16. Cited from the memoirs of the conductor Siegfried Ochs by Raymond Knapp, "The Finale of Brahms's Fourth Symphony: the Tale of the Subject," *19th-Century Music* 13 (1989): 4.

17. Raymond Knapp, "The Finale of Brahms's Fourth," especially pp. 4–11.

18. The prominent F♮ resolving to E brings back, quite consciously, the tonal world of the Andante. We recall that the final cadence of that movement consists of an unmediated Neapolitan-tonic cadence, F major to E major.

CHAPTER 7

1. See Carl Dahlhaus, *Foundations of Music History*, trans. J. B. Robinson (Cambridge: Cambridge University Press, 1983), especially chapters 5 and 9; and Leo Treitler, *Music and the Historical Imagination* (Cambridge, Mass.: Harvard University Press, 1989), especially chapters 1 and 2, on Beethoven's Ninth Symphony. For a full account of Dahlhaus's intellectual heritage, see James Hepokoski, "The Dahlhaus Project and its Extra-musicological Sources," *19th-Century Music* 14 (1991): 221–46.

2. Siegfried Kross, "The Establishment of a Brahms Repertoire, 1890–1902," in *Brahms 2: Biographical, Documentary, and Analytical Studies*, ed. Michael Musgrave (Cambridge: Cambridge University Press, 1987), pp. 30–31 and 37.

3. See the survey and collection of Viennese reviews of Brahms's First Symphony by Ingrid Fuchs, "Zeitgenössische Aufführungen der Ersten Symphonie Op. 68 von Johannes Brahms in Wien: Studien zur Wiener Brahms-Rezeption," in *Brahms-Kongreß Wien 1983*, ed. Susanne Antonicek and Otto Biba (Tutzing: Hans Schneider, 1988), pp. 167–86 and 489–515. On the reception of the First Symphony, see also Angelika Horstmann, *Untersuchungen zur Brahms-Rezeption der Jahre 1860–1880* (Hamburg: Wagner, 1986), pp. 248–79.

4. Norman Del Mar remarks that the Third Symphony is "uniquely problematic in its programming since it differs from its sister works in not being at all an obvious concert endpiece; many conductors indeed reject the idea of playing it as a closing item" (*Conducting Brahms* [Oxford: Clarendon Press, 1993], p. 42).

5. I am grateful to Barbara Haws, archivist of the New York Philharmonic, for providing me with data on performances of the Brahms symphonies.

6. Desmond Mark, *Zur Bestandaufnahme des Wiener Orchesterrepertoires* (Vienna: Universal, 1979).

7. See Mark's fig. 7 on p. 32 of his *Bestandaufnahme*.

8. An intelligent and well-documented study of this dimension of Brahms reception is contained in Albrecht Dümling, "Warum Schönberg Brahms für fortschrittlich hielt," in *38 Berliner Festwochen 88* (Berlin: Berliner Festspiele GmbH, 1988), pp. 12–33.

9. These statistics are taken from Mark, *Bestandaufnahme*, in which they are said to refer to "number of performances." The numbers seem rather low. Presumably they comprise not individual concerts, as in the New York Philharmonic figures cited above, but series of concerts at which the symphonies were played. For the period up to 1942, more precise statistics could be ferreted out from the lists in the book *Wiener Philharmoniker 1842–1942* (Vienna, 1942), which was prepared for the orchestra's centenary.

10. Figures compiled from the programs given in Peter Muck, *Einhundert Jahre Berliner Philharmonisches Orchester* (Tutzing: Hans Schneider, 1982), vol. 3. Included here are only regular subscription concerts, not special concerts or series—of which there are many and on which Brahms symphonies sometimes appear—or tour concerts. The number given represents not individual performances but the number of times the works were programmed for a group of concerts.

11. See, for example, Donald J. Grout and Claude Palisca, *A History of Western Music*, 4th ed. (New York: Norton, 1988), p. 714; Leon Plantinga, *Romantic Music* (New York: Norton, 1984), p. 421; Richard Crocker, *A History of Musical Style* (New York: McGraw Hill, 1966), p. 468. This historiographic tradition begins much earlier: see Guido Adler, *Handbuch der Musikgeschichte* (Berlin: Hesse, 1930), II, 969.

12. Fuchs, "Zeitgenössische Aufführungen," pp. 174–75.

13. Fuchs, "Zeitgenössische Aufführungen," appendix, pp. 496–97.

14. Cited in Raymond Knapp, "Brahms and the Problem of the Symphony" (Ph.D. diss., Duke University, 1987), p. 537; and Johannes Brahms, *1. Sinfonie c-Moll, op. 68*. Einführung und Analyse von Giselher Schubert mit Partitur (Munich and Mainz: Piper/Schott, 1981), p. 30. We cannot know how Pohl's expectations for the Second were met as he appears to have written no review of the work.

15. Cited in Knapp, "Brahms and the Problem of the Symphony," p. 544; and in Brahms, *1. Sinfonie*, ed. Schubert, p. 37.

16. See the reviews of the Third collected in *Musik gedeutet und gewertet: Dokumente zur Rezeptionsgeschichte von Musik*, ed. Hermann J. Busch and Werner

Klüppelholz (Munich: Deutscher Taschenbuch Verlag, 1983), pp. 206 (Theodor Helm), 208 (Richard Heuberger), 209 (Eduard Hanslick). For the Ninth, see the extensive compilation of reviews in Manfred Wagner, *Geschichte der österreichischen Musikkritik in Beispielen* (Tutzing: Hans Schneider, 1979), pp. 235–77.

17. "A.K.," critic of the *Fremden-Blatt*, printed in Wagner, *Geschichte*, p. 251.

18. Bekker, *Die Sinfonie von Beethoven bis Mahler* (Berlin: Schuster & Löffler, 1918), pp. 38–39.

19. Cited in Brahms, *1. Sinfonie*, ed. Schubert, p. 30.

20. Cited in Knapp, "Brahms and the Problem of the Symphony," p. 542.

21. Cited in Johannes Brahms, *Sinfonie Nr. 2, D-Dur, op. 73*. Einführung und Analyse von Constantin Floros (Munich and Mainz: Goldmann/Schott, 1984), p. 187.

22. Cited from Richard Wagner's *Prose Works*, trans. W. Ashton Ellis, vol. 6 (London: Paul, Trench, Trübner, 1897); reprinted as Wagner, *Religion and Art* [Lincoln: University of Nebraska Press, 1994]), p. 181. The original German is in Wagner, *Gesammelte Schriften und Dichtungen*, 5th ed. (Leipzig: Breitkopf & Härtel, 1911), X, 182–83.

23. Margaret Notley, "Brahms as Liberal: Genre, Style, and Politics in Late Nineteenth-Century Vienna," *19th-Century Music* 17 (1993): 107–23.

24. See also Leon Botstein, "Brahms and Nineteenth-Century Painting," *19th-Century Music* 14 (1990): especially 157–59.

25. Carl Schorske, *Fin-de-Siècle Vienna: Politics and Culture* (New York: Knopf, 1980), chapter 3.

26. Cited in Notley, "Brahms as Liberal," p. 118.

27. Bekker, *Die Sinfonie*, pp. 40–41. Cf. Bekker's remarks about the "society-forming" aspects of Beethoven's symphonies, cited in chapter 2.

28. For Adorno's remarks, see his *Einleitung in die Musiksoziologie* (Frankfurt: Suhrkamp, 1962), chapter 6, "Kammermusik."

29. Carl Dahlhaus, *Nineteenth-Century Music*, trans. J. Bradford Robinson (Berkeley and Los Angeles: University of California Press, 1989), pp. 269–71.

30. Dahlhaus, *Nineteenth-Century Music*, p. 269.

31. Leon Botstein, "Time and Memory: Concert Life, Science, and Music in Brahms's Vienna," in *Brahms and His World*, ed. Walter Frisch (Princeton: Princeton University Press, 1990), pp. 4–9.

32. Botstein, "Time and Memory," p. 9. J. Peter Burkholder ("Brahms and Twentieth-Century Classical Music," *19th-Century Music* 8 [1984]: 75–83) has suggested that Brahms was the direct forebear of the kind of uncompromising, idealistic twentieth-century modernism that has stretched from Schoenberg to Babbitt.

33. For further analysis of Schoenberg's orchestration of Brahms's op. 25, see Frisch, *Brahms and the Principle of Developing Variation* (Berkeley and Los Angeles: University of California Press, 1984), pp. 74–77; and Klaus Velten, *Schönbergs Instrumentation Bachscher und Brahmsscher Werke als Dokumente seines Traditionsverständnisses* (Regensburg: Bosse, 1976).

34. Eduard Hanslick, *Hanslick's Music Criticisms*, trans. and ed. Henry Pleasants (1950; reprint, New York: Dover, 1988), pp. 125–28.

35. Peter Gay, "Aimez-Vous Brahms? On Polarities in Modernism," in his *Freud, Jews, and Other Germans* (Oxford: Oxford University Press, 1978), pp. 248–49.

36. Cited in Knapp, "Brahms and the Problem of the Symphony," p. 574.

37. *Hanslick's Music Criticisms*, pp. 244–45.

38. *Johannes Brahms: The Herzogenberg Correspondence*, ed. Max Kalbeck, trans. Hannah Bryant (1909; reprint, New York: Da Capo, 1987), pp. 249–50.

39. *Herzogenberg Correspondence*, pp. 243–44.

40. Arnold Schoenberg, *Style and Idea*, ed. Leonard Stein (New York: St. Martin's, 1975), p. 54.

41. Schoenberg, *Style and Idea*, p. 75.

42. Schoenberg, *Style and Idea*, p. 407.

43. Cited in Knapp, "Brahms and the Problem of the Symphony," pp. 536–37. Horstmann observes that Pohl was just one of a group of critics who sensed a program in the First Symphony (*Untersuchungen zur Brahms-Rezeption*, p. 261).

44. Cited in Ludwig Koch, *Brahms-Bibliographie* (Budapest: Székesfőváros Házinyomdája, 1943), p. 58.

45. Leon Botstein, "Listening through Reading: Musical Literacy and the Concert Audience," *19th-Century Music* 16 (1992): 140.

46. On Kretschmar's *Führer*, see Botstein, "Listening through Reading," pp. 140–41; and *Music Analysis in the Nineteenth Century*, ed. Ian Bent (Cambridge: Cambridge University Press, 1994), II, 22–25.

47. Cited in *Music Analysis*, ed. Bent, p. 24. On Kretschmar's hermeneutics and their intellectual context, see ibid., pp. 22–24, and Edward Lippman, *A History of Western Musical Aesthetics* (Lincoln: University of Nebraska Press, 1992), pp. 353–59.

48. Botstein, "Listening through Reading," p. 140.

49. Kretschmar, *Führer durch den Concertsaal*, in Kretschmar, "The Brahms Symphonies," trans. Susan Gillespie, in *Brahms and His World*, ed. Walter Frisch (Princeton: Princeton University Press, 1990), pp. 128–29.

50. Philip Goepp, *Symphonies and Their Meaning*, 2nd series (Philadelphia: Lippincott, 1902), pp. 310–16.

51. Max Kalbeck, *Johannes Brahms*, rev. eds. (Berlin: Deutsche Brahms-Gesellschaft, 1912–21), III, 106–7.

52. Julius Harrison, *Brahms and His Four Symphonies* (1939; reprint, New York: Da Capo, 1971), pp. 156–62.

53. Susan McClary, "Narrative Agendas in 'Absolute' Music: Identity and Difference in Brahms's Third Symphony," in *Musicology and Difference*, ed. Ruth Solie (Berkeley and Los Angeles: University of California Press, 1993), p. 330.

54. McClary, "Narrative Agendas," p. 333.

55. McClary, "Narrative Agendas," p. 338.

56. Kretschmar, "The Brahms Symphonies," p. 136.

57. McClary, "Narrative Agendas," p. 340.

58. McClary, "Narrative Agendas," p. 341.

59. Robert Fink, "Desire, Repression, and Brahms's First Symphony," *repercussions* 2 (1993): 75–103.

60. Fink, "Desire, Repression," p. 82.

61. Fink, "Desire, Repression," p. 83.

CHAPTER 8

1. In 1889 Brahms recorded a wax cylinder for an assistant of Thomas Edison who was traveling around Europe to publicize the new invention. On the circumstances and content of this recording, see George S. Bozarth, "Brahms on Record," *American Brahms Society Newsletter* 5/1 (Spring 1987): 5–9, and the references cited there. See also Helmut Kowar, "Zum Fragment eines Walzers, gespielt von Johannes Brahms," in *Brahms-Kongreß Wien 1983*, ed. Susanne Antonicek and Otto Biba (Tutzing: Hans Schneider, 1988), pp. 281–90.

2. On Brahms, see especially George Bozarth, "Brahms's Pianos," in *Brahms and His World*, ed. Walter Frisch (Princeton: Princeton University Press, 1990), pp. 49–64; Will Crutchfield, "Brahms by Those Who Knew Him," *Opus* (August 1986): 12–21, 60; Jon W. Finson, "Performing Practice in the Late Nineteenth Century, with Special Reference to the Music of Brahms," *Musical Quarterly* 70 (1984): 457–75; and Robert Pascall, "Playing Brahms: A Study in 19th-Century Performance Practice," Papers in Musicology No. 1, Department of Music, University of Nottingham, 1991. A broader study of the nineteenth century is contained in *Performance Practice: Music after 1600*, ed. Howard Mayer Brown and Stanley Sadie (New York: Norton, 1990), pp. 323–458.

3. See the discussions in the anthology *Authenticity and Early Music*, ed. Nicholas Kenyon (Oxford: Oxford University Press, 1988); and in Richard Taruskin, *Text and Act: Essays on Music and Performance* (New York: Oxford University Press, 1995).

4. Daniel Koury, *Orchestral Performance Practices in the Nineteenth Century* (Ann Arbor: UMI Research Press, 1986), p. 148.

5. Cited in Koury, *Orchestral Performance Practices*, p. 141.

6. Koury, *Orchestral Performance Practices*, p. 141.

7. Koury, *Orchestral Performance Practices*, p. 149.

8. See Koury, *Orchestral Performance Practices*, chapter 12.

9. See Koury, *Orchestral Performance Practices*, pp. 226–28.

10. See Finson, "Performing Practice," p. 463.

11. Finson, "Performing Practice"; Robert Philip, *Early Recordings and Musical Style: Changing Tastes in Instrumental Performance, 1900–1950* (Cambridge: Cambridge University Press, 1992).

12. For example, in neither Furtwängler's 1947 recording of the First with the Lucerne Festival Orchestra (Music & Arts CD-804) nor his 1952 recording with the Berlin Philharmonic (Virtuoso 2699072) does the solo violinist use significant portamento.

13. Christopher Dyment, liner notes (1979) to LP release of Oskar Fried and Berlin State Opera Orchestra, Brahms, Symphony No. 1 (Past Masters, PM-32; originally DGG 66304–08 [1923]).

14. Cited in Christopher Fifield, *True Artist and True Friend: A Biography of Hans Richter* (Oxford: Clarendon Press, 1993), p. 468.

15. Cited in Fifield, *True Artist*, p. 467.

16. Cited in Fifield, *True Artist*, p. 466.

17. Cited in Fifield, *True Artist*, p. 468.

18. *Johannes Brahms Briefwechsel*, rev. eds. (Berlin: Deutsche Brahms-Gesellschaft, 1912–22; reprint, Tutzing: Hans Schneider, 1974), X, 100. *Mise* is a variant of *mies*, a Yiddish word.

19. Richard Heuberger, *Erinnerungen an Johannes Brahms* (Tutzing: Hans Schneider, 1971), p. 88.

20. Review excerpted in "Kritiken zu Zeitgenössischen Wiener Aufführungen der Ersten Symphonie von Johannes Brahms (Auswahl)," in *Brahms-Kongreß Wien 1983*, p. 515.

21. Heuberger, *Erinnerungen*, p. 88.

22. Eduard Hanslick, *Hanslick's Music Criticisms*, trans. and ed. Henry Pleasants (1950; reprint, New York: Dover, 1988), p. 234.

23. Another account of Bülow's conducting, written to Brahms by Elisabet von Herzogenberg in 1881, is even more critical of "affected little pauses before every new phrase, every notable change in harmony." See *Johannes Brahms: The Herzogenberg Correspondence*, ed. Max Kalbeck, trans. Hannah Bryant (1909; reprint, New York: Da Capo, 1987), p. 126.

24. Among the evidence for Brahms's attitudes toward tempo, phrasing, and rhythm are his remarks to George Henschel (*Personal Recollections of Johannes Brahms* [Boston: Badger, 1907], pp. 78–79) and the accounts of his piano playing and instruction by Florence May (*The Life of Johannes Brahms* [London: Reeves, 1948], pp. 1–46), Eugenie Schumann (*Memoirs of Eugenie Schumann*, trans. Marie Busch [London: Eulenberg, 1985], pp. 141–46), and Fanny Davies ("Some Personal Recollections of Brahms as Pianist and Composer," in *Cobbett's Cyclopedic Survey of Chamber Music*, 2nd ed. [London: Oxford University Press, 1963], I, 182–84).

25. Cited in Pascall, "Playing Brahms," p. 16.

26. Marie von Bülow, *Hans von Bülows Leben, dargestellt aus seinen Briefen*, 2nd ed. (Leipzig: Breitkopf & Härtel, 1921), p. 460.

27. Heuberger, *Erinnerungen*, p. 58. A very different impression of Richter's rehearsal techniques, as painstaking and meticulous, is given by Eva Ducat, who attended his London Symphony Orchestra concerts in 1904 (Fifield, *True Artist*, pp. 469–70).

28. Hans von Bülow, *Briefe und Schriften,* ed. Marie Bülow (Leipzig: Breitkopf & Härtel, 1895–1908), VII, 303, 305. In a letter of November 1887 to the Berlin concert agent Hermann Wolff, Bülow gave a timing for the Third Symphony that differed only slightly: 35 minutes (*Briefe,* VIII, 154).

29. Cited in Reinhold Brinkmann, *Late Idyll: The Second Symphony of Johannes Brahms,* trans. Peter Palmer (Cambridge, Mass.: Harvard University Press, 1995), p. 16.

30. Max Kalbeck, *Johannes Brahms,* rev. eds. (Berlin: Deutsche Brahms-Gesellschaft, 1912–21), IV, 81, 224.

31. *Brahms in der Meininger Tradition: Seine Symphonien und Haydn-Variationen in der Bezeichnung von Fritz Steinbach,* ed. Walter Blume ("Als Manuskript gedruckt"; Stuttgart: Ernst Surkamp, 1933).

32. *Brahms in der Meininger Tradition,* p. 19.

33. Norman del Mar, *Conducting Brahms* (Oxford: Clarendon Press, 1993), p. 6.

34. The liner notes prepared by Dyment for an LP release of the Fried recording (see above, n. 13) contain an illuminating discussion of his style and of his approach to the Brahms First.

35. Abendroth made another recording of the First with the Berlin Philharmonic in the mid-1930s.

36. A fine example of Abendroth's structural approach to tempo is his recording of the finale of Brahms's Fourth (Victor M31), where he remains quite consistent in tempo within the main groups of variations but makes noticeable shifts between them. Variations 1–9, the "first group," form a clear temporal unit without any breaks or changes. Abendroth slows considerably for variation 10, which begins the group of softer, quieter variations (the "second group"), and remains at a relatively consistent tempo up until the "return" at variation 16. Elsewhere in his recording of the Fourth, Abendroth will make a noticeable shift of tempo and then remain at the new tempo for a considerable period. In this sense he is, despite some similarities, a very different conductor from Fried, whose nuances seem more mercurial, less predictable.

37. *Brahms Briefwechsel,* X, 100. In the original German, Brahms writes for the third sentence, "Das wird mißverstanden und dasselbe Tempo wie in der Einleitung genommen." I take "werden" here to represent the passive voice rather than the future tense. (If it were future tense, Brahms would likely have written "Das wird mißverstanden werden" or "Das wird man mißverstehen.") Thus, Brahms is not saying "This *will be* misunderstood" (although that meaning is also implied), but that the Poco sostenuto *is* or *has been* misunderstood. The difference is important for my interpretation of his remarks.

38. Robert Pascall, "Brahms and the Definitive Text," *Brahms: Biographical, Documentary, and Analytical Studies,* ed. Robert Pascall (Cambridge: Cambridge University Press, 1983), pp. 73–74.

39. Del Mar, *Conducting Brahms,* p. 7.

40. An analogous effect, which Brahms would have studied closely, is the way in which the horn melody in the introduction to the first movement of Schubert's "Great" C-Major Symphony (D. 940) comes back at the end of the movement at its original tempo, also with proportionally altered note values.

41. *Letters from and to Joseph Joachim*, sel. and trans. Nora Bickley (1914; reprint, New York: Vienna House, 1972), p. 253.

42. Markings in the recently recovered engraver's model for the First Symphony, now at the Brahms-Institut in Lübeck, may support this hypothesis. This score, prepared by copyists, has corrections and emendations in Brahms's hand, presumably made in the spring or summer of 1877. The copyist had written *Sostenuto* at the beginning of the first movement and *Poco sostenuto* at the coda. Brahms changed the former marking to *Un poco sostenuto*, thus bringing it more into line with the coda.

43. Weingartner, *The Symphony since Beethoven*, trans. Maude Dutton (Boston: Ditson, 1904), p. 44. In this edition, dating from six years after the original publication, Weingartner also tempered his opinions in a footnote (p. 37).

44. *Brahms Briefwechsel*, XII, 169. In his *Buffets and Rewards: A Musician's Reminiscences* (London: Hutchinson, 1937), Weingartner gives details about his Vienna sojourn of 1895, including his personal contacts with Brahms and the composer's positive reactions to his conducting.

45. Cited in Peter Muck, *Einhundert Jahre Berliner Philharmonisches Orchester* (Tutzing: Hans Schneider, 1982), I, 220.

46. For details of Weingartner's recordings, see Christopher Dyment, *Felix Weingartner: Recollections and Recordings* (Rickmansworth: Triad Press, 1976). Prior to the complete series of symphonies made during 1938–40, Weingartner recorded the First Symphony twice, in 1923–24 and in 1928.

47. Liner notes to Weingartner's recording of Brahms symphonies (Centaur CRC 2124), p. 5.

48. Dyment, liner notes (see above, n. 13), p. 1.

49. Review included in Muck, *Einhundert Jahre*, II, 107.

50. For an authoritative discography, compiled by John Hunt, and an excellent survey of Furtwängler's recordings, see John Ardoin, *The Furtwängler Record* (Portland, Or.: Amadeus Press, 1994).

51. Furtwängler's 1952 performance of the Second Symphony with the Berlin Philharmonic (recorded in Munich) is considerably slower than that with Vienna in 1945. This later rendering is powerful but less refined and taut. The pacing and some of the climaxes and balances, which are heavy on the brass, seem more Brucknerian in spirit than Brahmsian.

52. Cited in Ardoin, *The Furtwängler Record*, p. 292.

53. Cited in Ardoin, *The Furtwängler Record*, p. 294.

54. Otto Strasser, "The Brahms Tradition of the Vienna Philharmonic: Karl Böhm Conducts the Orchestra," essay in the booklet accompanying Böhm recordings of 1976 (DGG 2563 587–90), p. 10.

55.   For a sensitive discussion of Norrington's recording of the First, see Raymond Knapp, "A Review of Norrington's Brahms," *American Brahms Society Newsletter* 11/1 (Spring 1993): 4–7.

56.   The London Classical Players, as listed on the recording, include a total of forty strings: ten first violins, ten second violins, eight violas, six cellos, and six double basses. With a total of twenty violins in the orchestra, it is somewhat misleading to claim an average of nine per "voice," since it appears from Norrington's math that only four "voices" are reckoned ($9 \times 4 = 36$). One must really count the first and second violins as *two* voices, which brings the total of strings to five voices. With forty players and five voices, as on the Norrington recording, the average is more accurately set at eight players per voice.

57.   Donald F. Tovey, *Essays in Musical Analysis:* Vol. I, Symphonies (London: Oxford University Press, 1935), p. 94.

APPENDIX II

1.   For details, see Margit McCorkle, *Johannes Brahms: Thematisch-Biblio-graphisches Werkverzeichnis* (Munich: Henle, 1984).

2.   Margit McCorkle, "The Role of Trial Performances for Brahms's Orchestral and Large Choral Works: Sources and Circumstances," in *Brahms Studies: Analytical and Historical Perspectives,* ed. George S. Bozarth (Oxford: Clarendon Press, 1990), pp. 295–328.

3.   See Robert Pascall, "Brahms and the Definitive Text," in *Brahms: Biographical, Documentary and Analytical Studies,* ed. Robert Pascall (Cambridge: Cambridge University Press, 1983), pp. 59–75; Pascall, "The Publication of Brahms's Third Symphony: A Crisis in Dissemination," in *Brahms Studies,* ed. Bozarth, pp. 283–94; and (primarily on the Third Symphony) *A Working Relationship: The Correspondence between Johannes Brahms and Robert Keller,* ed. George S. Bozarth (Lincoln: University of Nebraska Press, forthcoming).

4.   Pascall, "Brahms and the Definitive Text," pp. 72–74.

Selected Bibliography

———— ✌ ————

GENERAL

Bekker, Paul. *Die Sinfonie von Beethoven bis Mahler.* Berlin: Schuster & Löffler, 1918.

Bonds, Mark Evan. *After Beethoven: Imperatives of Originality in the Symphony.* Cambridge, Mass.: Harvard University Press, forthcoming.

Botstein, Leon. "Brahms and Nineteenth-Century Painting." *19th-Century Music* 14 (1990): 154–68.

————. "Listening through Reading: Musical Literacy and the Concert Audience." *19th-Century Music* 16 (1992): 129–45.

————. "Time and Memory: Concert Life, Science, and Music in Brahms's Vienna." In *Brahms and His World,* edited by Walter Frisch. Princeton: Princeton University Press, 1990, pp. 3–22.

Brodbeck, David. "Brahms." In *The Nineteenth-Century Symphony,* edited by D. Kern Holoman. New York: Schirmer Books, 1996.

Browne, P. A. *Brahms: The Symphonies.* London: Oxford University Press, 1933.

Burkholder, J. Peter. "Brahms and Twentieth-Century Classical Music." *19th-Century Music* 8 (1984): 75–83.

Dahlhaus, Carl. *Nineteenth-Century Music.* Translated by J. Bradford Robinson. Berkeley and Los Angeles: University of California Press, 1989.

————. "Symphonie und symphonischer Stil um 1850." *Jahrbuch des staatlichen Instituts für Musikforschung* 1983–84, pp. 34–58.

Del Mar, Norman. *Conducting Brahms.* Oxford: Clarendon Press, 1993.

Finson, Jon W. "Performing Practice in the Late Nineteenth Century, with Special Reference to the Music of Brahms." *Musical Quarterly* 70 (1984): 457–75.

Frisch, Walter. *Brahms and the Principle of Developing Variation.* Berkeley and Los Angeles: University of California Press, 1984.

Gay, Peter. "Aimez-Vous Brahms? On Polarities in Modernism." In his *Freud, Jews and Other Germans.* Oxford: Oxford University Press, 1978, pp. 231–56.

Hanslick, Eduard. *Hanslick's Music Criticisms.* Translated and edited by Henry Pleasants. 1950. Reprint, New York: Dover, 1988.

Harrison, Julius. *Brahms and His Four Symphonies.* 1939. Reprint, New York: Da Capo, 1971.

Heuberger, Richard. *Erinnerungen an Johannes Brahms*. Tutzing: Hans Schneider, 1971.

Horstmann, Angelika. *Untersuchungen zur Brahms-Rezeption der Jahre 1860–1880*. Hamburg: Karl Dieter Wagner, 1986.

Horton, John. *Brahms Orchestral Music*. London: BBC, 1968.

Kirby, F. E. "The Germanic Symphony of the Nineteenth Century: Genre, Form, Instrumentation, Expression." *Journal of Musicological Research* 14 (1995): 193–221.

Knapp, Raymond. *Brahms and the Challenge of the Symphony*. Stuyvesant, N.Y.: Pendragon Press, 1997.

Kretschmar, Hermann. "The Brahms Symphonies." Translated by Susan Gillespie. In *Brahms and His World*, edited by Walter Frisch. Princeton: Princeton University Press, 1990, pp. 123–43.

Kross, Siegfried. "Brahms the Symphonist." In *Brahms: Biographical, Documentary and Analytical Studies*, edited by Robert Pascall. Cambridge: Cambridge University Press, 1983, pp. 125–45.

———. "Das 'Zweite Zeitalter der Symphonie'—Ideologie und Realität." In *Probleme der Symphonischen Tradition im 19. Jahrhundert*, edited by Siegfried Kross. Tutzing: Hans Schneider, 1990, pp. 11–36.

———. "The Establishment of a Brahms Repertoire, 1890–1902." In *Brahms 2: Biographical, Documentary, and Analytical Studies*, edited by Michael Musgrave. Cambridge: Cambridge University Press, 1987, pp. 21–38.

McCorkle, Margit. "The Role of Trial Performances for Brahms's Orchestral and Large Choral Works: Sources and Circumstances." In *Brahms Studies: Analytical and Historical Perspectives*, edited by George S. Bozarth. Oxford: Clarendon Press, 1990, pp. 295–328.

Notley, Margaret. "Brahms as Liberal: Genre, Style, and Politics in Late Nineteenth-Century Vienna." *19th-Century Music* 17 (1993): 107–23.

Oechsle, Siegfried. *Symphonik nach Beethoven: Studien zu Schubert, Schumann, Mendelssohn und Gade*. Kassel: Bärenreiter, 1992.

Pascall, Robert. "Brahms and the Definitive Text." In *Brahms: Biographical, Documentary and Analytical Studies*, edited by Robert Pascall. Cambridge: Cambridge University Press, 1983, pp. 59–75.

———. "Some Special Uses of Sonata Form by Brahms." *Soundings* 4 (1974): 58–63.

Pedersen, Sanna. "On the Task of the Music Historian: The Myth of the Symphony after Beethoven." *repercussions* 2 (1993): 5–30.

Philip, Robert. *Early Recordings and Musical Style: Changing Tastes in Instrumental Performance, 1900–1950*. Cambridge: Cambridge University Press, 1992.

Reynolds, Christopher. "A Choral Symphony by Brahms?" *19th-Century Music* 9 (1985): 3–25.

Schubert, Giselher. "Themes and Double Themes: The Problem of the Symphonic in Brahms." *19th-Century Music* 18 (1994): 10–23.

Schumann, Robert. *On Music and Musicians.* Edited by Konrad Wolff, translated by Paul Rosenfeld. New York: Norton, 1969.

Sisman, Elaine R. "Brahms's Slow Movements: Reinventing the 'Closed' Forms." In *Brahms Studies: Analytical and Historical Perspectives,* edited by George S. Bozarth. Oxford: Clarendon Press, 1990, pp. 79–103.

Tovey, Donald F. *Essays in Musical Analysis.* Vol. I: Symphonies. London: Oxford University Press, 1935.

Wagner, Manfred. *Geschichte der österreichischen Musikkritik in Beispielen.* Tutzing: Hans Schneider, 1979.

Webster, James. "The General and the Particular in Brahms's Later Sonata Forms." In *Brahms Studies: Analytical and Historical Perspectives,* edited by George Bozarth. Oxford: Clarendon Press, 1990, pp. 49–78.

THE FIRST SYMPHONY

Brahms, Johannes. *1. Sinfonie c-Moll, op. 68.* Einführung und Analyse von Giselher Schubert mit Partitur. Munich and Mainz: Piper/Schott, 1981.

Brahms, Johannes. *Symphony No. 1 in C Minor, op. 68: The Autograph Score.* Introduction by Margit M. McCorkle. New York: Dover, 1986.

Brodbeck, David. *Brahms: Symphony No. 1.* Cambridge Music Handbooks. Cambridge: Cambridge University Press, 1997.

Fink, Robert. "Desire, Repression, and Brahms's First Symphony." *repercussions* 2 (1993): 75–103.

Fuchs, Ingrid. "Zeitgenössische Aufführungen der Ersten Symphonie op. 68 von Johannes Brahms in Wien. Studien zur Wiener Brahms-Rezeption." In *Brahms-Kongreß Wien 1983,* edited by Susanne Antonicek and Otto Biba. Tutzing: Hans Schneider, 1988, pp. 167–86.

Haas, Fritjof. "Die Erstfassung des langsamen Satzes der ersten Sinfonie von Johannes Brahms." *Musikforschung* 36 (1983): 200–211.

Knapp, Raymond. "Brahms's Revisions Revisited." *Musical Times* 129 (1988): 584–88.

"Kritiken zu zeitgenössischen Aufführungen der ersten Symphonie von Johannes Brahms (Auswahl)." In *Brahms-Kongreß Wien 1983,* edited by Susanne Antonicek and Otto Biba. Tutzing: Hans Schneider, pp. 489–515.

Musgrave, Michael. "Brahms's First Symphony: Thematic Coherence and Its Secret Origin." *Music Analysis* 2 (1983): 117–33.

Newman, S. T. M. "The Slow Movement of Brahms' First Symphony: A Reconstruction of the Version First Performed prior to Publication." *Music Review* 9 (1948): 4–12.

Pascall, Robert. "Brahms's First Symphony Andante—the Initial Performing Version," Papers in Musicology No. 2, Department of Music, University of Nottingham, 1992.

———. "Brahms's First Symphony Slow Movement: The Initial Performing Version." *Musical Times* 122 (1981): 664–67.

THE SECOND SYMPHONY

Brahms, Johannes. *Sinfonie Nr. 2, D-Dur, op. 73.* Einführung und Analyse von Constantin Floros. Munich and Mainz: Goldmann/Schott, 1984.

Brinkmann, Reinhold. *Late Idyll: The Second Symphony of Johannes Brahms.* Translated by Peter Palmer. Cambridge, Mass.: Harvard University Press, 1995.

Epstein, David. *Beyond Orpheus.* Cambridge, Mass.: MIT Press, 1979, pp. 162–75.

Schachter, Carl. "The First Movement of Brahms's Second Symphony: The Opening Theme and Its Consequences." *Music Analysis* 2 (1983): 55–68.

Steinbeck, Wolfram. "Liedthematik und symphonischer Prozeß: zum ersten Satz der 2. Symphonie." In *Brahms-Analysen,* edited by Friedhelm Krummacher and Wolfram Steinbeck. Kassel: Bärenreiter, 1984, pp. 166–82.

THE THIRD SYMPHONY

Bailey, Robert. "Musical Language and Structure in the Third Symphony." In *Brahms Studies: Analytical and Historical Perspectives,* edited by George S. Bozarth. Oxford: Clarendon Press, 1990, pp. 405–21.

Brahms, Johannes. *Sinfonie Nr. 3 F-Dur, op. 90.* Einführung und Analyse von Christian Martin Schmidt. Munich and Mainz: Goldmann/Schott, 1980.

Brodbeck, David. "Brahms, the Third Symphony, and the New German School." In *Brahms and His World,* edited by Walter Frisch. Princeton: Princeton University Press, 1990, pp. 65–80.

Brown, A. Peter. "Brahms' Third Symphony and the New German School." *Journal of Musicology* 2 (1983): 434–52.

McClary, Susan. "Narrative Agendas in 'Absolute' Music: Identity and Difference in Brahms's Third Symphony." In *Musicology and Difference,* edited by Ruth Solie. Berkeley and Los Angeles: University of California Press, 1993, pp. 326–44.

Pascall, Robert. "The Publication of Brahms's Third Symphony: A Crisis in Dissemination." In *Brahms Studies: Analytical and Historical Perspectives,* edited by George S. Bozarth. Oxford: Clarendon Press, 1990, pp. 283–94.

THE FOURTH SYMPHONY

Brahms, Johannes. *Sinfonie Nr. 4, e-moll, op. 98.* Einführung und Analyse von Christian Martin Schmidt. Munich and Mainz: Goldmann/Schott, 1980.

——. *Symphony No. 4. in E minor, op. 98.* Norton Critical Score. Edited by Kenneth Hull. New York: Norton, 2000.

Dunsby, Jonathan. *Structural Ambiguity in Brahms: Analytical Approaches to Four Works.* Ann Arbor: UMI Research Press, 1981, pp. 41–83.

Knapp, Raymond. "The Finale of Brahms's Fourth Symphony: The Tale of the Subject." *19th-Century Music* 13 (1989): 3–17.

Klein, Rudolf. "Die Doppelgerüsttechnik in der Passacaglia der IV. Symphonie von Brahms." *Österreichische Musikzeitschrift* 27 (1972): 641–48.

Litterick, Louise. "Brahms the Indecisive: Notes on the First Movement of the Fourth Symphony." In *Brahms 2: Biographical, Documentary, and Analytical Studies,* edited by Michael Musgrave. Cambridge: Cambridge University Press, 1987, pp. 223–35.

Mackelmann, Michael. *Johannes Brahms: IV. Symphonie e-Moll op. 98.* Munich: Fink, 1991.

Osmond-Smith, David. "The Retreat from Dynamism: A Study of Brahms's Fourth Symphony." In *Brahms: Biographical, Documentary and Analytical Studies,* edited by Robert Pascall. Cambridge: Cambridge University Press, 1983, pp. 147–65.

Pascall, Robert. "Genre and the Finale of Brahms's Fourth Symphony." *Music Analysis* 8 (1989): 233–45.

Vetter, Walther. "Der erste Satz von Brahms' e-moll Symphonie: ein Beitrag zur Erkenntnis moderner Symphonik." *Die Musik* 13/3 (1913–14): 3–15, 83–92, 131–45.

Weber, Horst. "Melancholia: Versuch über Brahms' Vierte." In *Neue Musik und Tradition: Festschrift für Rudolf Stephan zum 65. Geburtstag,* edited by Josef Kuckartz, et al. Kassel: Bärenreiter, 1984, pp. 166–82.

Index

A

Abendroth, Hermann, 165, 174–75, 176, 188
Adorno, Theodor, 35, 90, 150–51, 161
Aldrich, Richard, 182
Allgemeine musikalische Zeitung, 2, 11, 17, 19–20, 24, 146
art of transition, 54
Ashkenazy, Vladimir, 185
autonomy, 18

B

Bach, Johann Sebastian, 4, 130–31
Bagge, Selmar, 17
Barbirolli, John, 143
Barenboim, Daniel, 185
Beethoven, Ludwig van, 2, 3–4, 11, 12, 13, 17, 19, 27, 35, 36, 46, 68, 143, 144, 145–47, 167
  WORKS
  Leonore Overture No. 3, 178
  Symphony No. 1, 47–48
  Symphony No. 3 (*Eroica*), 16, 50, 131
  Symphony No. 5, 16, 45, 52, 58, 65, 144
  Symphony No. 8, 178
  Symphony No. 9, 15, 16, 18, 31, 32, 52, 58, 60, 64, 65, 145–47
Bekker, Paul, 35, 90, 147, 148, 150
Berlin Philharmonic, 18, 144, 178, 179, 182
Berlin State Opera Orchestra, 166, 174, 175
Berlioz, Hector, 4
Bernstein, Leonard, 143, 169
Billroth, Theodor, 116
Blume, Walter, 169, 173
Borodin, Alexander, 6

Boston Symphony Orchestra, 164, 182
Botstein, Leon, 151, 155, 156
Brahms, Johannes
  WORKS (OTHER THAN SYMPHONIES)
  Academic Festival Overture, op. 80, 91, 127
  Alto Rhapsody, op. 53, 35
  Clarinet Quintet, op. 115, 114, 150
  Es liebt sich so lieblich im Lenze!, op. 71, no. 1, 74
  German Requiem, op. 45, 30, 35–36
  Horn Trio, op. 40, 33
  Liebeslieder Waltzes, op. 52, 37
  Piano Concerto No. 1, op. 15, 30–31, 32, 35
  Piano Concerto No. 2, op. 83, 91
  Piano Quartets Nos. 1 and 2, opp. 25 and 26, 33, 34, 43, 151–52
  Piano Quartet No. 3, op. 60, 42–43
  Piano Quintet, op. 34, 33–34
  Piano Sonatas, opp. 1, 2, and 5, 29
  Rhapsody for piano, op. 79, 111
  Scherzo for piano, op. 4, 29
  Schicksalslied, op. 54, 35
  Serenades, op. 11 and 16, 12, 31, 32, 35, 38, 42
  Sextet No. 1, op. 18, 33
  Sextet No. 2, op. 36, 23, 33
  String Quartet No. 1, op. 51, no. 1, 36–38, 42, 43, 61–62
  String Quartet No. 2, op. 51, no. 2, 37, 43
  String Quartet No. 3, op. 67, 42–43, 114
  Tragic Overture, op. 81, 91
  Triumphlied, op. 55, 35
  Variations on a Theme by Haydn, op. 56, 36, 38–42, 43, 130
  Violin Concerto, op. 77, 91

breakthrough, 90
Brendel, Franz, 13
Brinkmann, Reinhold, 63–65, 68, 90
Bruch, Max, 11, 20–25, 26
Bruckner, Anton, 6, 15, 19, 20, 25–27, 133,
    143–44, 150
    WORKS
    Symphony No. 3, 147
    Symphony No. 4, 26–27
    Symphony No. 9, 147
Brüll, Ignaz, 115
Bülow, Hans von, 115, 116, 163, 166,
    167– 69, 175, 178, 179, 182
Buxtehude, Dietrich, 131

C

canon formation, 19
Cantelli, Guido, 143
chaconne, 130, 133–34, 136, 138–39
Chopin, Frédéric, 29, 45
Chrysander, Friedrich, 19–20, 24, 146
Cologne Concert Society, 19
Cone, Edward T., 117
congruence, 117, 121, 140
Cornelius, Peter, 13–14

D

Dahlhaus, Carl, 3, 6, 11, 14, 15–16, 17, 18,
    141, 151
Damrosch, Leopold, 21, 143
Deiters, Hermann, 12
Del Mar, Norman, 174, 176
Dessoff, Otto, 16, 67, 68, 163
developing variation, 33, 54, 75, 151
Dietrich, Albert, 12, 15, 33
Dömpke, Gustav, 116
Dvořák, Antonin, 6
Dyment, Christopher, 166, 182

E

Esser, Heinrich, 11, 15, 19

F

Fiedler, Max, 181, 182, 183, 184, 186
finale problem, 58
Fink, G. W., 2–3, 4, 11
Fink, Robert, 160–61

Finscher, Ludwig, 14
Finson, Jon, 4, 165
Franck, César, 6
Fried, Oskar, 174–75, 176
Fuchs, Ingrid, 145
Furtwängler, Wilhelm, 143, 175, 176, 181,
    183–85, 186, 188

G

Gay, Peter, 152
Gerber, E. L., 2
German unification, 36
Gesellschaft der Musikfreunde, 18, 19,
    166, 169
Giulini, Carlo Maria, 143
Goepp, Philip, 156–57
Grimm, J. O., 33
Gutmann, Albert, 168

H

Hamburg Philharmonic Society, 18
Hanslick, Eduard, 14, 19, 67, 116, 152,
    153, 154, 164, 167
Harrison, Julius, 156, 158–59
Haydn, Franz Josef, 2, 13, 19, 90
Helm, Theodor, 150
Henschel, George, 164
Herzogenberg, Elisabet von, 153
Heuberger, Richard, 166–67
Hiller, Ferdinand, 20
Hoffmann, E. T. A., 1–2, 16
Horstmann, Angelika, 145

J

Joachim, Joseph, 21, 29

K

Kalbeck, Max, 45, 116, 156, 157–58,
    160
Kirby, Frank E., 3, 5, 6, 7
Klemperer, Otto, 143, 166, 175, 176
Klitsch, Emanuel, 17, 21
Klughardt, August, 11
Knapp, Raymond, 130, 131
Konversations-Lexicon (Mendel's), 5–6
Koury, Daniel, 164
Kretschmar, Hermann, 155–56, 159

Kross, Siegfried, 6, 11, 142
Kubelik, Rafael, 143
Kurth, Ernst, 27

L

Lachner, Franz, 3
Lachner, Vincenz, 70
Lassen, Eduard, 17, 19
Leinsdorf, Erich, 143
Leipzig Gewandhaus Orchestra, 5, 18, 164, 174
Levi, Hermann, 16, 33, 148
Levine, James, 143
liberalism, 149–50
liquidation, 50
Liszt, Franz, 13, 15, 29, 45
Litterick, Louise, 117, 118
London Classical Players, 185–88
London Symphony Orchestra, 165, 174, 179
Louis, Rudolf, 151
Lueger, Karl, 149
Luther, Martin, 36
lyrical counterpoint, 68

M

Mahler, Gustav, 14, 36, 87, 90, 133, 143, 174
Mann, Thomas, 64
Mark, Desmond, 143, 144
Marx, A. B., 1–2
Mass for the Dead, 36
Masur, Kurt, 143
McClary, Susan, 159–60, 161
Mehta, Zubin, 143
Meiningen Orchestra, 115, 116, 164, 169, 173, 175
Mendelssohn, Felix, 4, 11, 12, 19, 27, 144
Mengelberg, Willem, 143
metrical ambiguity, 71, 95–99, 102, 107
metrical displacement, 54, 97, 101
metrical modulation, 82
middle classes (Bildungsbürgertum), 18, 149
Mitropoulos, Dimiti, 143
monumental style, 16, 26
Mottl, Felix, 178
Mozart, Wolfgang, 4, 12, 13, 19, 144
Musgrave, Michael, 160
musical idealism, 18

musical prose, 52
Musikalisches Wochenblatt, 142, 152

N

Newcomb, Anthony, 14, 45
Neue Zeitschrift für Musik, 3, 11, 13, 17, 21, 148
New German School, 13
Newman, Ernest, 166
New York Philharmonic, 143
Nicolai, Otto, 18
Niemann, Walter, 38, 39
Norrington, Roger, 174, 179, 181, 185–88
Notley, Margaret, 149

O

opera, 1–2
orchestral suite, 12
overture, 12

P

Pan-Germanism, 149
Pascall, Robert, 176, 177
passacaglia, 130
Philadelphia Orchestra, 181
Philip, Robert, 165
Philipp, Rudolf, 178
plot archetype, 45
Pohl, C. F., 116, 168–69
Pohl, Richard, 146, 155, 156
portamento, 165–66
Preyer, Gottfried, 3
program music, 12–15

R

Rabinowitz, Peter, 179
Reger, Max, 131
Reinecke, Carl, 11, 17
Reinthaler, Carl, 11–12, 36
Reißiger, Karl G., 3–4
Reynolds, Christopher, 30–31
Richter, Hans, 68, 116, 163, 166–69, 178, 179, 182
Ringer, Alexander, 19

S

Schachter, Carl, 71
Schmidt, Christian M., 91, 106

Schoenberg, Arnold, 33, 48, 50, 52, 94, 96, 117, 151–52, 154
Schorske, Carl, 150
Schubert, Franz, 11, 18, 19, 23, 27, 45, 68, 70, 122
    WORKS
    Symphony No. 9 ("Great"), 4, 5, 94, 144
Schubert, Giselher, 59, 63, 65
Schumann, Clara, 31, 33, 34, 35, 59, 67, 68, 148, 160, 177
Schumann, Robert, 3–5, 11, 12, 19, 27, 31, 80, 160
    "Neue Bahnen," 29, 30, 32, 35
    WORKS
    Symphony No. 2, 5
    Symphony No. 3, 6, 7, 14–15, 20
    Symphony No. 4, 144
sentence, 48
serenade, 12
Simrock, Fritz, 21, 169, 175
Solti, Georg, 143, 174, 181
Song of Roland, 157–58
Speidel, Ludwig, 155
Spohr, Louis, 4
Stanford, Charles Villiers, 166, 182
Steinbach, Fritz, 169, 173, 175
Stokowski, Leopold, 143, 181
Strasser, Otto, 185
Strauss, Richard, 116, 133, 178
Sulzer, J. G., 1
sublime, 1
symmetry, 56–57
symphonic poem, 13, 30
symphonic style, 15–17, 25, 26, 29, 32, 38, 46, 147
symphonic waves, 27
Symphony Society of New York, 21

T

Tchaikovsky, Peter I., 6
thematic-formal conflation, 72

thematic fulfillment, 49, 71, 97
thematic working, 16, 24
third relations, 23, 45–46, 93–95, 99, 104, 117, 119, 121–22, 124, 133, 138, 140
three-key exposition, 70–71, 94, 122
Toscanini, Arturo, 143
Tovey, Donald F., 33, 58, 64, 77, 87, 156, 187
Treitler, Leo, 141

V

vagrant chords, 117
Verdi, Giuseppe, 116
Vetter, Walther, 119
Vienna Philharmonic, 18, 68, 115, 143–44, 164, 165, 166, 168, 183, 185
Vivaldi, Antonio, 14
Volkmann, Robert, 12

W

Wagner, Richard, 13, 15, 27, 54, 56, 68, 110, 133, 148–49, 150, 151, 160
Walker, Alan, 127
Walter, Bruno, 143, 165, 186
Weber, William, 18
Webern, Anton, 131
Webster, James, 128
Weingartner, Felix, 169, 175, 176, 177–79, 181, 182, 183, 184, 185, 186, 188
Wiener Abendpost, 145
Wiener Morgen-Post, 145
Wiener Tagblatt, 167
Wiora, Walter, 14
Wolf, Hugo, 133
Wüerst, Richard, 13–14

Z

Zellner, Julius, 17
Zemlinsky, Alexander, 131
Zöpff, Hermann, 148